The Shell
Guide to Gardens

By The Same Author

The Amateur Gardener
Shrubs in Colour
Flowers in Colour
Garden Plants in Colour
Practical Gardening for Amateurs
Your New Garden
Your Garden Week by Week
Garden Pests and Diseases
Starting with Roses
Amateur Gardening Pocket Guide
The Encyclopaedia of Garden Work and Terms
Gardens to Visit in Britain
Your Lawn
Chrysanthemums for Everyone
Carters Book for Gardeners
All Colour Gardening Book
All Colour Book of Indoor and Greenhouse Plants
Picture Dictionary of Popular Flowering Plants
The Collingridge Encyclopaedia of Gardening
Practical Gardening Illustrated

The sunken garden, Great Dixter (p. 143)

The Shell
Guide to Gardens

THE FINEST BRITISH AND IRISH
GARDENS OPEN TO THE PUBLIC
DESCRIBED AND INTRODUCED BY

Arthur Hellyer

Heinemann : London

William Heinemann Ltd
15 Queen St, Mayfair, London W1X 8BE

LONDON MELBOURNE TORONTO
JOHANNESBURG AUCKLAND

First published 1977

Photoset and printed web offset
in Great Britain by
REDWOOD BURN LIMITED
Trowbridge & Esher

Contents

Colour Plates

Most of the photographs were taken by the author, but we are grateful to *Amateur Gardening* for permission to reproduce pictures on pages 109, 153, 156, and 170, to the British Tourist Authority on 89, Sheila Peacock on 92, and to *Country Life* on 118, 133, 142, 155 (Holkham Hall), 205 (Rudding Park) and 242.

The maps on pages 246–256 were specially drawn by Reginald Piggott.

Four Centuries of Garden Making

Gardens mean different things to different people. To some they represent history and to others design. Many are chiefly interested in the plants with which the gardens are stocked and though the majority of these probably think of little beyond the colour, form and beauty of the display, a minority will look also for rarity, exceptional size or superb cultivation.

So as the story of gardens in Britain and Ireland unfolds all these interests will be kept in mind and I shall try to direct readers' attention to the best examples in all these fields, especially, of course, to those that are reasonably accessible to the public, for it is of little use to know that something exceptional exists but not be able to see it. So most of the gardens I shall be writing about are open to the public fairly regularly, and even those few of which this is not true are open occasionally or can be seen by special request. These I have included only when they seemed to be in some way unique or so outstandingly good in a particular feature that those interested in this aspect of gardening would be willing to go to some trouble to see them.

The first gardens in Britain were made by the Romans nearly two millenia ago, but when they left the gardens quickly disappeared leaving little trace except that indicated by the foundations of buildings. But in one remarkable instance there was more to guide the archaeologists. When the site of a major military headquarters at Fishbourne near Chichester was discovered and cleared a few years ago it was found possible to trace the beds as well as the walls because the natural soil of the site was so poor that the Roman gardeners had found it necessary to import soil of better quality wherever they wanted to grow anything. The difference between this dark, porous, fertile soil and the yellow clay of the site is still plainly visible and so at Fishbourne it has been possible to replant a Roman garden much as it

1

must have been about A.D. 75. Not all the site is available since some of it was built over without knowledge of what lay below, but sufficient both of the garden and the buildings remains to be of great interest and a model has also been constructed showing what it is assumed the whole place looked like when it was at its prime.

What emerges is a very simple garden by present day standards, symmetrical and rectilinear, with large areas of grass bounded by trim hedges of box interspersed with rosemary.

After the Romans withdrew more than a thousand years were to pass before gardens began to play any significant part in the lives of the people. In monastries no doubt there were small plots set aside for herbs and medicinal plants, with perhaps a few grown simply for the beauty of their leaves or flowers, but no examples of this kind of garden remain and it requires a considerable effort of imagination to visualize what they were like.

As times became more settled, personal wealth and leisure increased and gardens began to be made again, but chiefly by kings, princes and the nobility or influential clergy who surrounded them. Yet again very little remains, certainly nothing at all complete until the beginning of the seventeenth century, though at Thornbury Castle in Gloucestershire some outlines of an early sixteenth century garden can be seen.

It is still possible to see several of the enclosures which were typical of gardens of this period. Ivy-covered remnants of the two-storey gallery can be seen, which contemporary accounts describe as encircling this garden. This little garden was ornamented with knots. Then there was another larger

garden enclosed by high walls and alongside this an orchard surrounded by alleys and arbours covered in thorn and hazel with a fence, ditches and a quickset hedge around the whole to keep out intruders, both human and animal. But considerable imagination is required even at Thornbury to visualize just what the series of little gardens looked like and no attempt has yet been made to reconstruct such a garden either at Thornbury or elsewhere.

For those who wish to study gardens as things still living and in use, the British story really starts towards the close of the sixteenth century. Before attempting to tell that story in some detail it may be helpful to take a much broader view of the major changes in fashion and interests that make it so unusually varied and fascinating.

Though it is an over simplification of what actually happened it is possible to see those four centuries of garden making as each dominated by quite different ideas about the purpose of gardens and the form they should take. We could say that the seventeenth century was chiefly concerned with order and rationality; that art and poetry largely determined the character of the eighteenth century gardens; whereas in the nineteenth century the great influx of new plants, some from the wild, some man-made by hybridization and selection, almost completely captured the imagination of garden makers. And what of the present century? It is always difficult to take a sufficiently detached view of one's own times, to disentangle what is important from what is only trivial or ephemeral, but my own guess would be that future historians will see the twentieth century contribution to gardening mainly as one of synthesis, of trying to extract the best features from each of the previous periods and combine them in a satisfactory way. They may well lay stress on the increasingly sensitive use of plants, for only in this century do garden makers seem to have attached great importance to the artistic and emotional effects which can be obtained by associations of plants, colours and forms. It is a movement that had its own origins at the close of the nineteenth century, stimulated no doubt by the work and ideals of impressionist painters, but in our own times it has received considerable impetus from the parallel development of flower arrangement as a hobby and art form. Much planting in recent years has been done by people who are also flower arrangers and I think it shows clearly in their work.

PATTERN AND ORDER

A feature of many sixteenth and seventeenth century gardens was the knot, or series of knots. These were an expression of the mediaeval passion for patterns and they were made with various plants kept closely clipped. The patterns themselves could be simple or complex and seem often to have been copied or adapted from embroidery. Frequently the 'over and

3

The link between old and new – York University (p. 244)

under' effect of such patterns worked in silk or wool was imitated in the garden knot by using plants of different colours – box, green- and golden-leaved thyme, lavender, hyssop, sage etc. Since these are all fairly short-lived plants no original knots survive, even from considerably later gardens, and all that one sees today are reconstructions. There are plenty of these about, one of the most successful, considered as a pattern, being in the Shakespeare Knot Garden at Stratford-on-Avon. But this, like the two charming little knot gardens at Hampton Court, suffers from inappropriate planting with many gay annuals and bedding plants, most of which were not available to sixteenth and seventeenth century gardeners. They do this kind of thing much better in some other countries, in America at Colonial Williamsburg, Virginia, for example, where the box-edged knots are filled with a patchwork of plants, mostly perennial, including periwinkles, ivies, jonquils and star of bethlehem.

The earliest complete garden I know in the British Isles is at Edzell Castle (Edzell, Tayside, Scotland). 'Complete' in this instance must be understood to mean that the whole garden is still there with its enclosing walls and that the work of restoration, for the most part admirably carried out by the Ministry of Public Building and Works (now absorbed by the Department of the Environment), was mainly concerned with the plan of the garden within those walls. For Edzell Castle is a ruin and only wild plants grew inside its beautiful garden walls when the work of remaking it began. No plans or records of what had been there existed, but the walls, with their quite elaborate carvings and niches, indicated what manner of garden it must have been when Sir David Lindsay completed it in 1604, and plans of other similar gardens in Scotland did exist. So a geometric pattern of beds was developed, partly from these old plans, partly by making use of Sir David's coat of arms, and a raised walk was made around the garden so that this pattern, outlined in box, could be seen clearly.

Edzell Castle is a gem which perfectly illustrates many of the most characteristic features of gardens of this period. It is small because there is still not a great deal of time or money for pure pleasure gardening. It is totally enclosed by quite high walls, partly for privacy, but also because the outside world still holds many dangers of beast as well as of man. It is also a strongly patterned garden, more so, probably, than the average, for even the niches in the walls are arranged in a chequer pattern. Tradition has it that they were filled with flowers in the armorial colours of the Lindsays, white and blue, with red added by the stone of the wall itself. Today flowers actually grow in summer in little trays lodged in the niches, blue lobelia and white alyssum, which illustrates one of the pitfalls that await restorers, for though sweet alyssum might have been available to Sir David lobelia certainly was not since it was not introduced from South Africa until the mid-seventeenth century. There are also anachronisms in the planting of the knots in the little parterre, for some of them are filled with floribunda roses, a twentieth century creation; and *Tropaeolum speciosum*, brought to Britain from Chile

4

during Victoria's reign, creeps through the drum-shaped yew that is the centrepiece of the garden. But these are minor blemishes which could easily be rectified and which it is equally easy to overlook either by visiting Edzell Castle at any period but summer or by using a little imagination to shut out the offending flowers. For me this is one of the most delightful small gardens in the British Isles, and I have yet to meet any visitor who did not fall under its spell.

Much larger than Edzell Castle, but rather lacking its finesse, is Pitmedden, another Scottish garden, near Old Meldrum to the west of Aberdeen. It differs from Edzell in several important details, one that it is viewed from much higher terraces which give an almost bird's eye view of the pattern,

The reconstructed fountain, Pitmedden House (p. 192)

the other that it is also overlooked by a pair of two-storey pavilions or gazebos, which are a good deal more elaborate than the simple little garden house tucked into one corner of Edzell. But the stone work at Pitmedden is nothing like so elegant and complex as that at Edzell Castle and the planting of the knots with highly coloured exotics is much more distracting.

The outside walls and gazebos on the east side of Montacute in Somerset may be even a few years older than those at Edzell Castle and are much more sophisticated in craftsmanship, being among the most beautiful of their kind in Britain. But though they now surround a garden this was not their original purpose, since when the mansion was built at the end of the sixteenth century this was the main entrance and forecourt and a gatehouse stood midway between the two elegant pavilions. The planting of the large green parterre to the north of this forecourt is a nineteenth century creation and so is much of the rest of the Montacute garden, a useful reminder that by no means all Victorian gardening was vulgar. These additions are sufficiently sensitive in style and expert in craftsmanship to deceive most uninformed visitors into believing that they are a genuine part of the original conception.

A feature of many early gardens was a mount. This might be a mound of soil placed more or less centrally, or a bank against one or more of the walls, but whichever type was used its purpose was the same, to enable those inside the garden to view the world outside without venturing into it. Very few genuine mounts remain, but there is a good one of the bank-against-wall type at Northbourne Court, near Deal.

The raised walks around the parterre at Montacute House may have been originally intended as mounts, but it is equally reasonable to regard them as terraces from which the parterre could be viewed, or they may have served both purposes.

At Cranborne Manor in Dorset there is a feature known as The Mount which may be the remains of a sixteenth century mount of the central, hillock type, but now it is very broad and only a few feet high. Possibly it has been eroded by rain and wind, but a more likely explanation is that it was deliberately spread out to make the site suitable for agriculture since Cranborne was not used as a residence by its owners, the Cecils, for something like two centuries, during which they preferred to live at Hatfield which is much grander and close to London.

Probably the best idea of what a mount of this kind really looked like is to be obtained from the Queen's Garden, in the Royal Botanic Gardens, Kew, since this was made in 1960 both as a fitting setting for Kew Palace and as a fairly elaborate reconstruction of a seventeenth century garden. It is a steep hillock overlooking the Thames, ascended by a spiral path and surmounted by a wrought iron pavilion. This garden also contains a formal parterre and pool and a herb garden surrounded by a raised walk which for part of its length is enclosed in a cloister-like pleached alley, another popular feature of early gardens. This one is of laburnum.

So strong was the desire for order in gardens of this period that even the trees and shrubs were trained or clipped to regular shapes. This art of topiary was very old, but its reappearance towards the end of the mediaeval age was not, I think, a conscious copying of an ancient fashion but rather a spontaneous acceptance of a system which enabled man to be in complete control of his garden, imposing on it his own rational ideas of pattern and symmetry. Nature was disorderly, chaotic and hostile since it had fallen with man when he sinned against God's rule in the Garden of Eden. Man's highest aim was to regain the lost paradise and in a tiny way he could anticipate that in the garden of his creation.

Many examples of seventeenth century topiary remain, some grown to such monstrous size with the centuries that they no longer serve the purpose originally assigned to them but have become romantic and strange. Such are the great columns and cones of yew at Packwood House in Warwickshire, said by some to have been planted to represent Christ delivering the sermon on the mount. But as one wanders around these immense shapes, oppressed by their size and mystified as to their meaning, it is wise to make the imaginative leap necessary to visualize them as they looked during the lifetime of John Fetherston, the Puritan who planted them. It is probable that none was then more than two metres high and collectively formed a pattern in solid geometry vastly different from that which appears today.

There is a similar change of scale in the immense yew buttresses which flank the ascent to Powis Castle at Welshpool and also in the fantastic yew and box shapes at Levens Hall, Cumbria. The Levens picture has been complicated by a good deal of later planting, some in the nineteenth century when topiary came back into fashion again after having suffered a century of derision. But that is another story.

The student of gardens could probably gain a more accurate idea of what seventeenth century garden makers really intended by looking at some much more recent reconstructions, such as the charming pool garden in Hampton Court or the tiny White Garden in Dutch style at Hidcote in Gloucestershire. Here the topiary specimens have not had time to grow out of scale and they do fulfil their purpose of converting largely flat patterns into solid geometry with a three dimensional instead of a two dimensional effect. There is another fine example of this in a notably different style at Penshurst Place in Kent, where box is trimmed into large slabs like masonry to decorate the parterre in front of the house.

The use of this new term 'parterre' indicates the growing influence of French ideas in garden making as England became more settled and the wealth of middle and upper classes increased. Parterre literally means a level area of ground and can be used for plain terrace or lawn, but is more commonly applied to areas in which beds, plants and ornaments are arranged in a perfectly symmetrical way. Frequently the beds themselves are exactly like the knots in older gardens, but whereas knots were used singly or in a completely random assortment the parterre was a carefully thought out and completely balanced composition, often on a very large scale. There are no parterres in Britain to compare with the finest French creations, as at Versailles and Vaux-le-Vicomte, and many of those that were made were destroyed a few years later by the landscape revolution of the eighteenth century. But some good parterres do remain, a few having existed more or less continuously since their inception, the majority being nineteenth or twentieth century reconstructions.

Water often played a major role in these large scale geometric compositions, just as it did in the Italian, French and Dutch gardens which they imitated. Splendid reconstructions of both types of parterre, plant and water, are to be seen at Blenheim Palace in Oxfordshire, and there are the remains of a genuine seventeenth century garden of this type, but with later additions, at Wrest Park in Bedfordshire. Here the parterres lead to a long, canal-like pool at the far end of which is a handsome pavilion which provides the terminal point of an impressive vista from the house.

Canal pools were a feature of numerous gardens at this period and a few still remain. The largest is the great canal, the Long Water, at Hampton Court, which is nearly a mile in length. Another very big canal is at Chatsworth, notable both for the impressive way in which it displays the house and for the gigantic single jet of the Emperor Fountain which was placed towards the house end of the pool at a much later date.

But in some ways the most interesting of all these seventeenth century canals, partly because of its relative complexity, partly because it is one of the few remaining in an area in which gardens of this type were at one time common, is at Westbury Court (Westbury-on-Severn, Gloucestershire).

Here there are two canals side by side, one perfectly straight and plain and centred on a slender two-storey pavilion, the other broader, T-shaped and with a Neptune statue at the intersection of the two arms. These twin canals are surrounded by low yew hedges and lawns, broken only by one small group of patterned beds. Westbury Court itself was demolished some years ago to make way for some old people's homes, but this does not matter greatly since it never played any important part in the garden design which centred on the gazebo. At one time this unique garden had fallen into such disrepair that it seemed it must disappear altogether, but it has been splendidly reconstructed by the National Trust. Flowers are confined to a couple of straight borders across one end and down one side, the group of beds on the largest lawn and to a little walled garden behind a single-storey pavilion which balances the tall gazebo in the opposite corner.

A few miles from Westbury Court is another of these west country canal pools at Frampton Court (Frampton-on-Severn, Gloucestershire). This one is simpler in design than that at Westbury Court, consisting of one pool only, but like it centred not on the house but on a two-storey pavilion, this one a rather elaborate example of the neo-Gothic style and sufficiently large to have been converted in recent years into a separate residence.

Another idea copied from the French and very popular with garden makers in the late seventeenth and early eighteenth centuries was the *allée*. The word of course means alley, and some would argue that it is precious to use a French word when an English one is available. I do not agree. There had been simple alleys and pleached alleys in British gardens for generations before the French conception became fashionable, and the French style is so different that it seems desirable to distinguish it by using the French name. At its simplest it was a straight walk through closely planted trees and shrubs, known as boskage, but usually there would be a number of such walks intersecting one another to form a regular plan, though this would only be fully revealed on paper or from the air, since to anyone on the ground it would seem more like a labyrinth. At the intersections there might be ornaments or statues, some of them standing in a circle from which the *allées* radiated like the spokes of a wheel.

There are *allées* of this kind at Wrest Park through blocks of trees that flank the canal on each side, channelling the vista to the pavilion. Many other gardens show remnants of such *allées*, though usually partially obliterated by neglect or changed use as at Lochinch or at Tyninghame.

But by far the best British example of the French *allée* is at Bramham in Yorkshire. Unhappily a great many of the enclosing trees were blown down by a great storm in 1962, but the garden has now been replanted and so visitors have the unique opportunity of seeing a garden of this kind somewhat as it must have looked to the generation that created it. Some imagination must still be exercised since not all the trees were destroyed and so old and large specimens remain among the new and relatively small ones. The effect is inevitably patchy and a little unsatisfactory though it is improving all the

9

The straight canal and pavilion, Westbury Court (p. 235)

time as the work of replanting proceeds. But what is so interesting and rather disconcerting is to see the raw way in which the various temples, pools, statues and other ornaments, formerly dominated by the trees, now stand out as major features in their own right. It must always be a fascinating speculation whether at any period garden makers who relied heavily on trees visualized and actively planned for the effect they would make at maturity or were primarily concerned with what would appear during the likely lifetime of their patrons.

Melbourne Hall in Derbyshire is interesting as a relatively small and largely unaltered example of an early eighteenth century garden made in the French style, complete with parterres, *allées* and a unique wrought iron pavilion (*see* page 260). Another fine example of this kind of garden making is at St Paul's Walden Bury (near Hitchin, Hertfordshire).

Tree avenues have been a much more typical and continuous feature of British and Irish gardens, often used as a means of displaying notably fine species. Reference to them will therefore recur in later sections, and here it will suffice to call attention to some early examples. At Levens Hall there is an oak avenue lining what was the original entrance driveway, nearly a mile in length. It must have been planted at the beginning of the eighteenth century since the bill for the acorns from which the saplings for it were produced has been found, dated 1695. The avenue of sycamore at Lanhydrock (near Bodmin, Cornwall) is said to have been planted in 1648, and the mile long avenue of horse chestnuts which runs through Bushey Park was planted about 1690 as part of Sir Christopher Wren's plan for the improvement of Hampton Court, which is just across the road. At Antony House (near Torpoint, Cornwall) is a remarkable series of radiating avenues, each formed of a different species, including horse chestnut, oak and lime, but it is not certain whether they were all planted at the same time. Some were planted about 1794 by Repton, French fashion, appearing like woodland which has had *allées* cut through to receive them, but others cross the open fields in the usual English fashion.

At Antony House the avenues radiate through the full 360 degrees of the compass. A more usual scheme when avenues or *allées* radiate is to restrict them to a segment of a circle, a scheme known as a *patte d'oie* because of its resemblance to the bone structure of a goose's foot. Such an arrangement was often used as a means of linking a parterre with the surrounding park or woodland, and a good example is to be seen at Hampton Court.

Most of the gardens so far named were made on level or gently sloping land and in Britain there are not many hillside gardens, so common in Italy. But one notable example from the seventeenth century does still exist in excellent condition at Powis Castle, Welshpool, just within the borders of Wales. Here the same desire for a formal, orderly design is apparent, but the pattern is vertical as well as horizontal, the garden rising in a series of terraces each different in width, depth and design. There is nothing quite like it anywhere else in the British Isles.

Gardens illustrating previous section include Adare Manor, Athelhampton, Bicton, Blenheim Palace, Blickling Hall, Bramham Park, Chatsworth, Compton Acres, Compton Wynyates, Cranborne, Chilham Castle, Drummond Castle, Edzell Castle, Frampton Court, Goldney, Hampton Court, Hatfield House, Kew (Queen's Garden), Knightshayes Court, Levens Hall, Lyme Park, Melbourne Hall, Montacute House, Newstead Abbey, Packwood House, Penshurst Place, Pitmedden, Powerscourt, Powis Castle, Thornbury Castle, Tyninghame, Westbury Court, Wilton House, Wrest Park.

CLASSICAL LANDSCAPES

Early in the eighteenth century the whole concept of the formal garden with its geometric patterns, regular shapes and axial symmetry began to be questioned. The assault came primarily from poets and writers, Pope and Addison prominent among them, and for the first time it was suggested that nature might after all be the best guide. Each site, it was argued, had its own character which should dictate the kind of garden that was made in it and both plan and planting should enhance, not obliterate the native genius of the place.

These were revolutionary doctrines, at that time unique to England in the Western World, though similar ideas had been pursued by Chinese garden makers. But as with most revolutions the changes proposed did not come immediately, indeed at the beginning it was not even entirely clear what those changes should be. There was, in fact, a considerable period of experiment and transition, lasting for more than a generation, during which some exceptionally beautiful gardens were made, of which my own favourite is Studley Royal in Yorkshire.

But before considering these matters in greater detail it is worth looking back at an older garden, already mentioned, in which maybe some of the first stirrings of these new ideas can be traced. This is Levens Hall, Cumbria, which readers will recollect has a fantastic topiary garden and a mile long avenue of oaks planted at the beginning of the eighteenth century. But what is remarkable about this avenue is that it does not proceed in a straight line from entrance gates to hall, as one would expect, but is centred on the River Kent here flowing through a beautiful gorge which turns it in a dog leg. This made it possible to align the avenue almost precisely on the upper reach of the river while the drive itself, now obliterated, must have turned sharply away to reach the road. It is as though the makers of the avenue were accepting the slight inconvenience to travellers for the express purpose of calling attention to the natural beauty of the place. That impression is enhanced by the fact that beeches were planted along the lip of the gorge as if to emphasize its shape and depth, and further clumps of trees were planted on the far side very much in the manner adopted by landscape designers half a century later.

On the other side of Levens Hall there is another tree avenue and this is separated from the formal garden, not by a wall or fence, as might be expected, but by a sunken ditch or ha-ha, a device much used by later landscapers.

There are many questions to be answered about Levens Hall, but the park and its avenue and trees are shown on a plan by Robert Skyring made about 1730, very much as they are today.

It is possible that historians will not accord Levens Hall any part in the landscape revolution despite the fascinating evidence of the features I have described. All would agree that Chiswick House in west London was a starting point, as was Pope's own garden at Twickenham, of which unhappily little remains, and the much vaster creations at Studley Royal and Castle Howard, both in Yorkshire, and both miraculously preserved.

The garden of Chiswick House was re-designed for Lord Burlington by William Kent, who was later to remake large parts of Stowe for Lord Cobham. There were at this period great changes in architecture as well as in gardening, with classical themes dominant. Every man of means or position had received a classical education and Rome was seen romantically as the centre of a golden age of the past. Added to all of this was the discovery by English travellers of the work of the seventeenth century school of landscape painters in Rome. The paintings of Claude Lorrain, Gaspar Poussin and Salvator Rosa suddenly became popular and their vision of an arcadian countryside rich with trees, lakes and ruins became a model for imitation in a real and not merely a canvas world.

So at Chiswick House Burlington designed a temple-like building in which he could display his art treasures, and Kent made alterations to the garden, which converted a formal canal into a meandering stream and in general softened the firm outlines and geometric shapes that already existed. Much of Kent's creation has now disappeared under a sea of suburban houses, but sufficient remains to give some idea of what he and his patron were about. Today it looks formal and not so greatly unlike the parterres and *allées* it was meant to displace, but to contemporary eyes it must have appeared very different.

Of Pope's garden so little remains that it is impossible to form any idea merely by looking at it what it was originally like. Even the grotto of which Pope was so proud, and which by a subterranean passageway linked a garden by the Thames with a second on the other side of the road, is now dull and dingy, a place completely lacking in magic. But good grottoes, so typical of this and later periods, do still exist, none better than one made in Bristol in 1747 by Thomas Goldney, a prosperous Quaker businessman who built himself a house in Clifton overlooking the city and River Avon, made a charming garden, more seventeenth than eighteenth century in character, and constructed an elaborate, shell-lined grotto. This, thanks to the care of the authorities of Bristol University, who now use Goldney House as a hall of residence, is still almost in mint condition.

Almost at the same time that Kent was altering the gardens at Chiswick House, John Aislabie was making an entirely new garden far to the north at Studley Royal. Here his invention was untrammelled by anything already in existence since he was working in a previously uncultivated valley out of sight of his house. For the first time a garden was being made as a complete end in itself, not as a setting for a building, still less as a stage on which crowds of important people could display themselves.

Aislabie's garden consists of large sheets of water set in smooth green turf and surrounded by trees with various classical buildings, one of which, a white colonnaded temple, is placed to be reflected in the mirror-like surface of the central circular pool. All the shapes are still regular, as they were in earlier gardens, but the effect is entirely different. Studley Royal is a magical place, intended to create a mood of contemplation and succeeding triumphantly in that purpose. Though very large it is best appreciated in complete solitude and it is said that John Aislabie liked most of all to visit it by moonlight.

Further up the valley and still further removed from any habitation are the ruins of Fountains Abbey. Again it is said that John Aislabie wished to purchase the abbey and incorporate it in his garden, but this was not possible in his lifetime. Not until years later was his son able to realize his father's dream and by then the English gardening revolution was complete, and what emerged was an idealized landscape owing nothing to rationality and geometry but everything to imagination and poetry. So in one short afternoon, by walking from Studley Royal to Fountains Abbey, the visitor can relive the years that changed the whole course of British garden making and were even to affect the character of the English landscape itself.

While John Aislabie was at work at Studley Royal, Lord Carlisle was embarking upon a very different experiment in garden making at Castle Howard not many miles away. John Vanbrugh had recently completed the mansion which stands on a ridge commanding extensive views both to north and south. At first garden making proceeded on conventionally formal lines, but soon Carlisle, assisted by various advisors, began to apply the new pictorial ideas and to embellish the landscape with a large lake and serpentine river, numerous buildings and trees disposed to make a natural setting for them, rather in the manner of a landscape painting by Claude Lorrain. Almost everything remains and the creator of this great landscape, the first garden really to merit that description, lies buried in the great domed mausoleum designed by Hawksmoor, which is both the largest and the most distant building he used to diversify it. Castle Howard has all the elements used by later landscapers, such as Henry Hoare at Stourhead, Lord Cobham assisted by Kent at Stowe, and Launcelot Brown in scores of gardens. Though it lacks the integrated composition of the best of these and has not the mysterious magic of Studley Royal, it is nevertheless an impressive achievement and fascinating as a precursor of what was to come.

Some time in the 1730s Kent began to work at Rousham in Oxfordshire,

A satyr at Rousham
House (p. 202)

redesigning the house and reshaping a garden already made by Bridgeman who had some regard for the new principles of design. But Bridgeman found it difficult to throw off the shackles of geometry and Kent's achievement at Rousham was to make the design conform much more closely to the natural characteristics of the land. Much of the garden is out of sight of the house and is intended to create a series of idyllic scenes which should be seen in a particular sequence so that each new vista opens up in its most effective way. There is a little valley enclosed by woodland, with two cascades feeding a large pool. A rill twists its way through woodland, filling a large stone-lined basin for bathing on its way. A wide avenue is centred at one end on a large statue of Hercules and at the other on a long, low temple set into the valley side. A grass slope with another temple looks out on the River Cherwell and the old stone bridge which crosses it. The whole garden is contained by the river which dictates its extent and separates it from the countryside of which it is an idealized reflection.

Yet at Rousham there were still echoes of the past. The cascades are clearly artificial, framed in stone and one bearing a statue of Venus with flanking swans. The avenue looks much like a wide French *allée* except that the trees are not trimmed, and even the serpentine rill, which was regarded

14

as a daring innovation at the time, is neatly channelled in a stone-lined trough. Apart from the fact that the trees are much larger and more dense than they could ever have been in Kent's day, Rousham remains much as it then was, rather overgrown in places but miraculously untouched by all the changing fashions that were to destroy or transform many other eighteenth century gardens.

Kent's greatest work was at Stowe in Buckinghamshire, where he worked for and with Lord Cobham, another aristocrat devotee of the new landscape style. This garden, too, had previously been laid out by Bridgeman, but the scale was much larger than at Rousham and the transformation to what we would regard as a natural style far more complete. Straight lines and circles were finally banished and by the time Stowe was completed, after the deaths of both Kent and Cobham, it had grown into what many experts still regard as the finest eighteenth century landscape garden in the classical manner.

Stowe has suffered more change than Rousham, but not of any fundamental kind. It is used today as a public school, some parts of the famous park have become playing fields and a golf course, and part of the lake is used for rowing and sailing. But none of this has necessitated any major alteration of the landscape and it is big enough to absorb minor ones with a minimum of disturbance. More serious is the intrusion of new buildings required for the college, but in the main these have been sited with discretion and from many parts of the garden are completely invisible.

The Temple of Ancient Virtue, Stowe (p. 217)

Stowe is remarkable for its size, its cohesion and the large number of temples, arches and other structures it contains. The original approach was from Buckingham up a mile long avenue of beech, through a huge Corinthian arch from which the first distant view of landscape and building was obtained, and then by a circuitous route around the perimeter of the park to reach the mansion on the far side by way of a handsome stone bridge and past two fine stone pavilions. Today one can still drive up the avenue, but the road turns left well before the arch and does not enter the park until the bridge is close at hand. In consequence the uninstructed visitor gets a totally different first impression. It need not be so, for the old track, rather rough but still usable, does continue to the Corinthian arch and, though it is impossible to continue through it, it is worth going up to it to absorb that first tremendous view, then return and explore the whole great landscape item by item.

Stowe possesses one of three similar bridges made at around this period as decorative structures for three different gardens, the other two being at Wilton House (near Salisbury, Wiltshire) and at Prior Park (Bath, Avon). All are elaborate, built of stone and roofed, and all are said to be based on an original drawing by Andrea Palladio, the Italian architect whose work inspired much of eighteenth century British architecture. Because of this supposed origin they are known as Palladian bridges. That at Stowe is the only one of the trio which serves a practical as well as an ornamental purpose, since one of the circulatory roads in the park actually crosses it.

The names of some of the principal features at Stowe, the Elysian Fields, the Grecian Valley, the Temple of Venus, the Temple of Virtue and the

The Palladian Bridge, Wilton House (p. 238)

1. The Pond Garden, Hampton Court (*see* page 145)

2. The moat and ruins, Scotney Castle (*see* page 208)

3, 4 & 5. Inverewe. *(top)* **The view across Loch Ewe;** *(bottom left)* *Primula* **Inverleith;** *(bottom right) Meconopsis grandis (see* **page 157)**

The Pantheon, Stourhead (p. 215)

Rotunda, emphasize the classical inspiration of the garden. In places such as this educated gentlemen could imagine themselves as Roman statesmen, philosophers or poets communing with great figures from a golden age.

Rousham and Stowe make their greatest appeal to those who have a similar knowledge and reverence for the past. Stourhead (near Mere, Wiltshire) has a universal attraction which requires neither classical nor specialist knowledge of any kind to be appreciated. It is, in consequence, the most popular eighteenth century landscape in Britain, and by any standard must be regarded as one of the most beautiful. It was made from 1745 onwards by Henry Hoare, a wealthy banker, and later altered and further developed by his grandson, Richard Colt Hoare, towards the end of the century. Since then it has acquired some new trees and shrubs, including rhododendrons which give it spring colour not available in Henry Hoare's day, and by some purists regarded as an unjustifiable intrusion. Yet the biggest crowds come at rhododendron time and it is probable that without them the National Trust would find it difficult to maintain the garden in its present superb condition. So it might seem wise to keep the late spring colour and suggest to those who are offended by it that they visit Stourhead at any other time of the year since it is constantly beautiful.

Again like Studley Royal and Rousham the main garden is not visible from the house and was intended as a tour, to be followed in an accepted way, so that one enchanting view would unfold after another. Today most visitors arrive at the church which should be the final point of the journey, but really it seems to matter very little for Stourhead is lovely from whichever angle one views it and in whatever order. Still, for those who wish to relive the past, the proper starting point is the house, across the lawn to enter a path which leads in one direction along the lip of the valley in which the garden lies, and in the other down the valley side. The first route, long overgrown, is being cleared to reopen the original view of a tall obelisk. The second route opens up almost immediately a vista of Apollo's Temple, apparently floating in the trees on the opposite side of the valley.

The walk continues transversely down the valley side to reach the upper end of the largest of three lakes which Hoare made by damming the valley at strategic points. From this point there are views up the valley across the top lake and into the countryside, and down the valley across the big lake, but still with the major objects that decorate it out of sight. These consist of temples, a rustic cottage, a large grotto and a stone bridge, with occasionally a distant glimpse of the obelisk as one proceeds around the lake on a well made path. At every point there is a new picture. The garden is a photographer's dream, though as one wryly remarked, 'It can cost you a fortune'.

Henry Hoare and Richard Colt Hoare were both amateurs and though they had professional assistance, Stourhead must be regarded as mainly their creation. Lancelot Brown was a professional, born and educated in the little village of Kirkharle and nearby Cambo in Northumberland, apprenticed as a gardener at Kirkharle, and then coming south to take charge of the kitchen garden at Stowe. There he learned enough about garden making to set up on his own account in 1751, and over the next thirty-two years he was to make more landscape gardens and in the process destroy more of the old formal gardens, than any single person before or since.

Brown (he acquired the sobriquet 'Capability' because it is said that when called in to advise he would often say that the estate had great capabilities) made or altered nearly two hundred gardens, many of which remain in some degree, though often with completely changed purpose, and sometimes transformed by new planting, as we shall see in a later chapter. But enough are sufficiently intact to give an exact idea of what he was about, and there is no doubt that more than any other single person he succeeded in changing the English landscape.

A criticism of Brown is that he worked to a formula, with lawns sweeping right up to the house, smoothly contoured land, a lake in the middle distance, maybe a temple or two as eye-catchers or focal points, clumps of trees to channel the views and belts of trees to contain them. This is in a measure true, but since every site is different and Brown was always ready to make good use of natural advantages there is great variety and they are rarely boring as the 'formula' theory would suggest.

Bowood (Studley, Wiltshire) perfectly illustrates Brown's principles with the one exception that the grass of the landscape no longer continues right to the house walls, having been replaced there in the mid-nineteenth century by level terraces with stone balustrades. But beyond these the prospect is almost entirely as Brown planned it, with a magnificent lake, fine trees well placed in belts, clumps and as isolated specimens, and one small temple strategically placed to catch the eye. Bowood is also supremely well maintained and is a very beautiful place. The water leaves the lake by a large cascade which falls over a very natural looking, though completely artificial rock face, honeycombed with subterranean passages and grottoes, but these have been closed for the safety of the public.

Another of Brown's great achievements can be seen at Blenheim Palace, though here he worked not on virgin land, but over one of the most elaborate of the early eighteenth century formal gardens, which he completely destroyed in the process. It was not until the twentieth century that Blenheim's parterres were restored, not as a reconstruction of the past, but to the entirely new designs of a Frenchman, Achille Duchêne, who specialized in this kind of thing. So today at Blenheim the visitor can see an amalgam of two entirely opposed styles, the formality of the early style of gardening around the mansion giving way to the 'natural' gardening of the eighteenth centuries in the outer policies.

Brown was followed by Humphry Repton, an impecunious gentleman artist who took up garden designing as a means of earning a living. Repton was as industrious as Brown and over two hundred parks and gardens are attributed to him, though most have suffered so much change that it is often difficult to determine just what is Repton's work and what the result of the depredations of time or the additions of later owners. However Repton introduced a unique method of conveying his ideas to his clients. He used his skill as an artist to paint the place as it was and then, by means of a series of vignettes which could be folded over or away from the picture, to indicate at a glance exactly what transformations his proposals would make. These pictures, with a written description of the proposed work, were bound into a slim volume between red covers, whence they are known as Repton's 'Red Books', and these have become valuable works of art, carefully preserved by owners or in libraries. A few have been assembled and reproduced as expensive limited edition books. It is desirable that more should be made available in this way, since they are fascinating in themselves and still provide useful instruction in the landscape designer's art.

Reptonian parks tend to have trees more dispersed than in Brown's work, often planted as individual specimens or in small groups. Repton also reintroduced terraces and avenues in the vicinity of the house and its approaches. His landscapes paved the way to the more plant conscious parks and gardens of the Victorian era.

Gardens illustrating previous section include Antony House, Blenheim Palace, Blickling Hall, Bowood, Castle Howard, Chilham Castle, Chiswick House, Claremont Woods, Corsham Court, Dodington House, Duncombe Park, Harewood House, Longleat, Luton Hoo, Prior Park, Rievaulx Terrace, Rousham House, Shugborough (Grecian influence), Stourhead, Stowe, Studley Royal (transition), Syon House, Trentham, Weston Park, West Wycombe Park, Wilton House, Woburn, Wrest Park.

PICTURESQUE LANDSCAPE

Many things were happening in the closing decades of the eighteenth century. Brown's style of smooth, sophisticated landscape was being widely criticized as tame and unimaginative. In architecture the classical style that had dominated so much of the Georgian period was giving way to a greater romanticism and this was also finding expression in gardens. The Gothic style was coming back into favour, and many gardens had gothic ruins, pavilions and other eye-catchers in place of the classical temples, rotundas, arches and bridges that had previously been in vogue. Some garden makers turned for romanticism to the Far East, making pagodas, tea houses and other buildings in what was believed to be the Chinese or Japanese manner. As early as 1757 Sir William Chambers wrote a book on the subject, though he had never visited any part of Asia. He designed the tall pagoda which is still a prominent landmark in the Royal Botanic Gardens, Kew. Among the many garden buildings at Shugborough, Staffordshire, mostly based on Grecian models, is one Chinese pavilion, and much earlier than this Henry Hoare had actually included a 'Turkish Tent' in his Stourhead decorations, though this does not seem to have remained for long, which is not surprising since it was made of canvas, the inside painted blue and white in mosaic, according to a contemporary account.

At Strawberry Hill, Twickenham, Horace Walpole was building his house as well as his garden buildings with such a delicate and light hearted version of the gothic style that it really started a style of its own, often referred to as Strawberry Hill gothic.

A little later Indian styles were tried; Nash built the Pavilion at Brighton for the Prince Regent; and Thomas Daniell, who had made a special study of Indian architecture and written a book about it, built Sezincote (Moreton-in-Marsh, Gloucestershire). It is said that Repton had a hand in the garden making here, which is one of the few remaining to illustrate this rather brief and not very popular phase. Certainly Sezincote is fascinating both as a house and garden, the former crowned by an onion-shaped dome, the latter with an Indian style temple, fountain and bridge, with a serpent ascending a pole as an additional ornament, the whole assembled around a stream which flows swiftly through a little glen. But the planting of this garden is very much of the twentieth century, with shrubs, herbaceous

20

plants and bamboos dominant, and the arrangement taking careful account of colour associations, a refinement which earlier generations of garden makers seem seldom, if ever, to have considered.

'Picturesque' was the fashionable word to describe these new trends, and if the garden was not picturesque, in the sense that a painter would have found in it variety of colour, texture and form to fire his imagination, it was not up to date.

Two further gardens may serve to illustrate what was happening by the early decades of the nineteenth century; one Alton Towers (near Uttoxeter, Staffordshire), which was commenced by the 15th Earl of Shrewsbury in 1814 and finished by his son, the 16th Earl, about 1835; the other Scotney Castle (Lamberhurst, Kent), made by Edward Hussey from 1836 onwards.

Both are largely the work of amateurs, though with professional help, especially in the design of the buildings which accompany them. Alton Towers is pure Gothic revival, the mansion a fantastic assemblage of turrets and towers designed at least in part by Pugin, who also had a hand in the Houses of Parliament. Built, like the garden, at enormous expense, it is today largely a ruin, which matters little since this rather enhances the romantic effect it was intended to make.

The garden fills a large valley to one side of this mansion and it contains a variety of strange structures, including a model of Stonehenge, a spiral fountain, a Roman colonnade, an elaborate conservatory, a Grecian temple and an elegant Chinese pagoda which spurts water into the air from its apex. Early prints show these disparate objects standing in an almost bare landscape, but now the small trees, already visible in these illustrations,

A picturesque landscape – Scotney Castle (p. 208)

have grown to maturity, many more have been added and the buildings have been so completely embedded in foliage that they no longer seem incongruous, but have become merely intriguing eye-catchers to be sought out and inspected one by one. Here is an outstanding example of time improving, not destroying, a garden, and Alton Towers has even been able to absorb the miniature railway, cable cars and other diversions which have converted it into one of the most successful amusement parks in Britain.

Scotney Castle could scarcely be more different and yet remain within the same picturesque school. It is romantic, but not gothic; it was made with the utmost good taste and though time has probably increased its beauty it must have been delightful from the moment it was completed.

The garden centres upon a group of genuine old buildings surrounded by a moat sufficiently wide at one side to be called a lake. There is the keep of a fourteenth century castle and the remains both of a sixteenth century reconstruction of part of the castle and of the adjacent seventeenth century villa, which (until 1836) was still the residence of Edward Hussey. Then he decided to build himself a fine new house overlooking the valley in which these buildings lie, and, by partial, carefully considered demolition, to convert the seventeenth century villa into romantic ruins which would make the focal point for a picturesque landscape, the finest view of which would be from the study windows of his new house. Woodland to contain the vista was already there in plenty; a quarry, opened just beneath the lip of the valley to provide stone for the new mansion, could easily be converted into a rock garden overlooked by a belvedere, and it only remained to introduce new trees and shrubs where required to embellish not only this main picture but a whole series of other delightful prospects to be revealed as the garden is explored.

Gardens illustrating this section include Alton Towers, Cliveden, Compton Acres, Cotehele House, Kew, Lanhydrock, Lochinch, Newstead Abbey, Portmeirion, Powerscourt, Rudding Park, Scotney Castle, Sezincote, Sheffield Park, Tatton Park, Woburn.

ARBORETUMS AND PINETUMS

While all these developments were taking place in what may be described as pictorial, in contrast to patterned, styles of garden making, other changes were occurring which were to have an equally profound effect on garden design throughout the British Isles. Distant parts of the world were being explored, new settlements were being made and as a result plant species were flowing back into Europe which had never been seen before. Some were of purely botanical interest, some had economic importance and many were plants of great beauty which gardeners were anxious to grow.

In the old formal gardens ornamental plants had found a place to embellish the knots and parterres or, if they required special conditions or care, they were grown in beds reserved for them. Gardeners had always been curious about new and strange plants and by the late seventeenth century numerous kinds had already been highly developed by breeding and selection. Tulips, hyacinths, anemones, ranunculus, carnations, pinks, auriculas and hollyhocks were among the plants which had prospered in this way, and which had provoked competition among gardeners who were often prepared to pay high prices for particularly desirable varieties.

Of course this kind of gardening continued throughout the eighteenth century and many gardeners did not depart from the old methods of garden making. But those who did adopt the new landscape principles found little or no place in them for such plants as these. Landscaping on the grand scale often involved planting many thousands of trees, and as a rule the cheapest and most easily produced native species were used. It is true that as landscapes became increasingly picturesque greater variety of colour might be deemed desirable, which could involve the use of exotic plants, but even so these would be almost exclusively woody plants with little or no place for herbaceous material.

So the pressure of plants grew and garden design was inevitably adapted to accommodate it. Humphry Repton was one of the first of the famous designers to restore a degree of formality in the region of the house, partly on aesthetic grounds, since many regarded it as ridiculous that fields should seemingly come right up to the windows and doors, partly because by restoring cultivated beds it was possible to grow a greater variety of plants.

Some garden makers became so obsessed with plants that they virtually abandoned design altogether and set out to establish collections of the kinds in which they were most keenly interested. So began the practice of making arboretums, which were really mixed woodlands in which a great variety of trees, many from foreign lands, could be grown. Pinetums followed as the

Picea brewerana at **Killerton** (p. 164)

number of coniferous trees increased, for the purpose of a pinetum is not, as its name might suggest, exclusively to grow pines, but any species belonging to the vast tribe of conifers of which pines are just one example.

An early example of an arboretum can be seen at Killerton (near Exeter, Devon), where planting was begun by Sir Thomas Acland, with the aid of John Veitch in 1792. The trees were planted mainly on a south facing hillside with extensive views towards Exeter. Arrangement is of the simplest, with one wide path zig-zagging up the steep slope and the trees arranged in a more or less random way with only an occasional grouping of related kinds in the manner common in botanic gardens. At the foot of the slope a more open, park-like style has been adopted, culminating on the southern boundary near the house in a long narrow rectangular garden laid out in formal beds filled with a great variety of woody and herbaceous plants. It is from this point that the finest view of the arboretum can be obtained and very impressive it is, with many mature conifers spearing their way through the more rounded shapes of broad-leaved trees.

John Veitch's grandson, Robert, was involved in the planting of a small arboretum, with special emphasis on conifers, on one of the Exeter estates that has now been absorbed into the campus of Exeter University, and here again there are some notable specimens, including some of the best *Torreya californica* in Britain. Elsewhere in the same campus are original Lucombe oaks, the famous hybrid between the cork oak, *Quercus suber* and the Turkey oak, *Q. cerris*, made by William Lucombe, an Exeter nurseryman in 1765 or thereabouts.

Not far away at Bicton (near Exmouth, Devon), attached to a garden made in the French grand manner in the eighteenth century (it is often wrongly attributed to the great French designer, Le Nôtre), is an extensive pinetum started in 1840 which contains many very large trees. Bicton is preserved by a private company as an amusement park.

The Holford family started to plant their arboretum at Westonbirt (near Tetbury, Gloucestershire) in 1829, and this has eventually grown to be the largest and probably the finest in the British Isles. Here again the main plan is simple, large blocks of trees separated by wide grass rides with many of the finest specimens planted beside these. One of the most spectacular features is a group of incense cedars (*Libocedrus decurrens*) now grown to great size and flanked by parrotias which colour brilliantly in the autumn. Westonbirt is particularly noted for its autumn colour and has one of the best groves of Japanese maples in the country, as well as thickets of a dogwood, *Cornus alba sibirica*, specially selected for the bright red colouring of the bark on its young stems.

One of the earliest British pinetums containing some original introductions by the Scottish plant collector, David Douglas, is at Scone Palace, Perth. Here there is a magnificent avenue of Western hemlocks (*Tsuga heterophylla*), as well as what is possibly the largest specimen of *Pinus jeffreyi* in the British Isles.

Though the pure arboretum and pinetum have tended to be superseded by other methods of making tree collections, some examples have continued to be made right up to the present time. The finest pinetum in the British Isles is the National Pinetum at Bedgebury, between Goudhurst and Lamberhurst in Kent. This was started in 1925 jointly by the Forestry Commission and the Royal Botanic Gardens, Kew, as soil and climate at Kew were not very satisfactory for some conifers. Bedgebury, extending over two valleys and the ridge separating them, offers a variety of sites plus clean air and a satisfactory, moderately acid soil. It is a naturally beautiful spot comparable with the valley, only a few miles away, in which the landscape of Scotney Castle was made; and, although the National Pinetum cannot compare with this in composition, it has been laid out with considerable thought for the effect the trees would make when mature. Because it is a botanical collection the different species of a genus are grouped together, yews and their relatives in one place, cedars in another, spruces in yet another and so on, but there are no straight lines, no hard drawn divisions between one group and another which merge in a seemingly natural way. There is also a useful admixture of deciduous-leaved trees to break up the rather solid mass of the mainly evergreen conifers.

Almost as large as publicly owned Bedgebury is the privately made Winkworth Arboretum which occupies a hillside near Godalming in Surrey. There is a large lake at the foot of the hill, but this does not enter as much as it might into the landscaping of this arboretum which seems to have been planned by its maker, Dr Wilfred Fox, primarily as a collection. It is particularly beautiful in the autumn because it contains an impressive number of berry-bearing trees and shrubs and species with good autumn foliage colour, but there is also fine colour at Winkworth in May when rhododendrons and azaleas are at their peak and there is a continuous carpet of bluebells in the woodland.

The most recent arboretum, that at Jermyns (near Romsey, Hampshire), is also privately made, by Harold Hillier. It really all started with a few trees left over in nursery beds, since Mr Hillier is also head of a great nursery firm. These trees, close to his home, provided the basis for a collection which has spread ever further until it now stretches across a considerable valley and has been continued on the other side of a road to give space for a special collection of rhododendrons. The latest addition is a kind of sub-tropical garden made in a disused sandpit.

Fine collections of trees are found in the following gardens: Batsford, Bedgebury Pinetum, Benmore, Bicton, Birr Castle, Borde Hill, Castlewellan, Chatsworth, Claremont Woods, Dawyck, Eastnor Castle, Exeter University, Hergest Croft, Jermyns Arboretum, Kew, Killerton, Leonardslee, Lochinch, Longleat, Mount Usher, Nuneham Courtenay Arboretum, Nymans, Powerscourt, Powis Castle, Scone Palace, Sheffield Park, Stourhead, Syon Park, Valley Gardens, Wakehurst Place, Westonbirt Arboretum, Winkworth Arboretum, Wisley.

PLANTS FROM WARMER CLIMATES

The changes we have been considering in garden aims and styles were profound, but there was yet another that was to have equally potent (and some might consider less desirable) effects on garden design. Many of the new plants came from climates far warmer than our own. They could not be grown with safety out of doors throughout the year, though some were quite happy outside during the summer months. So if they were to be grown at all, some means must be found to protect them at least in winter.

For the start of this particular story we must go back to the seventeenth century or earlier. The first partially tender plant (or half-hardy to use the currently accepted garden description) to capture the imagination of British gardeners was the orange, which arrived at the end of the sixteenth century. No doubt the interest was in part due to the mythical and legendary associations of this eastern fruit, but there were good practical reasons too, for the orange is a handsome evergreen and the British Isles are woefully short of native evergreen trees and shrubs. So by the end of the seventeenth century everybody who was anybody in the gardening world grew oranges. They were cultivated in ornamental tubs or other containers in which they could be placed outdoors in summer and then, before there was danger of severe frost in autumn, could be carried into some reasonably light but sheltered place. So the orangery was born, precursor of the conservatory and greenhouse, which in Victorian times were to attain a pinnacle of excellence with only technical improvements to follow in our own times.

The early orangeries were inevitably rather inefficient as places in which to create a controlled climate for plants, though they were often very handsome buildings in their own right. Usually they were built of stone, though at Saltram House near Plymouth, there is a fine example constructed mainly of wood. They were roofed like a house and their illumination came from large windows, usually confined to front and sides, with a solid wall behind. Heating, if any, would be from coal or wood fires with flues in floor or back walls. Probably the largest ever made is at Margam House, Port Talbot, and now the property of West Glamorgan County Council. Built in 1789 this mammoth structure is 100 metres in length. Such buildings served well enough for fairly tough plants such as oranges, especially as these could go outdoors during most of the period from May to September when they were making their growth, but they proved unsatisfactory for more difficult plants as these were introduced.

So architects went to work to design more satisfactory buildings, better lit and heated and capable of keeping plants in good condition throughout the year, if that were necessary. Some very attractive conservatories were produced, none finer than that at Syon House, on the western outskirts of London. In this, although the structure is framed in stone, both front and

Evolution of the greenhouse – *(left)*
Tatton Park orangery (p. 222), *(right)*
Bicton conservatory (p. 87), *(below)*
Edinburgh Botanic Garden plant
house (p. 131)

roof are glazed and there is sufficient light to meet the requirements of a great variety of plants, including many from South Africa and Australasia which do not mind a fairly dry atmosphere.

But even the Syon conservatory was originally flue heated, and it was the use of cast iron water pipes with consequent better distribution of heat, reduced danger of fumes damaging to plants and less drying of the air that made further progress possible. Then came narrow iron girders and glazing bars and beautiful structures such as the great palm house in the Royal Botanic Gardens, Kew, and a lovely conservatory with curving roof against a wall in Bicton Gardens (Exmouth, Devon). Chatsworth in Derbyshire also had a vast conservatory designed by the then head gardener, Joseph Paxton, later knighted; a building which was the prototype for the Crystal Palace in which the Great Exhibition of 1851 was housed. The Chatsworth conservatory had to be demolished in 1919, but plant cases against a wall, another nineteenth century invention, still remain.

Recently Chatsworth has taken the lead again with the first privately owned plant house built on a new principle, first used in the Edinburgh Botanic Garden, in which much of the weight of the glass is supported from outside by steel cables attached to slender gantry-like structures. By this means fewer glazing bars can be used, insuring minimum interference with light, while inside supports can be eliminated, leaving the space entirely free for plants to be disposed in any way desired. Such modern greenhouses have thermostatically controlled heating, usually by small bore steam pipes and automatic ventilation so that any desired climatic conditions can be maintained with a minimum of uncertainty.

Gardens to illustrate this section include Bicton (conservatory), Blickling Hall (orangery), Bristol Zoo, Cambridge Botanic Garden, Charlecote Park (orangery), Chatsworth, Culzean (orangery), Dodington House (conservatory), Edinburgh Botanic Garden, Glasgow Botanic Garden, Glasnevin Botanic Garden, Hampton Court, Hyde Hall, Kew, Lyme Park (orangery), Montacute House (orangery), Powis Castle (orangery), Saltram House (orangery), Syon Park (conservatory), Tatton Park, Threave, Wallington, Wisley, Woburn Abbey.

Victorian Display

The development of glasshouses solved one problem but produced a new one of its own. In these improved conditions plants could be multiplied with a speed and precision previously impossible. Annuals and 'easy' plants such as pelargoniums, heliotropes and marguerites, as well as bright foliage plants, such as alternantheras and iresines, could be produced in their thousands. But what to do with them when the greenhouses and conservatories were full to overflowing?

The answer came in a system of plant rotation which came to be known as bedding out. Plants were put outdoors when conditions were favourable for them and when they were at the height of their beauty. Some would stay outdoors for several months at a time, others might be retained for much shorter periods, perhaps no more than a week or so. They would be used mainly for the purpose of mass display, packed tightly together in beds, often forming coloured patterns within the overall pattern created by the shapes and arrangement of the beds themselves.

Impetus was given to this fashion by the arrival of many new annual plants, particularly the half-hardy annuals from South Africa, South and Central America and other warm climates since these almost all had an extended flowering period. They could be raised easily in tens of thousands each spring in the new glasshouses and acclimatized, or hardened off to use the gardening term, in time to be planted out in late May or early June when there was little further danger of frost sufficiently severe or prolonged to kill them. Other plants, not strictly annuals, could be multiplied in the same cheap and prolific way and it was not long before a considerable and profitable trade had emerged in the commercial exploitation of these seed-raised bedding plants.

The terraces which Humphry Repton and others of his period had reintroduced to gardens were ideal for this kind of display gardening and by the mid-nineteenth century terraces were the fashion and everyone was adding them to their gardens if they were not there already.

Landscapes by Lancelot Brown, as at Harewood House, near Leeds, and Trentham, near Stoke on Trent, acquired terraces in the Italian Renaissance style. Great formal gardens such as Powerscourt, south of Dublin, and Waddesdon Manor, near Aylesbury, brimmed over with pelargoniums and all the other popular favourites. W. A. Nesfield, who with Charles Barry designed the terraces at Trentham, also laid out the formal area around the Palm House at Kew, expressly for the purpose of bedding out.

Examples could be multiplied indefinitely, but most have fallen into disuse, killed by the mounting expense of producing and caring for such vast numbers of plants. Bedding out on the grand scale is now almost restricted to public parks, where it remains as popular as ever. Specially fine examples are to be seen in many of the London parks, including Regent's Park, Hyde Park, St. James's Park and the Embankment Gardens, at Hampton Court Palace and in the Brighton parks, but there is scarcely a park's department throughout the country that does not pride itself on this kind of gardening. Interesting to the historian, because a genuine example of a Victorian garden made with bedding out in mind, is Bristol Zoo, which still remains a small but notable example of the genre.

The art of carpet bedding is also preserved in a few parks and public gardens. In this special form of bedding out all plants used are either naturally very short or are kept short by frequent pinching out of shoot tips. By this means a close carpet of growth is produced and the plants are arranged to

29

make patterns, reproduce coats of arms, mottoes or other messages or even to form clock faces complete with floral hands rotated by clockwork or electrical mechanism concealed beneath the bed. Floral clocks are still a feature of some parks in Britain and fine examples of carpet bedding are to be seen in Waverley Gardens, Edinburgh, in Rouken Glen Park, Glasgow, and at Victoria Park, also in Glasgow, and in several of the London borough parks.

Gardens illustrating this section include Ascott, Bristol Zoo, Chatsworth, Cliveden, Chester Zoo, Drummond Castle, Dunrobin Castle, Holker Hall, Kew, Lanhydrock, Tatton Park, Trentham, Waddesdon Manor, Wrest Park.

PUBLIC PARKS

It is appropriate that public parks should be the final repository for Victorian specialities such as bedding out and carpet bedding since they were themselves virtually a Victorian invention. Parks open to the public had existed before but they were Crown property such as Hyde Park, Regent's Park and St. James's Park and were not owned, let alone created, by municipalities as was the flood of new parks which started at about the time Victoria came to the throne. The first appears to have been made in Derby and still exists, though it is now one of the minor open spaces of that great midland city. It is known as Derby Arboretum, though it was not planned primarily as a collection of trees but as a place in which citizens could walk and so get healthy exercise. It is one of the very few gardens designed by John Claudius Loudon, one of the most prolific and influential horticultural writers of the time, and it is really a rather curious place. The site, presumably more or less level when work began, has been worked into a number of low ridges and hillocks with trees scattered all over the place, not obviously to any particular plan. It is not very inspiring, though it probably does still fulfil fairly well its original purpose of providing a green and leafy promenade for residents in a rather dreary part of the city, and nowadays it has a good bowling green and other facilities for sport which its creators almost certainly did not envisage.

Derby Arboretum was completed in 1840. Two years later another famous writer, Samuel Curtis, proprietor and editor of *Curtis's Botanical Magazine*, was busy working on a much more ambitious and exciting park in east London which prevented him for several years from joining his daughter in Jersey. But I will come back to this.

In Victoria Park, east London, the image of the public park was really created. There was a large lake with islands, plenty of grass and trees for recreation, flower borders and bedding out. It remains to this day an attractive and entertaining place, admirably serving the purpose for which it was created.

Other parks followed in rapid succession until every town of any size and consequence had at least one, and many of the larger cities had several. Some were created expressly as parks from more or less bare sites. Others were old, privately owned parks purchased by or donated to local authorities and adapted by them for their new role. Yet others were gardens which could no longer be maintained by their owners. Some very famous places have been saved for posterity in this way, notably Newstead Abbey (Ravenshead, Nottinghamshire), once the home of Lord Byron and now a park belonging to Nottingham Corporation; Pollok House (Glasgow), maintained by Glasgow Corporation; and Highdown (Goring-by-Sea, Sussex), Britain's best known chalk garden, now maintained by Worthing Corporation. In other instances there has been a sharing of responsibilities which has enabled fine gardens to be maintained. Tatton Park (Knutsford, Cheshire), Lyme Park (Disley, Greater Manchester) and Shugborough (near Stoke-on-Trent, Staffordshire) all belong to the National Trust, but are leased for use as parks, to Cheshire County Council, Stockport Corporation and Staffordshire County Council respectively.

Some of these will be found described in greater detail in other parts of this book, but there are now so many good parks in the British Isles that it would be impossible to include them all here. This is a subject for a separate book and it is really rather surprising that no one has yet written it.

Help from the Gulf Stream

Better greenhouses were not the only Victorian answer to the problem of growing tender exotic plants. It soon became apparent that the milder climate of certain parts of the country could be exploited for this purpose provided certain difficulties could be overcome. In the British Isles the highest winter temperatures occur near the coast, and particularly in the coastal regions of south-west England, western Scotland and most of the Irish coast. All these benefit from the equable temperatures of the North Atlantic Drift, which is the northerly branch of the Gulf Stream, and known to most people by that name, which is therefore used here. This water varies little in temperature between summer and winter and washes all these shores.

The problems arise because these same maritime districts are nearly all exposed to fierce gales, often accompanied by salt drift which may penetrate many miles inland. Because of these hazards these areas are often relatively treeless, which increases the exposure of smaller plants. For all these reasons natural vegetation is usually sparse, there is often little depth of soil over the rock and what there is is poor.

Nowhere in the British Isles were all these advantages and drawbacks more vividly contrasted than at Gairloch on the north-west coast of Scotland, but it was here, on a little peninsula of almost barren rock, near the

31

village of Poolewe, that Osgood Mackenzie started to make the garden of Inverewe in 1862. Even soil had to be carried to the site to make cultivation possible, and to protect the garden from the fierce gales shelter belts had to be established. For this purpose Scots fir and Corsican pine were first used, a particularly hardy variety of the former being obtained from the mountain sides around nearby Loch Maree. As these trees began to take hold and provide some protection inner belts of *Rhododendron ponticum* were established and other trees introduced, including birch, oak, mountain ash, *Cupressus macrocarpa* and some of the north-western American conifers, such as western hemlock, Douglas fir and noble fir (*Abies procera*).

So successful was Osgood Mackenzie that once the shelter belt had grown to sufficient size many more tender exotic plants could be grown in the garden, and today, under the care of the National Trust for Scotland, it is one of the finest of its kind in the British Isles, particularly renowned for its collection of rhododendrons, meconopses and celmisias.

At about the same time, but about 560 miles to the south, Augustus Smith was starting a similar experiment on Tresco in the Isles of Scilly. Here there was the same problem of wind and a similar solution by means of a shelter belt, mainly of *Cupressus macrocarpa* and *Pinus radiata*, which took many years to grow sufficiently high and thick to provide adequate shelter. But there the similarity between Inverewe and Tresco Abbey ends. Conditions in the two places are very different, the soil at Inverewe meagre and acid, that at Tresco plentiful but sandy; the climate in Scotland moist, the Isles of Scilly relatively dry. So it was not the rhododendrons and other new shrubs from the Himalaya that thrived best at Tresco, but those from drier regions, including the Canary Islands, South Africa, some regions of Central and South America and Australasia. In fact at Tresco the number of exotic species grown is probably greater than at Inverewe. The two gardens look totally dissimilar, Inverewe largely a woodland garden with many plants growing in semi-shade, Tresco open and sunny with succulents clinging to its warm terrace walls, pelargoniums sprawling down its steep banks, and palms, giant agaves and primitive proteaceous* plants enhancing the impression that one must have strayed right out of the British Isles into some sub-tropical region.

Inverewe and Tresco represent extremes of climate and situation between which there are hundreds of intermediates providing a unique opportunity for growing plants from practically all regions of the world. Indeed so successful has this nineteenth century experiment proved that today many visitors consider these maritime gardens the most interesting in the British Isles. In a journey of no more than a few hundred miles they can see plants

---

* Proteaceous: plants belonging to the Protea family, which includes not only the genus protea but also leucadendron, leucospermum, persoonia, grevillea, embothrium, hakea, banksia, helicia, roupala and telopea. They have a wide distribution in the Southern Hemisphere and may have survived from very early times.

growing under seemingly natural conditions that in other places would necessitate travelling as many thousands. At Logan, Galloway, the Asiatic primulas are so much at home that they have strayed far outside the garden and greet the visitor beside the lane that leads to it, while in a damp woodland site beyond the garden South American *Gunnera manicata* has become a weed. In the damp, mild air of western Ireland, tiny Garinish Island in Bantry Bay houses another remarkable collection of half-hardy plants, but this garden is as famous for its design features as for its plants, and that is part of another story that is told in a later section.

A few sites were already so naturally beautiful and also so favourable in soil and climate that little needed to be done except to cut tracks and establish exotic plants. Perhaps the finest example of this is Crarae Lodge, south of Inverary, beside Loch Fyne. Here a stream coming down from the hills has cut itself a deep gorge through the rock before it enters the loch. Sir George Campbell, a twentieth century plant lover, chose this site for his collection of trees, but he became involved in making a 'natural' garden, in the sense that very little needed to be altered and only the plants had to be added. His friends sent him so many interesting things that he soon had a collection, including many Asiatic rhododendrons, eucalyptus species, embothriums, eucryphias, malus species, primulas and many other exotics. So well do some of them enjoy the conditions that they have become completely naturalized and renew themselves by self-sown seedlings. The natural effect of this garden is enhanced by the restricted use of wide paths, access being mainly by narrow tracks which wind in and out among the trees and shrubs. At one point a little wooden bridge across the gorge provides some of the finest views of this unique garden.

Derreen in south-west Eire also occupies a site of great beauty on a little peninsula jutting out into the Kenmare River. But here a great deal of art and a lot of fine planting have been used to exploit the natural advantages of the site. There are many semi-tender rhododendrons, embothriums and also fine trees, including a giant cryptomeria which has partly collapsed under its own weight, and some very big eucalyptus. But for the plant lover the greatest excitement at Derreen is provided by the tree ferns, *Dicksonia antarctica*, which are so much at home that they spread by their wind-blown spores which seem to grow most freely in the damp drainage channels cut to take surplus water out of the peaty soil.

At Achamore House, on the little island of Gigha, off the coast of Argyll, the late Sir James Horlick also succeeded in establishing many of the more tender and difficult rhododendrons. He bequeathed all his plants to the National Trust for Scotland and scions from them are being established in other Scottish west coast gardens, including Brodick Castle on the Isle of Arran, where conditions are also exceptionally favourable and one of the best collections of large leaved rhododendrons has been thriving for many years. But the light intensity in Gigha, the long days in summer and short days in winter, do not suit all plants. It would be quite impossible to grow

Rhododendron macabeanum at **Achamore House (p. 71)**

there the great range of succulents and sunlovers that thrive at Tresco Abbey. Even *Camellia japonica*, a shrub that enjoys a measure of shade, does not flower well at Gigha, though the hybrids between it and *C. saluenensis*, the useful man-made forms of *C. williamsii*, do well, apparently because they have a different light controlled bud formation mechanism.

Five hundred miles to the south, at Caerhays Castle on the coast of Cornwall, all types of camellia grow and flower well. It was here that *C. williamsii* was first made, taking its name from the owner, Mr J. C. Williams, and here also is probably the largest *C. reticulata* in the whole of the British Isles. At Caerhays Castle there are also exceptionally fine magnolia trees, some of the largest michelias in the country, as well as rhododendrons in thousands and many other treasures.

The Channel Islands also benefit from a mild maritime climate, a fact which was appreciated by Samuel Curtis as early as 1841 when he purchased a site on the side of a very sheltered valley at Rozel, Jersey, and started to build a house there. It would seem that La Chaire was intended as much for his daughter, Mrs Fothergill, as for himself, but he spent the last years of his life there and planted many exotic species. The house has gone and so have most of the plants, but the terraces he made for them remain and some of the great Monterey cypresses which crown the ridge were probably planted by him. So maybe was an immense *Eucryphia cordifolia*, but the very fine *Magnolia campbellii* must have been planted later, since it had not been discovered when he died in 1860.

So the list could be extended sufficiently to fill a whole volume, and for the student of these matters there is one book devoted to the subject, long out of print but available in reference libraries and occasionally to be picked up secondhand. *Shrubs for the Milder Counties* by the late Arnold Foster is concerned primarily with Devon and Cornwall, where he lived, but has application to all the western maritime regions of the British Isles.

Gardens illustrating the section include Achamore House, Brodick Castle, Castlewellan, Crarae Lodge, Derreen, Exeter University, Garinish Island, Glendurgan, Inverewe, Kiloran, Lochinch, Logan, Mount Stewart, Mount Usher, Rowallane, Sharpitor, Trelissick, Trengwainton, Tresco Abbey, Trewithen.

Daffodils and cabbage palms, Achamore House (p. 71)

COLLECTORS' GARDENS

In the main, and with a few notable exceptions, such as Garinish Island, these gardens interest plant lovers rather than those attracted by good design. They have been made by collectors concerned primarily with making the plants of their choice happy and their first consideration has usually been 'Where will this plant grow best?', rather than 'Where will it look best?', or even more forbiddingly 'Does my garden really need this plant at all?'.

Where good design and good plant collections have gone hand in hand it has often been because the collector inherited a garden that had already been fully laid out yet retained space for further planting without serious injury to its form or proportions. This happened at Tregothnan (near Truro, Cornwall), where camellias, rhododendrons (including some of the earliest and largest specimens of *Rhododendron arboreum*) and many other exotic trees and shrubs have been introduced to a landscape garden originally designed by Humphry Repton. Not far away at Lanhydrock a fine eighteenth century park and earlier seventeenth century house, faithfully restored after a damaging fire, form the setting for another good though less extensive plant collection.

Rhododendrons, azaleas and other shrubs in vast numbers have transformed Lochinch (near Stranraer, Dumfries and Galloway), converting what must formerly have been a neglected and rather rustic imitation of a seventeenth century French garden into one of the most visually exciting gardens in Scotland.

Perhaps the finest example of all – some would say the finest garden in England – is at Sheffield Park (near Uckfield, East Sussex), where Lancelot Brown laid out the original landscape which later grew to include four, instead of the original two, lakes, and which finally acquired a superbly rich clothing of exotic trees and shrubs which fill it with colour each spring and autumn and give it an entirely new kind of beauty and interest throughout the rest of the year.

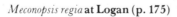

Meconopsis regia at **Logan (p. 175)**

Some collectors, who were not fortunate enough to possess ready made landscape gardens in which to display their treasures, made landscapes of their own or adopted a park-like style in which the unifying feature was usually mown turf running in lawns, rides or walks between plants massed in irregular beds, usually with some individual trees and shrubs isolated as specimens. The most important rule in such gardens seems to have been to avoid at all costs straight lines made either by the shape of beds or the disposition of the trees. It could be parodied as 'curving is beautiful', and so long as the curves were well chosen and had some relationship to one another the result could be very satisfactory. Trouble arose when wiggles and twists were introduced solely for their own sake, as they often were by garden makers without much eye for a picture.

Fine examples of this kind of garden making are to be found in hundreds of gardens made from 1890 onwards. Wakehurst Place (Ardingly, West Sussex) is an exceptionally lovely one, because of the skill with which the beds have been placed in a well landscaped setting. There are pools and a

Rhododendron falconeri at **Trengwainton (p. 225)**

In the woodland, Savill Garden
(p. 206)

lake, one of the former flanked by a considerable rock garden, but the lake is rather hidden by woodland, though there are plans to improve this.

Wakehurst occupies a ridge of land with valleys on each side and the good air drainage into these valleys makes them exceptionally free of late spring frosts for this part of England. It is this and the moderately acid soil that have made them so suitable for big collections of trees and shrubs from many parts of the world, an advantage exploited with particular brilliance at Wakehurst.

Mount Usher (near Wicklow, Eire) is a supremely satisfactory example of the 'park' solution applied to the assemblage of a great collection of plants. Made since 1860 by four generations of Walpoles, it has been constantly maintained and renewed and is now one of the most beautiful and interesting gardens of its kind in the British Isles. The site is fairly flat but a wide stream flows through it and by use of some low weirs to create cascades, and some cleverly placed bridges, charming pictorial effects have been created. It is around this stream that the plant collection has been built up in irregular beds, small coppices and as isolated specimens. The eucalyptus are some of the best in the British Isles; there are magnificent eucryphias, some of them hybrids bred at Mount Usher; and there are a great many other rare trees and shrubs, including magnolias, embothriums, ceanothus, nothofagus, podocarpus, nothopanax, lomatia, drimys, telopea and dacrydium.

Yet despite these and many other fine collectors' gardens, all made by amateurs, professional designers, who often have only a sketchy knowledge of plants, came to despise the plantsmen, who in turn have been mystified by designers who appeared to be more interested in masonry than in plants. 'I don't call that a garden', has been a frequent complaint from both sides, which is a pity since the perfect garden should surely contain both elements. It could be argued that twentieth century garden making has been largely concerned with the resolution of these differences, but that is another aspect of our garden history that must wait for a later section. Before that it is necessary to look at some other nineteenth century developments which were to affect garden making in profound ways.

Gardens illustrating the section include Abbotsbury Sub-Tropical Garden, Achamore House, Annes Grove, Benmore, Bodnant, Borde Hill, Brodick Castle, Castlewellan, Crathes Castle, Derreen, Exeter University, Glendurgan, Harlow Car, Highdown, Inverewe, Jermyns, Kiloran, Knightshayes Court, Lanhydrock, Leonardslee, Lochinch, Logan, Mount Stewart, Mount Usher, Muncaster Castle, Nymans, Rowallane, Sharpitor, Sheffield Park, Trengwainton, Tresco Abbey, Trewithen, Wakehurst Place.

WOODLAND GARDENS

Another Victorian invention which was to have great influence on the subsequent development of garden making in the British Isles was the woodland garden. This grew naturally out of the tree clumps and coppices which were the joint heritage of the mediaeval park and the landscape movement. The process of integrating these more closely into the garden was stimulated by the arrival of more and more rhododendrons, many of which succeeded best in the dappled summer shade and winter cover provided by thinly planted evergreen and deciduous trees.

Many of the new Asiatic rhododendrons were not only spectacular in bloom, but were fairly easily raised from seed. Hybridists, both amateur and professional, quickly went to work on them and since rhododendron seed is small and freely produced, garden owners found themselves with thousands of seedlings and no room in the garden proper to grow them on. The obvious solution was to go out into the surrounding policies planting rhododendrons wherever there was suitable cover for them, and so the idea of woodland gardening as a thing apart was born.

One of these nineteenth century plantations which remains in good order and is constantly accessible to the public is attached to The Hirsel, home of the Earls of Home (near Coldstream, Borders), known as Dundock Wood. So little artifice has been put into the planting that it seems entirely natural, as though the rhododendrons, and the accompanying azaleas which fill the air with their rich perfume in May and early June, had always grown there.

But these are relatively tough and common kinds. The more opulent varieties which were bred from species such as *R. griffithianum*, *arboreum*, *thomsonii*, *griersonianum*, *barbatum*, *fortunei*, *dicroanthum*, *campylocarpum* and *cinnabarinum* required better treatment and more protection from vandalism or theft. Nor was it only rhododendrons and azaleas that thrived in these conditions. Camellias, previously considered mainly as greenhouse shrubs, also took to the woodlands and proved to be almost completely hardy in leaf and stem, though their flowers were readily destroyed by frost.

Other shrubs followed them into the equable shelter of the trees, crinodendrons, eucryphias, pieris, gaultherias, mahonias and many more. Some herbaceous plants accompanied them, including lily of the valley, violets, Solomon's seal (polygonatum), libertia, trilliums, epimediums, hardy cyclamen, primroses, polyanthus, foxgloves, hostas, the willow gentian and the wood anemones. By the end of the nineteenth century woodland gardens were being made in many parts of the country, and this has continued to be a fashionable style. In some places, such as at Leonardslee (near Horsham, West Sussex) and Achamore House (Isle of Gigha, Strathclyde) they are almost complete entities on their own; in others as in Park Wood, Hergest Croft (Kington, Hereford and Worcester) or Wakehurst Place (Ardingly, West Sussex) and Bodnant (near Conwy, Gwynedd, N. Wales), they are additional attractions attached to gardens with other features.

Leonardslee remains the most spectacular woodland garden in private ownership, but the Valley Gardens and Savill Garden still being extended in Windsor Great Park and initiated by Prince Albert (later to become George VI) and Eric Savill (later knighted) in the 1930s surpass Leonardslee in size and variety and probably constitute the finest woodland

The herbaceous borders at Arley Hall (p. 77)

landscapes in the British Isles. Landscape is justly applied to both Leonardslee and the Windsor complex of gardens, for unlike the little woodland planting at Dundock Wood all have been planted with careful consideration for the overall effect that would be produced as trees and shrubs grew to maturity. Both places enjoy many natural advantages, interestingly contoured land, lakes which though originally man-made have existed so long that they have been completely assimilated into the landscape, native tree cover and moderately acid soil. Leonardslee and Windsor must be considered as the greatest achievements in a style of gardening which is almost as British in its origins as the eighteenth century landscape, though there was a parallel but seemingly unrelated development in the south-eastern states of the U.S.A.

Gardens illustrating this section include Achamore House, Annes Grove, Benmore, Bodnant, Borde Hill, Cliveden, Clyne Castle, Crarae Lodge, Dawyck, Dundock Wood, Howick Hall, Hergest Croft, Heaselands, Inverewe, Isabella Plantation, Kiloran, Knightshayes Court, Leonardslee, Mount Usher, Muncaster Castle, Rudding Park, Savill Garden, Sheffield Park, Trelissick, Trewithen, Valley Gardens, Wakehurst Place, Waterhouse Plantation.

HERBACEOUS BORDERS AND ISLAND BEDS

No one knows when or by whom the herbaceous border was invented. Certainly it was not by William Robinson, as many people seem to believe, though he undoubtedly did a great deal to popularize this method of growing herbaceous perennials. The most probable explanation is that herbaceous borders never were invented but simply evolved as a perfectly natural development from the kind of mixed planting that has existed from the earliest gardening times in Britain. We have already noted that the original knots and parterres, if they were planted at all, were probably filled with a mixture of plants as in the reconstructed seventeenth century gardens in Colonial Williamsburg. Where there were neither knots or parterres flowers seem to have been grown mainly in simple rectangular beds, again in mixture rather than segregated or in patterns.

When the eighteenth century landscape movement banished flowers altogether from the vicinity of the house they were grown in the kitchen garden, no doubt in straight borders as one can still see in many such gardens in Scotland. It is only necessary to imagine such kitchen garden planting restricted to hardy herbaceous perennials and the herbaceous border is born; and maybe even that restriction is not really necessary since herbaceous borders have rarely been rigorously confined to hardy herbaceous perennials as the purists would insist, but seem always to have admitted a variety of non-woody plants.

41

Be that as it may, fine herbaceous borders were certainly being made before 1850 and described as such. At Arley Hall (near Nantwich, Cheshire) there is a plan dated 1846 which includes twin herbaceous borders separated by a wide gravel walk and they still occupy exactly the same place.

A water colour painting of the great parterre at Drummond Castle (Crieff, Tayside), made by T. B. Vacher probably some time in the 1860s, shows large herbaceous borders delineating some of the pattern, but these have long since disappeared, probably because of the cost and labour of maintenance.

That, in fact, is what has happened to most privately owned herbaceous borders, though good examples remain in many public parks as well as in gardens that seek to attract the public, such as the Royal Horticultural Society's garden at Wisley (Surrey), Nymans (Handcross, West Sussex), Falkland Palace (Fife) and Crathes Castle (Banchory, Grampian). Scottish borders still existing in kitchen gardens are to be seen at Williamston (Insch, Grampian) and at Kincorth (Forres, Grampian).

There is also a gem of a border, perfectly portraying the essential artificiality of this kind of planting, at Manderston (Duns, Borders). It is quite small and planted for August–September effect. All the rules have been followed, the plants grouped and arranged according to height, but what really makes it so special is the careful thought that has been given to colour, everything just right and in precisely the best spot, with never an awkward clash or disconcerting break in continuity. As a final touch of sophistication a charming marble bowl, with ducks and cherubs, is placed on a pedestal at exactly the right height to appear to float on the flowers.

The herbaceous border and its derivatives, island beds and mixed borders of herbaceous plants, shrubs, annuals, etc., did for soft-stemmed plants what arboretums, pinetums and woodland gardens did for woody plants. All these forms provided reasonably coherent frameworks within which a great variety of plants could be displayed. They suited both the out-and-out collector and the garden maker who was simply attracted by the form and colour of plants. But, though many herbaceous plants will live indefinitely, herbaceous borders need to be remade quite frequently if they are to be kept in good order and so it is never possible to see exactly what the original creators intended, unless they left detailed planting plans and it is still possible to obtain the varieties they used. In most cases neither condition can be met and the borders, if they are maintained at all, are planted to suit current taste and not to satisfy historical verity.

It was probably the curving shrub borders of gardens such as Wakehurst Place that suggested the idea of applying a similar formula to beds for herbaceous perennials, instead of nearly always growing them in long borders. Island beds, as they have come to be known, were much publicized in the 1950s by Alan Bloom and others and one of the largest and most satisfactory examples of this style is to be seen in Mr Bloom's own garden at

6. Pool in the woodland, Achamore House (*see* page 71)

7. *Rosa gallica officinalis*, **Harlow Car** (*see* **page 147**)

8. **The red borders, Hidcote Manor** (*see* **page 151**)

Bressingham Hall (near Diss, Norfolk). In this garden the emphasis is firmly on herbaceous plants, both the border and the rock garden kinds, plus some bog plants and aquatics. The garden is undulating, beds are of ample size and simple outline, the grass paths and open spaces are of good proportion and the whole effect coherent and pleasing.

At Threave School of Practical Gardening (near Castle Douglas, Dumfries and Galloway) the island bed system has been used on a much more comprehensive scale to take in almost the entire garden, including rose garden, herbaceous beds, heather garden, rock garden and scree. If it were not divided and diversified by some coppices and small areas of woodland this insistence on one method might become boring, and even in its present form one is occasionally reminded of a golf course with its long fairways, bunkers, tree clumps and greens.

At Syon Park the island bed system has also been used, but here exclusively for perennials in a grassed area known as Flora's Lawn, and there is also a small area of island beds at Wisley, grouped near the restaurant.

Gardens illustrating the section include Arley Hall, Bressingham Hall, Burford House, Clare College, Crathes Castle, Falkland Palace, Hascombe Court, Leith Hall, Newby Hall, Oxford Botanic Garden, Pusey House, Rudding Park, Syon House, Threave, Wisley.

MAN-MADE PLANTS

Plant breeding and plant selection had no doubt gone on for centuries, but the great inflow of previously unknown species from the mid-eighteenth century onwards gave it an entirely new impetus. Breeders not only had a great wealth of new material with which to work, but almost for the first time found that they could make many interspecific crosses, which really gave them the power to create new plant races, unknown in the wild and completely dependant on man for their maintenance. Hybridization, which was a trickle in the eighteenth century, had become a flood by the time Queen Victoria came to the throne and today has grown into an industry on which vast sums of money are spent and many livelihoods depend. Techniques have developed to such an extent that much breeding and propagation is now carried out in test tubes in laboratories and it is even found possible in some cases to transfer individual genes from one organism to another. 'Genetic engineering' is the name given to these new aims and methods and where they will eventually lead is by no means clear, but the revolution in plant material due to straightforward hybridization and selection in greenhouse, garden and field is plain for all to see.

This is not the place to examine it in depth, but it must be touched on because of its influence on garden making and gardening interests. A few examples will suffice to show how profound and far reaching these were.

43

The rose garden, Syon Park (p. 221)

First the rose. Until the early nineteenth century virtually all roses flowered once a year, usually for a few weeks, after which their display was finished. Then with the importation of China and Tea roses came the possibility to breed varieties that would give two, three or even more flushes of bloom each summer.

It was not long before rose lovers were attempting to combine this repeat flowering characteristic of the early China and Tea roses with the flower size and colour range of traditional roses. First came the Bourbon race, soon followed by the Hybrid Perpetuals which had magnificent flowers but were often awkward in habit and were not as a rule anything like so continuous flowering as their name implied. The next step seems to have been almost an accident. In 1864 a French nurseryman sowed a lot of Tea rose seeds and from the resultant seedlings named one La France. It combined a quality of bloom and a continuity of flower production which were eventually to cause rose lovers to accord it a class of its own, called Hybrid Tea, and this has dominated the rose world ever since, though its supremacy has long been challenged by another later group of hybrids, often known as Floribundas.

Once roses were made to flower most of the summer and well into the autumn in addition, the stage was set for a take over by the rose of territory previously exclusively held by bedding plants. Whereas these had to be replaced, sometimes several times a year, roses were permanent and both less troublesome and less costly to maintain. Roses were no longer confined to rose gardens, but invaded all the beds and borders, finding a place among herbaceous perennials, shrubs or indeed in any situation in which continuous summer colour was desired.

It is for this reason that it is difficult today to point to many 'rose gardens' as such, though there are few gardens in which roses do not find a place. Those looking for roses on their own should visit, any time between June and September, such places as Queen Mary's Garden in Regent's Park (London), the Royal National Rose Society's display garden at Chiswell Green (St. Albans), the rose garden and rose borders at the Royal Horticultural Society's garden (Wisley, Surrey), the Northern Horticultural Society's garden at Harlow Car (Harrogate, West Yorkshire), the big display garden at Syon House (Isleworth, Greater London), and numerous other rose gardens in public parks and rose nurseries. Sizeable privately owned (or at any rate privately made) rose gardens, mainly of the Edwardian period, are to be found at Luton Hoo (Luton, Bedfordshire), Polesden Lacey (near Great Bookham, Surrey) and a few other places, but in general roses will be found incidental to other features.

Yet the new roses created a new race of gardeners, the rosarians, devoted above all to one flower, just as man-made races of chrysanthemums produced chrysanthemum specialists, man-made dahlias produced dahlia specialists, sweet peas produced sweet pea specialists, orchids produced orchid specialists and so on through a long list of plants, many of which had not existed at all in their present form and variety before the nineteenth century. It was, in a way, the story of tulip mania, which swept Europe in the early seventeenth century, all over again with much the same enthusiasm, but without the accompanying hysteria, probably because the interest was divided between so many plants instead of being concentrated on one.

Yet for the garden visitor to the British Isles who has succumbed to one of these specialist interests it will be important to know where they can best be seen. Trials of many of these flowers, including chrysanthemums, dahlias, delphiniums, irises, daffodils, carnations, sweet peas, and day lilies (Hemerocallis) are held in the Royal Horticultural Society's gardens at Wisley, and there are fine displays of chrysanthemums, dahlias etc. in many parks. Hybrid fuchsias, another man-made race, are also park favourites with specially good collections in the Quarry Park at Shrewsbury and in Trentham Gardens, Staffordshire. There is usually a glasshouse full of indoor varieties of fuchsias at Wisley, and at Trentham.

But when it comes to looking for private collections of these man-made specialities it is more difficult to give advice since most have been made primarily for the purpose of competitive exhibition at flower shows, many are in quite small gardens or even on allotments and few are ever open to the public. So perhaps the best advice that can be given to interested visitors is to get in touch with the secretaries of the various specialist societies that look after their special interests, whose addresses can be obtained from the

Royal Horticultural Society, Vincent Square, London SW1P 2PE. Most are run by honorary secretaries operating from their own homes, so addresses are apt to change fairly frequently.

Gardens illustrating this section include Arley Hall, Barrington Court, Charleston Manor, Chatsworth, Harlow Car, Hascombe Court, Hyde Hall, Kiftsgate Court, Luton Hoo, Polesden Lacey, Queen Mary's Rose Garden, Royal National Rose Society, Syon Park, Threave, Wisley, and in most public parks.

ALPINES AND ROCK GARDENS

Another new interest we owe to the Victorians is rock gardening, or more accurately the cultivation of rock plants, which is not quite the same thing. Rocky structures in the garden might be said to date back to the grottoes of the seventeenth and eighteenth century gardens and we have seen that landscape designers also used rocks, as at Bowood in Wiltshire and Chatsworth in Derbyshire. But all these early examples were intended to induce a mood or create a picture and no thought was given to the cultivation of plants other than a few ferns or something of the kind. It was left to the Victorians to discover the beauty of alpine plants, just as they discovered the beauty of mountains and invented the sports of mountaineering and skiing.

By the end of the nineteenth century rock plants (a description which included any plants naturally found in rocky places, whatever the altitude or lack of it) and rock gardens were in full fashion, and the principles of 'natural' rock gardening were being formulated. The correct system, one was told, was to study and follow nature (how often has this kind of advice produced the strangest and most incongruous results when translated to the garden), and to arrange rocks so that they seemed to be native to the site, appearing through the soil as natural outcrops. Stratified rock formations were the most admired models and if the rock was both weather-and water-worn so much the better. As a result considerable areas of the Cumbrian and Mendip Hills were searched for suitable stone and limestone rock gardens sprang up in all parts of the country, even though there was no limestone in the vicinity nor even rock formations of any kind, and with little thought for the fact that many rock plants grow on granite, sandstone or other non-alkaline stone and are poisoned by excessive calcium.

Nevertheless though most of these classic rock gardens failed in their primary purpose, which was to provide ideal conditions for the admired mountain and rock flora, many were beautiful in their own right, though often most incongruously placed. Nearly all proved very costly to maintain and for this reason few have survived in private ownership, though there are some fine examples in public and National Trust gardens.

The largest, and in many ways the most satisfactory as well as the most spectacular, is in The Royal Botanic Garden, Edinburgh. The site is ideal, on the summit of a hill with magnificent views of the city of Edinburgh, with the steep hill known as Arthur's Seat as a backdrop. Non-calcareous rock is used and there is an adjacent peat garden for plants requiring specially acid conditions. As a result this garden is successful both as a spectacle and as a place in which to cultivate a vast range of rock plants.

There are also notable rock gardens in the Royal Botanic Gardens, Kew, and in Cambridge Botanic Garden, the latter made in two parts, one with non-calcareous rock, the other of limestone, specially for the cultivation of lime-loving plants, and reproducing many of the peculiar structural and ecological features of natural limestone formations.

Another famous rock garden is that in the Royal Horticultural Society's gardens at Wisley. This was made in 1911 by Pulham and Sons to a design by Edward White. It is constructed of sandstone, much of it in very large blocks, and is, unusually, on a north facing slope. But since then it has been frequently altered and enlarged and an additional much admired feature is an alpine meadow filled with tiny hoop petti-coat daffodils (*Narcissus bulbocodium*) in spring.

These are all large scale constructions. On a much smaller scale and showing what private garden owners were doing early in the present century is an excellently maintained limestone rock garden at Sizergh Castle (near Kendal, Cumbria), but here all attempt at growing rock plants has long since been abandoned, if indeed it ever succeeded, and the garden is stocked with ferns, herbaceous perennials and aquatics.

Semi-natural rock garden, Muckross House (p. 184)

There are several well made rock gardens and screes in the Northern Horticultural Society's garden at Harlow Car (Harrogate) and also at the school of the National Trust for Scotland at Threave (near Castle Douglas, Dumfries and Galloway). The National Trust for Scotland also owns a period piece at Leith Hall (Kennethmont, Grampian), a garden made largely in Edwardian times with a rock garden that does most of the 'wrong things', is romantic rather than natural, yet has a charm of its own which it would be a pity to disturb.

Another early rock garden is at Liverpool University Botanic Garden, Ness (Neston, Cheshire). This was made early in the twentieth century by A. K. Bulley, a rich man who was also a socialist. With the object of interesting working men in ornamental plants he opened his garden free to the public, possibly the first person in Britain to do so as a regular thing, though it is said that he did not enjoy mixing with people and surrounded his house with gorse bushes so that the public should not be encouraged to approach too closely. The garden contained shrub and herbaceous borders as well as the rock garden which was made in a damp and rather cold hollow, not really a very suitable place to grow alpines. The rock garden remains much as it always was, but other parts of the garden have been altered and on the hillside behind Mr Bulley's house there is now a fine heather garden.

But nowadays few enthusiasts make rock gardens, finding it far more satisfactory and a good deal cheaper to grow rock plants in raised beds, dry walls, blocks of tufa, trough gardens or pots and pans which can be protected from excessive winter rain in a frame or unheated greenhouse, should that be necessary. New rock gardens are mainly on a miniature scale, complete with plastic lined pools and cascades and confined to villa gardens where their artificiality perhaps satisfies some need by recalling real mountains, rivers and lakes enjoyed on holiday.

Gardens illustrating the section include Aberdeen Botanic Garden, Cambridge Botanic Garden, Edinburgh Botanic Garden, Harlow Car, Inverewe, Kew, Leith Hall, Liverpool University Botanic Garden, Luton Hoo, Mount Usher, Muckross, Oxford Botanic Garden, Rowallane, Sizergh Castle, Threave, Wakehurst Place, Wallington, White Craggs, Wisley.

One of the rock gardens at Harlow Car (p. 147)

THE JEKYLL STYLE

So by the close of the nineteenth century we have a number of gardening styles existing side by side with no very clear connections between them and sometimes seemingly in direct opposition. Some garden makers favoured formality, others naturalness, some wanted colour heaped upon colour, others sought the coolness of woodland glades or delighted in collections of native ferns. This was the period of the great disputation between William Robinson, author of numerous books and founder editor of several gardening magazines, and Reginald Blomfield, architect and garden designer, one extolling the virtues of herbaceous borders, rock gardens and woodland gardens, the other the necessity for firm design and a solid architectural framework. Looked at in retrospect there seems to be a curious unreality about all this thunder, for in the home parts of his own garden at Gravetye Manor (near East Grinstead, West Sussex) Robinson adopted a plan so basically formal that even Blomfield would have approved, while in some of his gardens, as at Trinity Manor (Jersey, Channel Islands), Blomfield admitted just the sort of semi-wild features that Robinson advocated.

What seems to have been happening throughout this period and has continued to happen ever since, is that garden makers were trying to bring together all the desirable and useful features that had been introduced up to that time. Taking this view one may see the twentieth century in the British Isles as a period of consolidation and synthesis rather than of innovation, which is probably why to some outsiders, familiar with the experiments of Burle Marx in South America and many other American and Scandinavian designers, we in Britain seem to have been standing still. A closer look at what has actually been achieved will prove that this is not true.

The principal architect of change, whose influence is still felt perhaps even more effectively than when she was alive, was a retiring Victorian spinster named Gertrude Jekyll. Comfortably off and with no necessity to earn a living, Miss Jekyll spent much of her early life painting in water colours. She knew and was greatly influenced by William Morris and John Ruskin and like them she believed firmly in the virtues of traditional craftsmanship as opposed to the new trend towards mass production. She admired the work of the impressionist painters and it was no doubt this and her own work as an artist that gave her a deep interest in colour and the effects it could produce in the garden.

In middle life and largely owing to failing eyesight Miss Jekyll abandoned painting and devoted herself to gardening. She became friendly with the young architect Edwin Lutyens and during the next forty years they collaborated in the making of many gardens, Lutyens drawing the design plans and Jekyll the planting plans. But she also worked with other architects and for garden owners and was probably involved in greater or lesser degree in over two hundred gardens.

49

In the light of this great output of work it seems strange that so few Jekyll gardens remain today. Part of the explanation is that she worked with plants, frequently with herbaceous plants, which even when perennial are relatively ephemeral, often needing to be lifted, divided and replanted every few years, with every time the opportunity for change. But this built-in instability was probably increased by the character of the properties themselves, mostly of medium size, built for successful business and professional men and of a kind to be much in demand, readily saleable and fairly frequently changing hands.

A few do remain more or less intact. This is the case at Barrington Court (near Ilminster, Somerset), though this is not perhaps very typical Jekyll, and it seems doubtful whether she ever saw it.

Folly Farm (Sulhamstead, near Reading, Berkshire), built by Lutyens and planted by Jekyll, is possibly as good an example of her style as any, but Hestercombe, near Taunton in Somerset, when fully restored may come even closer to the original.

Her own home, Munstead Wood (Godalming, Surrey), specially designed for her by Lutyens, remains in the building much as it was in her day, but the garden is a travesty of what she made. Much better is nearby Orchards, also a Lutyens/Jekyll collaboration and much better preserved than most. Vann, a few miles away at Hambledon, looks just like the pictures of Jekyll gardens and was originally planted by her for the original Lutyens house, but both house and garden have been greatly altered and so one can only now say of Vann that it is in the Jekyll manner.

What that manner was is difficult to crystallize in a few words. Miss Jekyll wrote freely and in numerous books and articles expounded her ideas. Because Miss Jekyll so often worked with architects she nearly always had a firm architectural design to carry her planting. One of her most noteworthy skills was to soften the harsh lines of masonry without losing the underlying sense of form. Lutyens, in particular, used stonework brilliantly, giving his paths elaborate patterns, constantly varying the character of his steps, exploiting the lights and shades of recessed pools, allowing water to fill pools almost to the brim so that they lay like silver mirrors on his terraces. A favourite device was to confine straight narrow rills of water between flagstoned edges, but allow them to break out at regular intervals into wider pools which he called 'tanks', and these Miss Jekyll would discreetly decorate with irises, rushes or other suitable plants. He also made splendid pergolas with massive stone pillars and heavy cross beams and these Miss Jekyll clothed with vines, clematis, honeysuckles, roses and other climbers.

She derived a great deal of her inspiration from cottage gardens, particularly those of Surrey south of the Hogsback where she lived, just as many of the architects for whom she worked derived their inspiration from traditional country houses. But it was the profusion of the cottage garden, not its confusion, that attracted her. Jekyll borders might look so right that

The Lutyens pergola, Hestercombe (p. 150)

there seemed no other way to make them, but every plant had been placed with care to produce a precise effect.

The density and variety of her planting tended to disguise the firm architectural lines which often underlay it, but she appreciated good design as much as colour and always ensured that it made its effect, much as good bone formation contributes to the beauty of a well made body.

Jekyll gardens, like those of the seventeenth century, were often divided into numerous enclosures, rather like a series of outdoor rooms, but

51

whereas in olden times the design of each section would have been clearly based on pattern, Miss Jekyll was as ready to accept pictorial as geometrical concepts and her compartments were as different, one from another, as ingenuity and good taste could make them. Even when the beds or borders were strictly geometric in shape Miss Jekyll's planting nearly always flowed in an apparently artless, highly pictorial way. She was one of the first to use all manner of plants in association to produce the effects she wanted, annuals, herbaceous perennials, roses, shrubs, climbers and even bedding plants, including the new man-made races of dahlia and antirrhinum which she found useful because of their colour range and long flowering season.

Whether Miss Jekyll was really the originator of all these ideas seems doubtful. More probably she was an especially gifted interpreter of gardening trends that were already under way and she had the ability, both by writing and by practical example, to make those trends more widely known. Perhaps her own most distinctive contribution was in the use of colour; certainly no one, either before or since her day, has written with greater clarity or understanding about it. It was she who seems first to have advocated the use of a restricted colour range in particular borders or sections of the garden. It was she, too, who pointed out the quite different effects produced by association of harmonizing or contrasting colours. When she used a wide range of colours in one border she usually arranged them in a definite sequence like the colours in a rainbow, and she was also probably the originator of the single colour border, of which we have seen considerable use in recent times.

But to whatever extent Miss Jekyll originated or influenced ideas of this kind it is clear that early in the twentieth century some or all of them were being incorporated in many new gardens. One of the most celebrated, and undoubtedly a potent trend setter, was that made by Major Lawrence Johnston at Hidcote Manor, high up on the Cotswold Hills, near Chipping Campden in Gloucestershire. When Major Johnston bought this old stone built house it virtually had no garden and the situation seemed too exposed to encourage anyone to try to make one. Major Johnston thought otherwise and immediately began to plant hedges which would give protection and cut the area up into a number of separate compartments. Briefly his plan was to make a wide central walk through the length of the garden, enclosed by hedges, with a second walk at right angles to it and then to tuck a number of smaller divisions into the spaces on each side of this great T.

But it is the way in which he filled in the design and in particular the skill with which he diversified the style and planting of each of his outdoor 'rooms' that really make Hidcote such a success. The scene constantly changes from wide open, almost empty space, to small densely planted enclosures, some strongly based on pattern and geometry, others lush and cottage-like, yet others seemingly natural except for the plants, few of which are native.

Colour he handled almost as carefully as Miss Jekyll herself and she would have approved of Hidcote, though it is doubtful that she ever saw it or even met Major Johnston. But what really matters is that whereas Miss Jekyll's gardens so often found new, less perceptive owners, Hidcote passed from Major Johnston's ownership directly into that of the National Trust, and so has been maintained and renewed (something that all plant gardens require) in the way he would have wished.

Though Miss Jekyll was not directly concerned in the creation of Great Dixter (near Northiam, East Sussex), Lutyens was. He was engaged in 1910 by Nathaniel Lloyd to renovate and enlarge a fifteenth century house, and he also designed some of the main features of the garden. Again it was divided into several separate sections, some of them completely enclosed and really complete gardens in their own right. There is a sunken garden, a little courtyard garden, a topiary garden, a rose garden, an orchard with fritillaries and other bulbs naturalized in the grass, and a magnificent mixed border of herbaceous perennials, shrubs and climbers. This garden, so characteristic of its period, has remained in the possession of the same family throughout and has been splendidly maintained, enlarged and improved. The planting shows all the qualities that Miss Jekyll extolled, including richness, variety and carefully considered use of colour and form.

Crathes Castle is an old mansion in the Scottish baronial style, perched on a steep hillside near Banchory, Grampian. Like Hidcote this is not, at first sight, a very favourable place in which to make a garden, since it would appear to be both cold and exposed. But when in 1932 Lady Burnett of Leys took it in hand it already had some very large yew hedges, reputedly nearly 250 years old, which gave a degree of shelter to the upper part of the garden and by extending these and further dividing the lower garden with walls and belts of shrubs and tall plants, a series of enclosures was created which have made it possible to grow in this garden – or more accurately series of gardens – an extraordinarily wide range of plants, some of them usually regarded as distinctly tender.

In plan, with its numerous more or less rectangular subdivisions, the garden of Crathes Castle bears a considerable similarity to a mediaeval garden. On the ground nothing could be more dissimilar, because of the great variety of treatment and of plants. Shrubs and herbaceous plants dominate even the more formal sections and limited colour schemes are common. This is certainly a garden that Gertrude Jekyll would have approved, but she had no direct hand in making it.

Nor can she be directly credited with any share in Nymans (Handcross, West Sussex), but she visited the gifted Messels who made it and her ideas, if not her handiwork, are clearly to be seen. But Nymans also illustrates other influences of the period, including a good pinetum and fine collections of rhododendrons, magnolias, camellias and other shrubs, some of them hybrids made there. One alone, *Eucryphia nymansensis*, will ensure that the name of this lovely garden is known to thousands of plant lovers who have never visited it.

The White Garden, Sissinghurst Castle (p. 213)

Before leaving Miss Jekyll's manner and studying other influences more closely, two more recent gardens must be recorded, Sissinghurst Castle made by Sir Harold Nicholson and his wife, Vita Sackville West, between 1930 and her death in 1962; and Cranborne, which though it has had a garden for centuries has been virtually remade in the last twenty years. Both are supremely successful examples of the virtues of splitting gardens into numerous sections, each with its own treatment, using the widest range of suitable plants, but associating them with great thought for the effects of colour and form. Both have a white garden, though they are totally different in character. Both have herb gardens, again quite unlike, that at Cranborne being more clearly intended to be mediaeval in mood if not precisely in manner.

Another interesting difference is that the main divisions at Cranborne were already laid down when the garden was first made at the beginning of the seventeenth century, whereas when the Nicholsons acquired Sissinghurst it had no garden and they had to start from scratch. Possibly as a result of this, and also no doubt because it covers a lesser area, the compartments at Sissinghurst are more closely and ingeniously integrated than those at Cranborne. Yet the likeness is sufficient to reveal the common source of inspiration.

Sissinghurst, perhaps more completely than any other garden in the British Isles, illustrates the delightful and varied effects that can be produced by skilful plant associations. Many other gardens have them, but Sissinghurst brims over with them, so much so that any student of plant colour and form could spend days there at different times of the year, since it is planned for pleasure from January to December.

Vita Sackville West once described her ideal garden as combining the maximum formality of design with the maximum informality in planting. If

54

one bears in mind that informality here does not mean either disarray or carelessness, it is an apt description of the ideas of Miss Jekyll and all her followers.

Gardens illustrating this section include Barrington Court, Coates Manor, Castle Drogo, Cranborne, Gravetye Manor, Great Dixter, Hestercombe, Hidcote Manor, Nymans, Sissinghurst Castle, Tintinhull House.

TWENTIETH CENTURY SYNTHESIS

Other influences besides those commonly associated with Gertrude Jekyll were at work during the early years of the twentieth century. While Sir Reginald Blomfield (he was knighted for his services to architecture) was continuing his arguments with William Robinson, Harold Peto, an architect often overlooked in the gardening annals of these times, was using architectural ideas borrowed from the Italian renaissance to create new gardens in an unquestionably British style.

The two most accessible of Peto's gardens are Buscot Park (between Faringdon and Lechlade, Berkshire) and Garinish Island (Glengariff, in south-western Ireland). Two more different sites it would be difficult to imagine, Buscot Park being in good English farming country, well wooded, pleasant but totally undramatic, while Garinish Island is a tiny islet in Bantry Bay, surrounded by wild water and wilder mountains and entirely uncultivated (indeed to all appearances uncultivable) until Annan Bryce, a Belfast merchant, purchased it in 1910, and engaged Harold Peto to design a house there and make a garden. As a result of a succession of delays and misfortunes the house was never built, but the garden was made and is now the property of the government of Eire.

Garinish Island from near the Martello Tower (p. 138)

What Peto planned was an Italianate mansion on a little hill at one end of Garinish Island, overlooking a garden that would combine both formal Italian and woodland features. To make this possible soil had to be transported to the island and a shelter belt of trees established, just as had been done sixty years earlier at Inverewe, which in many ways this barren site resembled. The result in the two places is totally different because of the very different intentions of Osgood Mackenzie and Harold Peto. Where the former was entirely dedicated to the idea of building up a great collection of exotic plants in a favourably mild and moist climate, Peto (and presumably his patron Bryce) were intent on using exotic plants to create a series of beautiful linked gardens. In this Peto's aim was similar to that of Johnston at Hidcote, but the methods were different, the emphasis on architecture at Garinish Island greater (it would be dominating had the mansion been built) and plants used much more as a subsidiary element in design.

A woodland garden, more accurately a woodland glade, runs the length of the tiny island from the base of the hill at the east to the sea at the west, where it terminates in a roofless temple. The centre of the island is open lawn flanked by trees and shrubs separated from the hill by large mixed borders which bisect a walled kitchen garden and leading to the focal point of the whole design, a rectangular garden with a pavilion at one end which makes the viewing point for a superb prospect of mountain and sea framed in a colonnaded archway at the other end. It is a daring confrontation between extreme sophistication and untamed nature and there is no denying the drama.

At Buscot Park Peto used similar methods to produce quite different effects as befitted the very different nature of the site. The house already existed, a Georgian mansion of great dignity, placed on top of one of the rounded contours typical of this country. Some distance away to the east is a considerable lake, and Peto's task was to link one with the other. This he did by a series of balustraded steps leading down to a long straight *allée* or avenue

Pleached alleys and temple, Barnsley House (p. 81)

through the wood. The ingenuity lay in his treatment of this *allée*, which has architectural features throughout its length, linked by a stream of water which at one stage falls in cascades, at another flows so slowly as to seem quite still, but is always rigidly confined between flagstoned banks. Architectural features punctuate the walk through a green tunnel of trees framing the silver water of the lake, becoming ever larger as one approaches it and with a little Temple centrally placed on its far bank. Again there is drama, but in a much more subdued key.

At about this time, but apparently with no connection of any kind, Lord Aberconway was applying similar Italian methods to the improvement of his mother's garden at Bodnant, near Conwy. Here the house stands on a hillside with superb views up the Conway valley to the mountains of Snowdonia. When Lord Aberconway took charge this slope was still in its natural state, but with two large cedars spaced to frame the view from the house.

His aim was to produce a more striking effect, to give the house a more solid base and to provide himself with a variety of sites on which to grow plants. This he did by converting the slope into a series of terraces in the Italian manner with imposing flights of stone stairs, balustrades and pools. As a focal point for the lowest terrace on which he had made a long narrow canal pool, he purchased a charming eighteenth century pavilion.

The result is one of the finest garden prospects in the British Isles, enhanced by generous planting which includes many rare and beautiful plants. The terraces are only one of the many features at Bodnant, others being a woodland garden made with great skill in the glen, lawns and borders around the house, a wonderful pleached alley of laburnums and a huge collection of rhododendrons, many of them raised at Bodnant.

This fine garden which must, both for its design and plant collection, rank as one of the best in the country, has been constantly maintained, enlarged and improved and, though it now belongs to the National Trust, it is still, under the terms of the bequest, managed by Lord Aberconway's son, the third baron.

The particular style of gardening which we call 'picturesque' and which we left at the height of its flowering at Scotney Castle in 1836 never completely disappeared, though it ceased to be in the mainstream of development. Yet many twentieth century gardens have picturesque features and the importance of painterly qualities in gardens were implicit in almost all that Miss Jekyll and others like her were doing.

It was also a search for picturesqueness rather than any real interest in Japanese philosophy and symbolism that brought Japanese gardens into fashion around the turn of the century. It is doubtful whether any genuine Japanese gardens, with their restricted use of plants and large element of mysticism, have ever been made in Britain except as show pieces. What appealed to British gardeners was the romantic appearance of Japanese buildings and ornaments and of the plants associated with them. Japanese style pavilions, bridges, moon walls, stone lanterns and other features, usually arranged around a pool or stream planted with cherries, waterside irises, wisterias, bamboos, Japanese maples and other Asiatic plants began to appear in many British gardens and can still be seen at Tatton Park (Knutsford, Cheshire), Newstead Abbey (near Nottingham), Cliveden (near Taplow, Buckinghamshire), Hascombe Court (near Godalming, Surrey), Compton Acres (Poole, Dorset) and Powerscourt (Co. Wicklow, Eire) and on a smaller scale in many other places.

Perhaps the best twentieth century example of pure romanticism is to be seen at Portmeirion (Gwynedd, in north Wales). This little cove with a semi-derelict house and garden was purchased about 1925 by the writer and architect, Clough Williams-Ellis. He decided to put into effect there an idea he had already expressed in an article, suggesting that large properties which were becoming a liability could be made profitable by being adapted for more general use. Such schemes have since become commonplace, but Portmeirion was a pioneer and remains unique in the methods adopted. What its new owner set out to do was to exploit the romantic nature of the site to the full by creating in it a kind of idealized village with a strong Mediterranean flavour. Portmeirion is often described as an Italian village in Wales, and certainly some of its buildings, most of all the slender campanile which dominates it, are modelled on Italian originals. But there are buildings in many different styles and of different periods, gothic, baroque, classical and vernacular; some brought here from other places or assembled from a miscellany of old pieces. The whole of this extraordinary collection is bound together by the gardens which surround them and the little park which forms its centrepiece. Flowers embower the place, rhododendrons and azaleas in spring, followed by embothriums, hydrangeas and gay bedding plants in summer. There is nothing in the least like it anywhere else in the British Isles and probably nowhere else in the world.

Also romantic in character is the garden at Mount Stewart, beside Strangford Lough in Northern Ireland, made by Lady Londonderry. This had already been landscaped in the eighteenth century, and on a little hill to the south of the house there still stands an attractive garden building of the period, made in the Grecian style and known as the Temple of the Winds. But it was with the garden immediately surrounding the house that Lady Londonderry was chiefly concerned. In front of the house she made an Italian style terrace with geometric beds for bedding plants. Beyond this she made a sunken garden with an oval pool and a pavilion in Spanish style. Another section became an iris garden, a fourth was surrounded by a hedge and filled with topiary, a fifth was made in the form of a Tudor rose and so the invention continued.

All this sounds very much in the manner of many gardens being made about this time, but Mount Stewart is distinguished from all by its strong element of humour. This has been a rare quality in British gardens, for even in the early days we seldom seem to have gone in for the squirting pavements and other primitive water jokes so common in Italy. At Chatsworth there is a bronze willow tree that spurts water from its branches, but this seems to be more an exhibition of technical skill than a piece of fun.

Lady Londonderry saw to it that Mount Stewart was different. She engaged a local craftsman to make a number of strange animals and objects with which to decorate her garden, designed, it is said, as caricatures of friends.

The topiary garden is humorous too, full of strange shapes including an Irish harp, the Red Hand of Ulster, and a fantastic hunt – and again all the figures represent members of the Londonderry family.

Many of the features characteristic of twentieth century gardens can be seen in the Savill Garden, the first and also the most complex of the gardens made by Sir Eric Savill. When started in 1932 the intention was simply to make a water and bog garden in a damp glade through which a stream flowed. After the war the scheme was extended, a wall was erected at one end of the site to represent a dwelling and a series of gardens (or perhaps more accurately in this instance garden features, since they are not concealed one from another) was planned, increasing in formality in the region of this dummy house. The wall itself is well clothed with climbers, then on a terrace a series of rectangular raised beds has been constructed for alpines, and the design continues with flower borders, a rose garden, lawns with specimen trees and shrubs, a woodland garden, an alpine meadow in which daffodils are naturalized, and a large greenhouse for slightly tender shrubs.

But it is not simply the design that is interesting in this garden, but also the plants which are exceptionally varied and well grown. The soil is acid, rhododendrons and other ericaceous plants thrive, as do meconopses, primulas, gentians, and many other choice plants. The Savill Garden combines all the interest and expertise of a collector's garden with the beauty of a composition containing many well ordered parts logically put together.

No doubt an equal amount of skill and artistry went into the construction of the Valley Gardens, the quite separate series of gardens flanking Virginia Water, to which Sir Eric Savill applied his talents when he had more or less completed the Savill Garden. But these are planned as 'natural' landscapes, a style which should conceal rather than display man's handiwork, and though they are remarkably varied in character they do not include any formal elements.

When and to whom the idea first occurred of using heathers on their own to form a separate garden or garden feature is not clear, but it probably arose as a side development from rock gardening. Heathers are well suited to rock garden planting and are often used in this way, though their readiness to spread fast, overrunning any less vigorous plants that may be in their way, can be a hazard. Planted on their own this smothering habit becomes a virtue since weeds are killed, weed seeds are prevented from germinating, labour of maintenance is reduced and an interesting evergreen covering of green, yellow or copper foliage is produced, parts of which burst into flower colour at different times of the year (since heathers are available to flower successively from July to April). In addition to dwarf species there are also much taller tree heathers and these, with other congenial shrubs and a few trees such as birches, pines and cypresses, can be used to create very pleasing effects.

The heather garden in the Valley Garden illustrates all these good features, and there are also fine examples at Wisley, Threave (Castle Douglas), University of Liverpool Botanic Garden (Ness) and the Royal Botanic Gardens (Kew). There are attractive small heather gardens made by Adrian Bloom at Bressingham Hall (Diss, Norfolk), and here too will be found one of the best mini-pinetums in the country.

Maybe it was the excellent weed smothering properties of heathers that gave rise to the idea of using other spreading, low growing plants as ground cover. Certainly by the 1950s this had become a characteristic of much garden planting, and whole books have been devoted to the selection and management of ground cover. It is to be seen in many gardens, but perhaps nowhere more effectively used for beauty as well as utility as in a little woodland garden at Threave.

Gardens illustrating the section include Arley Hall, Anglesey Abbey, Balbithan House, Barnsley House, Barrington Court, Birr Castle, Blickling Hall, Bodnant, Borde Hill, Branklyn, Burford House, Buscot Park, Charleston Manor, Clare College, Cranborne, Crathes Castle, Crittenden House, Dartington Hall, The Garden House, Garinish Island, Harlow Car, Hascombe Court, Heaselands, Hever Castle, Hidcote Manor, Hodnet Hall, Kiftsgate Court, Liverpool Botanic Garden, Mount Stewart, Newby Hall, Pusey House, Savill Garden, Sissinghurst Castle, Sutton Park, Tyninghame, Wallington.

Heather gardens illustrating the latter part of the section include Bicton, Bressingham Hall, Furzey, Kew, Liverpool Botanic Garden, Threave, Valley Gardens, Wisley.

WATER AND BOG GARDENS

In the seventeenth and eighteenth century water was used mainly for its own sake, as a mirror to catch the light or to reflect a beautiful building or scene, in fountains and cascades for its movement and music, or in the eighteenth century landscape as a silver surface to contrast with the undulations of grazed turf and the rougher shapes and textures of trees. Water as a place in which to grow plants of a special character seems to have been a comparatively late development, perhaps another that derived stimulus from the interest in rock gardens, since planted pools are often in association with these.

Whatever its origins, when it did arrive water gardening and its logical companion, bog gardening, rapidly became popular and developed a trade of their own, both in specialist nurseries producing, and sometimes breeding, aquatics and moisture-loving plants, and in manufacturers providing materials to be used in pool contruction.

As a result water and bog gardens are to be found in a great many British gardens today, notably at the Northern Horticultural Society's garden (Harlow Car, West Yorkshire), at the Royal Horticultural Society's garden at Wisley (Surrey) and in the Savill Garden (Windsor Great Park).

But in all these places water and bog are simply features taking their place among many others. Burnby Hall (Pocklington, Humberside) is unique in having a water garden as its main reason for existence. This remarkable garden was made by Major P. M. Stewart, whose principal delights were shooting big game and fishing. For the latter purpose he made two very large lakes lined with concrete, linked them with a stream flowing through a rock garden and then proceeded to plant them with every variety of water lily he could acquire. By the time of his death he had amassed a collection of about fifty-eight varieties which had proved satisfactory; many of them have now grown into large colonies, so that they make a really spectacular display on sunny summer days.

Another garden which makes excellent use of water both for its own sake and as a medium in which to grow plants is Hodnet Hall (Shropshire). This was planned and made from 1922 onwards by Brigadier Heber Percy. The

The water garden, Hodnet Hall (p. 154)

house overlooks a shallow valley through which a stream flows, and by damming this at several different points the Brigadier created a chain of lakes in and around which he has made his garden. Apart from this considerable emphasis on water and water-loving plants, the planting is very much like that of many other twentieth century park gardens, with good trees to provide elevation and shelter, irregular borders for shrubs and perennial plants, massed rhododendrons and azaleas for late spring and early summer colour, rose beds, peony beds etc. This would be a fine garden without water; with it it is outstanding.

But the most exciting recent use of water in a garden is in the campus of York University. The new university is built on land adjoining an Elizabethan house which was itself acquired by the university authority together with its very old (but not Elizabethan) topiary garden. In the eighteenth century this garden had been enlarged on landscape lines and had acquired a small lake. Much of the rest of the land on which the university buildings were to be erected was rather marshy, though it rose gently to a low hill top on one side.

The late Frank Clarke, Reader in Architecture at Edinburgh University, had the brilliant idea that the cheapest way to get rid of the surplus water and the most effective means of creating a unique university setting would be to drain all the water into an immense river-like lake, which would completely fill the lowest level, and then to arrange the buildings around this.

This dream was eventually turned into reality by a committee of architects and advisers, and it is difficult to know to whom the greatest credit is due. Mr. Clarke was not himself completely happy about the way in which the buildings were disposed irregularly around (and in one case actually in) this lake, and some have criticized the use of a prefabricated building system to produce highly interesting shapes for which it was not intended. But while the experts disagree ordinary mortals delight in one of the most brilliantly imaginative landscapes (perhaps waterscape would be a more appropriate word) created in the British Isles since the eighteenth century.

Modern technology has helped not only in the economical construction of the buildings but also of the fourteen acre lake which was entirely lined with black plastic welded on site. By the time this immense sheet began to break up, the soil had become so consolidated by the weight of the water that there was little seepage and, in fact, the fish which had been introduced to the lake actually benefited from the mineral salts which reached the water from the soil. It is also interesting to note that many of the thousands of semi-mature trees that have been planted each autumn to fill in the landscape have come from Castle Howard, which readers will recollect was one of the first great eighteenth century landscapes.

Gardens illustrating this section include Achamore House, Brodick Castle, Burnby Hall, Edinburgh Botanic Garden, Harlow Car, Hodnet Hall, Logan, Oxford Botanic Garden, Savill Garden, Waterhouse Plantation, Wisley, York University.

THE PROFESSIONALS

Looking back it is strange how few professional designers or architects figure in this account of the development of British gardens. For some reason amateurs, though seldom willing to design their own houses, feel entirely competent to plan their own gardens and a great deal of the variety of our gardens is undoubtedly due to this unfettered, untutored, individual approach. However during the first half of the twentieth century a rapidly expanding class of successful professional and business men anxious to provide themselves with properties of suitable dignity has created a demand for professional assistance. A number of nursery firms established thriving 'landscape' departments; J. Cheal and Sons of Crawley were employed by Lord Astor to plan, make and plant parts of his garden at Hever Castle, and at Polesden Lacey this firm made a series of integrated gardens, including a rose garden, iris garden, lavender garden and peony walk.

Pulham and Sons specialized in water and rockwork. They made the massive rock garden at Wisley, also the upper two lakes and connecting rock garden at Sheffield Park. George G. Whitelegg of Sevenoaks, Kent, also made many fine rock gardens. Harry Veitch and Sons of Chelsea made gardens as well as seeking out and growing new plants, and an example of their work can be seen at Ascott (Wing, Berkshire). William Wood and Sons of Taplow were particularly active in constructing gardens, terraces and courtyards for small to medium sized gardens.

There were also freelance architects, such as Edward White who laid out the garden at Samares Manor, Jersey, for Sir James Knott and included Japanese features in it. He also advised Pulhams at Wisley.

But the most prolific of these professional designers, working in the private sector, yet one of the least publicized, was Percy Cane, who for something like fifty years designed gardens in many parts of Britain and also a few abroad. He was also, between the wars, a frequent exhibitor at the Chelsea Flower Show, and there is no doubt that these exhibits, and the example of many gardens actually created for important private owners, did have an effect on the course of garden design.

His Chelsea exhibits frequently took a form which he may almost be said to have invented. This he called a 'garden glade', by which he meant an area of mown grass more or less enclosed by trees and shrubs, so as to create a closed vista. Where Percy Cane's idea of a glade differed from the usual woodland glade of this period was in the degree of its grooming. It could be described as such a glade tidied up to make it fit into the most urban setting. Though based on the natural, it was quite obviously and intentionally manmade, with well trimmed verges, well cultivated borders and plants carefully selected for the effect they would produce. He liked to break up his areas of grass with little groups of birch trees and when these grew too large they were to be replaced with young ones.

He liked terraces and good stonework around the house, often included herbaceous borders and formal pools of water in his designs and was a little overfond of striking contrasts between columnar and horizontal conifers, such as *Chamaecyparis lawsoniana Allumii* and *Juniperus media Pfitzeriana*. Most of these features can be seen at either Dartington Hall (Totnes, Devon) or Falkland Palace in Scotland. At the former, where he followed the American professional, Beatrix Farrand, there are typical stone stairways leading down into and out of the great tiltyard, another mammoth staircase leading up to the belvedere and grass terrace above the tiltyard, and above this again a typical glade linking these essentially formal features with the outer woodland. There is a lot of Pfitzer's juniper too, but here they are contrasted not with an erect form of Lawson's cypress but with the old Irish yews, the twelve apostles, which have long been a feature of Dartington.

At Falkland Palace we observe the same well laid, well proportioned flag-stone paths and terraces, plus borders skilfully angled to focus attention on some of the most exciting features of the palace, and parts of the ac-companying ruins have been cleverly emphasized with rose and heather beds.

Nearly all the more famous free-lance designers have been engaged mainly on town planning, industrial landscapes and similar large scale work, where the scope and the money available have been so much greater than in private gardens. Much of this has been too big to appear to have much relevance to the problems of ordinary householders, and when one such planner, charged with the landscaping of a satellite town, was invited to write a series of articles advising tenants of the new authority how to lay out their own gardens, he admitted that he had not even started to design his own since it was so small he did not know what to do with it. Pressed further he agreed to supply a few plans provided someone else added the plants, since his knowledge of these was limited.

This highlights a fundamental difference in approach between many present day professional architects and private gardeners. Many of the former believe that exotic plants, and particularly conspicuous plants such as trees and large shrubs, should be excluded from a landscape to which they are foreign not only in origin but also in character. Only native plants should be used, though that definition seems often to be stretched to in-clude any that have become familiar by long usage or those which so closely resemble native species that it requires expert knowledge to identify them as foreign. Whatever their aesthetic validity such arguments have little appeal for gardeners, most of whom are too keenly interested in colour, form and rarity to allow themselves to be confined to the very restricted British native flora.

In this connection it is worth noting that there is disagreement among large scale planners as to whether theories that may seem appropriate in a rural setting should also apply in an urban area. Some argue that where the whole environment is obviously man-made exotic plants are acceptable if they fit into the overall style that is being created. An example of this kind of conflict has occured at Exeter University where a considerable garden has been created during the last twenty years or so, partly by preserving the best established planting in a series of nineteenth century estates which were acquired by the university as development land, but also by taking in en-tirely new areas.

Since the nineteenth century garden makers were quite uninhibited by any notion that native plants were superior to exotics, but on the contrary were anxious to stock their gardens with the most fashionable trees and shrubs then available, and since also it has been a policy of many town councils to build up the image of south Devon as an ideal holiday area with an exceptionally mild climate, to which end they frequently used hardy palms, cordylines, yuccas and similar tropical-looking plants in their public

65

The tiltyard, Dartington Hall (p. 122)

planting, it seemed sensible to the university authorities to continue planting in the same style. As a result the campus of Exeter University now has
one of the finest collections of exotic trees, shrubs and climbers to be seen
anywhere in the country. It includes comprehensive collections of
eucalypts, acacias, eucryphias and pittosporums, as well as many plants
seldom seen outdoors elsewhere, such as *Cassia corymbosa*, freely used as a
wall covering for buildings, *Vallea stipularis*, *Tibouchina semidecandra* and *Lobelia tupa*.

But when an eminent landscape architect was called in to advise on a
further extension of this campus she strongly opposed the idea of including
any exotic material in the planting and insisted that it should be entirely in-
digenous.

Nevertheless there has been good use of exotic plants in some new town
development, perhaps most notably at Crawley where J.St. Bodfan Gruffyd
has introduced many fine trees, including sweet gums, various poplars,
robinias, acers and sorbus species, and has planted exotic and native shrubs
in bold groups to give colour and variety of flower, leaf and stem throughout
the year.

In the Royal Horticultural Society's garden at Wisley, Surrey, Geoffrey
Jellicoe and Lanning Roper, both professionals, have combined to produce
a new feature which has completely changed the aspect of the garden in the
region of the house, a long, low building in the vernacular style popular at
the close of the nineteenth century. The garden was originally laid out by
the owner, G. F. Wilson, a knowledgeable plant lover. Much of it he then
planted as woodland for the cultivation of rhododendrons, azaleas and
other shrubs and also of primulas and shade-loving perennials.

Since its acquisition by the Royal Horticultural Society it has been
almost continuously developed and extended so that today it comprises
nearly all the features characteristic of twentieth century gardens, including rock garden, stream, lakes, a new and more favourably situated woodland, herbaceous borders, heather garden, pinetum, model vegetable, fruit
and small gardens, fine modern glasshouses and an area reserved for the
trial of new plants and vegetables.

But one thing it lacked was any really formal feature and it was this that
Messrs Jellicoe and Roper were asked to add. An old range of glasshouses in
front of the house was demolished, a potting and tool shed beyond them was
altered to make a pleasant garden building, arched in the centre so that a
vista could be obtained through it, and the old frame yard and nursery
beyond were converted into a walled garden.

The major feature of this new development is a large canal pool fed with
water by bubbling fountains in raised stone tanks and gushing wall fountains. A large multi-jet fountain is set in the pool itself and to one side there
is an avenue of Western hemlocks which, as they grow sufficiently large, are
to be pleached to form a covered alley held aloft on bare stilt-like trunks.

The walled garden is equally formal, divided by a hedge into two equal sections, both filled with simple geometric beds, but that nearest to the pool used for bedding plants in season, the other for more permanent planting of herbaceous perennials, shrubs and roses. It is in this section, designed by Lanning Roper, that the greatest sensitivity in the association of plants is shown, a really fine example of our present preoccupation with plant colour and form, considerations which Miss Jekyll advocated so persuasively three quarters of a century ago.

Gardens illustrating the section include Dartington Hall, Falkland Palace, Polesden Lacey, Sandringham, Wisley, York University.

A promenade beside the water – York University (p. 244)

Recommended
Gardens

At least 2,000 gardens in Britain and Ireland are open to the public at some time each year, though with many it is for no more than half a day in aid of charity. On top of this there are a great many public parks and botanic gardens, as well as the grounds of numerous universities and other establishments. Probably nowhere else in the world is there such a concentration of interest for the garden-loving visitor, nor such a diversity of styles and plants; for, as I hope I have shown in the first part of this book, in the British Isles fashions in garden making have changed frequently and profoundly, and the climate and soil are so diverse that it is possible to grow an enormous range of plants.

Clearly all these gardens cannot be mentioned individually in this book. My selection has been guided by two main objectives; one, that the gardens must contain something of real interest to gardeners, whether by way of history, design or plants, and the other that it must be possible to visit them. Other things being equal I have therefore favoured those gardens that are open frequently, and have only included a few of the one-or-two-day-per-annum type where they appear to be almost unique in some respect and therefore worth a special effort.

As far as practicable I have indicated the frequency and main periods of opening, but it is impossible to give precise dates and times in a book which will not be revised and re-issued annually, since these can and do change. In the case of gardens in private ownership there is also the possibility that the owner no longer feels able to open or that the property changes hands and the new owners do not wish to continue in the old way. All I can say, therefore, is that **at the time of writing the information given is to the best of my knowledge correct, but that it would be wise to check, and certainly to look up actual dates and times of opening in the various guides and lists that are published annually.** One of the most comprehensive is *Historic Houses,*

Castles and Gardens in Great Britain and Ireland, published by ABC Travel Guides Ltd., Dunstable, Bedfordshire, and obtainable from most book-shops and newsagents. The National Trust publishes an annual, *Properties Open in 19—*, which is obtainable from regional offices or the head office, 42 Queen Anne's Gate, London SW1H 9AS. A comparable guide is issued by the National Trust for Scotland from its offices, 5 Charlotte Square, Edin-burgh; and in collaboration with the Scottish Tourist Board it also issues a more comprehensive guide, *Seeing Scotland.*

Four principal charities organizing garden openings in Britain are the National Gardens Scheme, 57 Lower Belgrave Street, London SW1W 0LR; Scotland's Garden Scheme, 26 Carlisle Terrace, Edinburgh EH1 2EL; Gardeners' Sunday, White Witches, Claygate Road, Dorking, Surrey; and the British Red Cross Society, 9 Grosvenor Crescent, London SW1X 7EJ. Their guides, known respectively as *Gardens of England and Wales Open to the Public, Scotland's Gardens, Gardens to Visit,* and *Open Gardens Guide,* are available from the respective head offices and also from many bookstalls and newsagents.

For Ireland there is *Castles, Houses and Gardens of Ireland,* published by the Historic Irish Tourist Houses and Gardens Association, Rookwood, Bally-boden, Dublin 14; also a smaller brochure, *Castles, Houses and Gardens* from the same source.

In addition both the National Trust and the National Trust for Scotland publish individual guides for most of the properties they own, and some, but by no means all, of these contain moderately comprehensive lists of excep-tionally fine or rare plants growing in the gardens.

One of the best detailed surveys of plants is *Conifers in the British Isles,* pub-lished by the Royal Horticultural Society, Vincent Square, London SW1P 2PE, but as its name indicates this is concerned solely with coniferous trees and shrubs. I do not know of any comparable work on broad-leaved trees, though in *A Field Guide to the Trees of Britain and Northern Europe,* Alan Mit-chell has compressed a vast amount of useful information into a volume suf-ficiently small to be carried around for field reference. I strongly recommend it to all lovers of trees. Mr Mitchell is now in charge of both Westonbirt Arboretum and the National Pinetum at Bedgebury. He knows more about the whereabouts and dimensions of good trees in Britain than anyone living and has contributed much of the tree data appearing in *Coni-fers in the British Isles.* Where I have quoted tree sizes they are frequently from his measurements.

It is clearly much easier to pin-point woody plants than herbaceous plants because of their much greater permanence. For the latter all that is usually possible is to give general indications as to the type of plant for which a garden is particularly noted, e.g. that celmisias grow well there, or maybe lilies, gentians or meconopses. But even trees can disappear, blown down by storms, killed by disease or just worn out by old age. Nor do trees always get taller. In preparing these descriptions I have frequently noticed that the most recent available measurements are less than those made 20 or 30 years earlier. Perhaps in the meantime the trees have lost some of their topmost branches and must therefore be presumed to be in a state of decline – or could it be that the earlier estimates were less accurate than those made today?

ABBEY LEIX HOUSE, *Abbeyleix, Co. Laois, Eire. 1 mile south-west of Abbeyleix on the L31. No peak season. Privately owned. Open daily from Easter to the end of September.*

This large garden and park, made on both sides of the River Nore, is chiefly interesting for its collection of trees, including a fine lime avenue, some big larches, possibly among the first planted in Ireland, and also many good conifers. A very big Sitka spruce (*Picea sitchensis*) was planted in 1836 from original Douglas seed, there are good specimens of *P. smithiana*, and a well grown *Pinus wallichiana* planted in 1861. The terraced garden in front of the mansion is not open to the public, but nearby, in front of what was once a dairy, is a little circular pool with a ledge around its edge, which was used for cooling the milk, and this is fed by an amusing little fountain consisting of two children huddled beneath an umbrella which constantly drips water.

ABBOTSBURY SUB-TROPICAL GARDENS, *Abbotsbury, Dorset. Off B3157, on by-road to Chesil Beach, ½ mile west of Abbotsbury. Peak season spring. Privately owned. Open daily from mid-March to late September.*

Here can be seen one of the early plant collections started by Lord Ilchester about 1815, and constantly added to for at least a century after that. Much of it is in woodland which has become very overgrown, but the core of the collection is in a big rectangular walled garden and this has been maintained and is easily accessible. There are some magnificent old trees and shrubs, including many rhododendrons and camellias, some with names that have been almost forgotten. There is a very large pterocarya and many acacias, tricuspidarias, hydrangeas, cordylines, hardy palms (trachycarpus), as well as cannas, kniphofias and numerous other herbaceous perennials.

Exotic plants in Abbotsbury Subtropical Garden

ABERDEEN BOTANIC GARDEN, *Aberdeen, Grampian. In Chanonry, Old Aberdeen. Peak season May to August. University of Aberdeen. Open all the year.*

The 'natural' rock garden, Aberdeen Botanic Garden

This eight acre garden beside the Botany Department buildings of Aberdeen University was started in 1898 as a result of a bequest by Andrew Cruickshank, for which reason it is often known as the Cruickshank Botanic Garden. It has a good collection of herbaceous plants and shrubs, but is chiefly remarkable for two large rock gardens, one made about 1918 by the rather unusual process of excavating deep paths so that much of it is sunk below normal ground level; the other started in 1966 and a copybook example of the 'natural' outcrop method of construction. The old rock garden is now largely planted with shrubs, but the new one contains many good alpines and moisture-loving plants, including *Penstemon pinifolius, Diascea cordata,* numerous gentians and roscoeas.

ACHAMORE HOUSE, *the Isle of Gigha, Strathclyde. By ferry from Tayinloan 3 miles away on A83. Peak season April to June. Privately owned. Open daily from spring to early autumn.*

There was little more than poor woodland around Achamore House when, in 1944, the late Sir James Horlick purchased the whole island of Gigha in order to possess this place and make a garden there. He judged that the mild climate, moist air, ample rainfall and acid soil would be just right for the more difficult rhododendrons that he had been unable to grow in his garden at Titness Park, Berkshire, and the next thirty years were to prove just how right he was. The island is only 6 miles long, 1½ miles across at its widest, but it has one low hill and Achamore House nestles in the lea of this on the landward side, a little sheltered from the worst fury of Atlantic gales, though even so the wind can at times be fearsome. To the

existing trees Sir James added great shelter belts of evergreens such as griselinia, various escallonias, *Rhododendron ponticum, Senecio rotundifolius, Olearia macrodonta, O. forsteri (paniculata)* and *Cupressocyparis leylandii* which divided the garden into numerous sections, though this is not immediately apparent since many of the hedges are concealed by the woodland. Then by leaving some open glades, making many paths and wider rides, and cleverly planting a large pool, he succeeded, with the advice of James Russell, in creating a very delightful woodland landscape, though his primary objective had simply been to build up a vast collection of rare plants.

In this he also succeeded for the climate is sufficiently mild for even quite

71

Woodland pool at Achamore House

tender plants such as *Rhododendron burmanicum*, *R. lindleyi* and *R. fragrantissimum* to thrive. Some of the large-leaved species such as *R. macabeanum*, *R. falconeri*, *R. hodgsonii* and *R. sinogrande* are among the finest specimens of their kind in the British Isles, and a list of the species and hybrids grown at Achamore House reads like the pages of the *Rhododendron Handbook*. (*See* illustration on page 34.)

But this is far more than a rhododendron garden. There are plants at Gigha of a great number of genera from many parts of the world, though the climate is too damp and the light intensity too low for succulents to thrive as they do at Tresco Abbey in the Isles of Scilly. Yet the garden is given a sub-tropical look by large tree-like specimens of *Cordyline australis* and smaller, but still considerable, plants of the much more tender *C. indivisa*.

Around the pond and in many of the damper parts of the garden Asiatic 'candelabra' primulas are completely naturalized so that the problem is not to grow them but to keep them from becoming too crowded or spreading too far. *Camellia japonica* varieties grow but do not flower very well, but the hybrid *C. williamsii* succeeds well and there is a grove of the variety Donation that is a wonderful sight in spring. There is a fine specimen of *Pinus montezumae* in the walled garden behind the house, and the strange Chilean bromeliad *Puya alpestris* grows and flowers in the south walled garden nearby. But really there is no end to the good things that can be found in this remarkable place.

Though it is possible to travel to and from Gigha in a day and see the garden, anyone desiring to study the plants in any detail should arrange to stay at least one night at the little hotel. The views, especially of Jura to the west, are magnificent.

See illustration on page 35 and Colour Plate 6 opposite page 42.

Please check actual dates and times of opening in the various guides and lists given on pages 68–69.

Acorn Bank herb garden

ACORN BANK, *Temple Sowerby, Cumbria. On B6412, off A66. 6 miles east of Penrith. No peak season. National Trust. Frequent spring to autumn opening.*

Here it is chiefly the old walled kitchen garden that is of interest, now transformed into a herb garden with a comprehensive collection of culinary and medicinal kinds.

There are also pleasant herbaceous borders, rose beds, specimen trees and extensive woodland with a mill and gypsum quarry.

ADARE MANOR, *Adare, Co. Limerick, Eire. On L28, 4 miles south-east of junction with T11. No peak season. Privately owned. Open frequently from May to September.*

Here we have a fine example of the neo-Tudor style of architecture accompanied by a large formal parterre designed in the mid-nineteenth century by P. C. Hardwick, the last of the three architects to be employed on the mansion which had taken thirty years to build. The other two were James Pain, a local man, and A. W. N. Pugin, who designed the much more romantic Gothic mansion of Alton Towers. The site is a fine one, with the River Maigue flowing past the house, extensive park and woodland to the north and romantic ruins seemingly dotted all over the place. To all this the elaborately patterned, perfectly maintained parterre makes a striking contrast. The scale is

Box parterre at Adare Manor

appropriately large, the design symmetrical but varied, some sections plain grass, others elaborate *parterre de broderie* cut in box, with long ribbon-like patterns enclosing the whole on each side. Large Irish yews provide the vertical lines in this elaborate composition which can be viewed most effectively from a raised terrace walk on the south side.

Parterres of this kind were a feature of many nineteenth century gardens, but almost all have disappeared because of lack of labour and the high cost of maintenance. This one at Adare Manor is probably the best remaining of its type and period in the British Isles.

ALTON TOWERS, *near Alton, Staffordshire. On the road from Alton to Farley, off B5022, 4 miles east of its junction with A522 near Cheadle. No peak season. Alton Towers Ltd. Open daily from Easter to October.*

This extraordinary garden, made by the 15th and 16th Earls of Shrewsbury at fabulous expense between 1814 and about 1835, portrays the romantic element in garden making at its zenith. Even in its own time it aroused controversy, J. C. Loudon describing it in 1833 as 'in excessively bad taste, or rather, perhaps, as the work of a morbid imagination joined to the command of unlimited resources'.

It is made in the steep sided valley of the River Churnet, quite bare when work began, but now almost entirely filled with trees. The intention of the 15th Earl, who started it all, was to create a fairy-tale garden full of strange buildings and other objects copied from far off lands and distant times. The master plan was his, but he engaged specialists, including Thomas Allason and Robert Abraham, to design some of the buildings. They included an elaborate conservatory, a Roman colonnade and bath, a Grecian temple, a Gothic tower, a Chinese pagoda, a Swiss cottage, and a Druidical stone circle in the style of Stonehenge. He also made lakes of various shapes and sizes by damming or diverting the river, and he created tributary streams, cascades and lots of fountains, including one very strange affair made in the shape of a screw.

It must indeed have looked a motley assortment when it was all done and when, in 1831, as a final gesture to romanticism, the 16th Earl, who had by then succeeded his father, engaged A. W. N. Pugin to design a neo-gothic mansion overlooking the valley, a dark mysterious looking building, all turrets, towers and castellations.

Time, however, has wrought a miraculous change. The mansion has become a ruin. The other buildings have become so deeply embedded in the trees, which were small when Loudon wrote his condemnation, that they only just appear or are even completely concealed until one approaches them closely. Instead of being eyesores they are now fascinating focal points for particular scenes, to be discovered one after another and not taken in at a glance.

Most fascinating of all is the Chinese pagoda in the depths of the valley, standing on a little island in the centre of a pool and spouting a 20-metre column of water into the air.

There are many horticultural delights also to be discovered at Alton Towers. There is a very large rock garden made beneath the causeway that crosses the head of the valley. There is an excellent rose collection, the conservatory is well stocked, the cedars are magnificent and

74

there are splendid trees of many different kinds. Nowadays the place is an amusement park and one can see it, if one so wishes, from the coaches of a model railway or from cars swinging from an overhead cable. These modern distractions have been as successfully absorbed by the trees as the 15th Earl's original 'follies'.

The Chinese pagoda, Alton Towers

ANGLESEY ABBEY, *Stow-cum-Quy, Cambridgeshire. On B1102, 2 miles from its junction with A45. No peak season. National Trust. Open frequently from spring to autumn.*

Huttlestone Broughton, 1st Baron Fairhaven, was a collector of fine art from all parts of the world, and a man obsessed by the garden style of the late seventeenth century. He virtually recreated Anglesey Abbey to house his art treasures and he exploited to the full the flat fenland countryside to set out avenues on a scale worthy of the period he so much admired. One of them, the trees of horse chestnut and plane four deep on each side, extends for half a mile to the west and is crossed at right angles by a second avenue of similar composition which is only a little shorter. Two more avenues run in parallel to the east of the house, and beyond them is an *allée*, cut through Norway spruce which has proved difficult to control; and beyond that again is a wider and more open *allée* backed by the same spruce trees but framed on the other side by more readily trimmed yew.

Lord Fairhaven used all these avenues and formal walks to display statuary and other ornaments of which he made a great collection, and in one formerly marshy spot he built a kind of temple of classical columns framed in a

yew circle to contain a fine marble copy of the Bernini David. In fact wherever one goes in this astonishing garden one is constantly stumbling upon new

Entrance to rose garden, Anglesey Abbey

objects to admire – satyrs leering from the trim yew entrance to the rose garden; lovely vases displayed against dark yew hedges or placed where they will be reflected in water; a remarkable temple in the Chinese style housing a huge, polished porphyry bowl and many more.

All this was done between 1926, when he acquired the place, and the mid-1950s. Then late in life he appeared to change his style, to become a collector of trees as well as of *objets d'art*, and he commenced to establish an arboretum in the avenues to the east and a pinetum in a previously unused area in the extreme south-east corner of the estate. The effect of these additions is to increase the horticultural interest but to blur some of the clean lines of the original design.

There are several other interesting and beautiful things to see in this highly original garden, including a large, semi-circular herbaceous garden designed by a personal friend, Col. Vernon Daniell, and an enclosed parterre planted with blue and white hyacinths in spring, followed by red and yellow dahlias in summer.

ANNES GROVE, *Castletownroach, Co. Cork, Eire. On by-road north out of Castletown-roach on T30. Peak season May to July. Privately owned. Open occasionally or view by appointment.*

Here the principles of woodland and wild gardening have been exploited with great skill by the late Richard Grove Annesley who personally designed and extended this garden over a period of more than half a century. The site is ideal, a steep sided valley through which the Awbeg River flows, dividing and rejoining around low, swampy islands. The house looks down on this valley which has been given an almost jungle-like profusion of mainly exotic vegetation. The variety is not only bewildering but also at times extraordinary.

Who would have expected to find plants one usually associates with rather dry ground, cordylines, for example, phormiums, yuccas, crocosmias and *Curtonus paniculatus*, thriving side by side with obviously wet ground species such as gunneras, rheums, bamboos, lysichitums and Asiatic primulas. On the better drained land of the valley side there are thousands of rhododendrons, species as well as hybrids. There are also fine specimens of *Drimys winteri, Stransvesia davidiana* and several species of aesculus.

In complete contrast to all this informality there is a walled garden of considerable size beside the drive, perhaps the old kitchen garden before Richard Annesley took charge, which now has double herbaceous borders leading to a little summerhouse and long formal beds edged with box and filled with bedding plants in season. Beside this, but cut off as a separate feature, is a water garden with some fine meconopsis species growing around it, including good pink and rose forms of *Meconopsis nepaulensis*. Outside, sheltered by the wall, is an exceptionally large

Streamside planting at Annes Grove

9. The Cottage Garden, Sissinghurst Castle (*see* page 213)

10. The rock garden behind the Pin Mill, Bodnant (*see* page 91)

11. Astilbes in a damp spot, Branklyn (*see* page 96)

Hoheria lyallii and a very good *Sophora microphylla*. The mild and moist climate encourage rapid growth and there are some notably large conifers at Annes Grove, even though they are not very old. These include *Abies magnifica, Cedrus deodara, Cupressus macrocarpa, Pinus wallichiana, Thuya plicata* and *Tsuga heterophylla*.

ANTONY HOUSE, *Antony, Cornwall. On A374, 2 miles west of Torpoint. No peak season. National Trust. Open fairly frequently from April to September.*

For garden lovers Antony House is interesting for its towering candle snuffer shaped arbour cut out of yew, its very tall *Ginkgo biloba, Cryptomeria japonica, Carya ovata* and *Quercus suber*, its Burmese temple bell displayed at the end of a wide alley, and, most of all, for its series of radiating tree avenues. On the north a very large lawn and tree plantations separate the house from the estuary of the River Lynher, and these appear to have been planned by Humphry Repton about 1794. The plantations form radiating avenues, that to the north-east lined with horse chestnuts, and further avenues each composed of one kind of tree, oak, lime etc., radiate like the spokes of a huge wheel around the house. It is not clear whether these were also part of Repton's scheme, but they are quite different in style from those to the north, being open to the country in the English style, not enclosed in woodland in the French manner.

The Burmese temple bell, Antony House

ARLEY HALL, *Northwich, Cheshire. On by-road north from Great Dudworth on A559. Peak season May to August. Privately owned. Open fairly frequently from late spring to autumn.*

There are very old buildings at Arley Hall including a huge tithe barn that may well date back to the fourteenth century. The casual visitor might easily imagine that the house itself was also old, but it is, in fact, nineteenth century, built in the Jacobean style. Its creator, Rowland Eyles Egerton-Warburton and his wife Mary, also laid out the gardens and a plan dated 1846 shows them in outline very much as they are today, though not surprisingly the use made of the various parts has changed. There is, for example, a very large walled garden which was originally a kitchen garden but is now laid out with lawns and flower beds. An old 'tea cottage' is shown looking out on formal beds of a typically Victorian character. The little garden house remains but all formality

The Flag Garden and tithe barn, Arley Hall

has disappeared and curving island beds are filled with a profusion of old-fashioned and shrub roses.

Other changes might be noted, including the planting of many good rhododendron and azaleas, the creation of two little 'secret' gardens, one for herbs, the other mainly for bedding roses, and also of an entirely new woodland garden in an area where formerly there was no garden at all.

The perceptive visitor will also note the very careful use of plants in this garden, particularly the thoughtful associations of colour and form so typical of much twentieth century planting and scarcely at all of the nineteenth century, certainly not of a period as early as 1846. Yet this plan does indicate clearly, exactly where they are today, what is still one of the great glories of Arley Hall, a magnificent pair of herbaceous borders terminated by a handsomely decorated stone pavilion (*see* page 40). They must have been among the first borders of their kind planted anywhere.

ASCOTT, *Wing, Buckinghamshire. On A418, 2 miles south-west of Leighton Buzzard. No peak season. National Trust. Open fairly frequently from spring to early autumn.*

Much of the interest of this garden is that it is one of the very few readily accessible examples of the design work of the famous Chelsea nursery firm, James Veitch and Son. It was made by them towards the close of the nineteenth century for Leopold de Rothschild and shows a curious intermingling of the styles then fashionable though usually regarded as mutually antagonistic. Parts of the garden are formal and clearly intended for Victorian bedding out, but other parts follow the more natural style then being advocated by William Robinson and his followers. There are some handsome fountains, two rock gardens (one made of tufa stone), an arboretum, a topiary garden and a huge sundial laid out on a lawn with gnomen, hours and an inscription cut in box and yew. Perhaps the oddest thing is that these disparate features are not segregated but are mixed in a somewhat haphazard way. However there is

Venus in a shell chariot, Ascott

compensation for this lack of overall coherence in the charm of much of the detail, the many fine trees and other plants, and the fine views over the Vale of Aylesbury.

The topiary sundial, Ascott

79

ATHELHAMPTON, *Puddletown, Dorset. On A35, 1 mile east of Puddletown. No peak season. Privately owned. Open spring to autumn fairly frequently.*

Athelhampton is a Tudor house with what is virtually a twentieth century garden since work did not commence on it until 1891 and there have been constant improvements and additions since. But the new garden has been designed in an old style, with several more or less rectangular enclosures, liberal use of topiary and large hedges, good stone work (it is Ham stone, the same as that used for Montacute), wrought iron gates and suitable fountains, statues and ornaments. It all looks so convincing with its raised terrace from which to view the largest of the parterres, its stone gazebos and all the trappings of a genuine seventeenth century garden, that it is hard to believe that none of it except the house and a fine dovecote is yet a century old. A more obviously modern garden has been made beside the river which flows behind the house and also between this and a subsidiary stream. In this part there are flower borders and a large lawn leading to an area of rough grass with shrub

The largest enclosure at Athelhampton

roses and moisture-loving plants in the damper spots.

BALBITHAN HOUSE, *Kintore, Grampian. On a by-road north-east from Kintore, which is on A96. Peak season May to August. Privately owned. Occasionally open.*

This is a romantic looking house, high and narrow, with jutting turrets and steep crow-stepped gables. It was built some time in the seventeenth century and has remained largely unaltered.

Even the garden, divided into two enclosures by high stone walls, remains in outline much as it must have been for three centuries, but its planting has been completely transformed in the last decade by its present owner, Mrs Mary McMurtrie. She is a flower painter with a special interest in old or choice plants and in a few years she has amassed a considerable collection at Balbithan House and started a little nursery garden from which they can be sold to other flower lovers. The walls are covered with climbers and other plants that enjoy shelter, long rock beds line

A long rock bed, Balbithan House

one of the main paths and are filled with small plants and shrubs which make an almost continuous tapestry of cover as they do at Branklyn. There is a pretty herb garden and beds specially made for old-fashioned pinks, of which Mrs McMurtrie has an unusually comprehensive collection. There is also a lawn surrounded by curving beds filled with *Rosa gallica versicolor* and other old varieties backed by *Campanula lactiflora*, potentillas and other perennials.

In short this is a flower lover's paradise in miniature, charmingly placed beside the River Don in a remote and sheltered valley where its very existence could pass unsuspected until you were led to its gates.

BARNSLEY HOUSE, *Barnsley, Gloucestershire. On A433, 4 miles north-west of Cirencester. No peak season. Privately owned. Open fairly frequently during spring and summer.*

In this little garden, only about 2½ acres in extent, may be seen all the changing styles that have characterized English garden making over the past four centuries, but here they are not left overs from the past nor for the most part deliberate reconstructions of it, but the result of these influences moulding the ideas of Mr and Mrs David Verey, who have completely remade it since 1952.

The stone house was built in 1697 in the Queen Anne style. In 1762 a little Gothic summer-house was erected on the far side of the lawn to the west of the house, and then about 1820 the house itself was given a third storey and a stone colonnaded verandah with a castellated roof which gave the whole building a romantic Tudor instead of a classic Palladian appearance.

This was the framework around which the Vereys went to work and in a few years they had completely transformed the garden to include a formal parterre on the south side, a pleached laburnum alley (*see* illustration on page 56), a tiny picturesque landscape with the Gothic summer-house as the focal point, and a little wilderness of trees and shrubs growing in rough cut grass. They were even able to obtain the facade of a Tuscan Doric 'temple' from an eighteenth century landscape as a terminal feature for one grass walk, and they also purchased a modern fountain by Simon

Barnsley House from the pleached lime walk

Verity with two Cotswold sheep carved in relief from Purbeck stone and sprayed with water by frogs. The whole garden, with the exception of the little landscape which is kept suitably green, is filled with flowers in the beds, up the walls and in containers of many kinds, but all chosen and associated with the careful thought for colour and form which characterizes so much twentieth century planting. Recent additions are two small knots in front of the Tudor style verandah.

BARRINGTON COURT, *near Ilminster, Somerset. From Ilminster follow B3168 and just north of Puckington turn right for Barrington. Peak season May to September. National Trust. Open about once a week all the year.*

The garden, or more accurately gardens, since there are several of them linked together, are beautiful and interesting as an example of the late work of Gertrude Jekyll. She was already over eighty when garden making started here and it seems unlikely that she ever visited the place, but she submitted plans by post for various features, including the formal iris garden, the mixed borders, the walled garden and the moat garden. Before this period it would appear that Barrington Court had virtually no garden, though the two linked houses are both very old, one of honey coloured Ham stone built in the early sixteenth century, the other of red brick built about 1670 and originally used as a stable, though it has now been converted to a dwelling house.

It is interesting to see how the garden sections have been designed to suit these very different buildings and yet to retain a harmony and logical sequence of their own. Around the Tudor house everything has been kept deliberately plain and simple, with lawns sweeping virtually to the house walls and gardening restricted mainly to the planting of aquatics in the old moat and in a stone basin above it.

Much more elaborate are the gardens around the Caroline house. Numerous outbuildings, many of them old and attractive in themselves, invite division into several distinct sections, one a kitchen garden with flower borders, another good mixed borders of perennials and bedding plants extending at one end into an orchard bordered with rose beds. There is an iris garden laid out in formal, box-edged beds, some of which are filled with lavender and further decorated with purple clematis trained over metal frames; and a lavender walk leading to the most elaborate garden of all in front of the Caroline block. This is rectangular, completely enclosed by a high brick wall which is covered with plants and has as its central feature a large lily pool. There are also slightly raised beds filled with crinums, azaleas and other plants, the whole very characteristic of Jekyll's fondness for a formal setting with a lavish display of flowers to clothe but not conceal the underlying design.

The iris garden, Barrington Court

BATSFORD PARK, *Moreton-in-Marsh, Gloucestershire. At intersection of A44 and A429. No peak season. Privately owned. Open occasionally.*

Here is one of the great nineteenth century arboretums, made on a Cotswold hillside with extensive views and notable for its magnificent trees and considerable collection of bamboos. Batsford Park was made from the 1880s

82

onwards by Lord Redesdale, who had been British Ambassador to Japan and was a friend of Sir Joseph Hooker. He was therefore well placed to obtain rare trees and shrubs, which he arranged with great skill, maintaining open rides to display them without losing the fine outward views. He decorated these rides with ornaments, including bronze deer, a bronze Buddha and an elegant Japanese rest house. He also made use of a stream and imported rocks to form pools, cascades and rock gardens.

Cedars and weeping beech in Batsford Park

Only a few of the hundreds of trees can be mentioned, but an excellent catalogue and plan is available and the trees are well identified. There are two exceptionally large specimens, probably the best in the British Isles, of *Cedrus deodara albo-spica*, a tree usually regarded as so slow growing as to be suitable for a rock garden. There is a very fine group of blue Atlas Cedars, a magnificent weep-

ing beech and a huge and very beautiful western hemlock (*Tsuga heterophylla*). On an island in a lake is a particularly slender *Picea omorika pendula*, and other trees worthy of inclusion in this short selection are *Abies grandis*, *Catalpa bignonioides*, *Fraxinus americanus*, several trees of *Juglans ailantifolia*, *Quercus velutina* and old specimens of *Magnolia obovata* and *M. veitchii*.

BEDGEBURY PINETUM, *Goudhurst, Kent. On B2079, 2½ miles south of its junction with A262 at Goudhurst. No peak season. Forestry Commission. Open all the year.*

There has been forest in the Bedgebury district for centuries and in the nineteenth century in some parts of the Bedgebury Estate exotic conifers were planted. This was the estate which in 1924 was jointly acquired by the Forestry Commission and the Royal Botanic Gardens, Kew, as a site for a national Pinetum, since many conifers did not grow well on the dry, poor soil at Kew. Since 1945 the management of the pinetum has been solely the responsibility of the Forestry Commission. Much of the early design was the work of William Dallimore.

With more recent additions the pinetum now covers nearly 100 acres and includes over 200 species of coniferous trees as well as about 250 varieties. The site is itself beautiful, including two valleys, the streams which flow through

them and feed a large lake at their confluence, and the high ridge between them. These natural landscape qualities have been enhanced by the planting, since though for scientific purposes related genera and species are grouped together, they are in irregular interlocking plantations and they are interplanted with many deciduous trees, including maples, oaks, birches, southern beeches (nothofagus) and liquidambar carefully placed to break up the solid masses of evergreen foliage and produce delightful pictorial effects. Nowhere is this care in association seen better than around the lake where a mixed planting of taxodiums and *Metasequoia glyptostroboides* provide delightful contrasts in colour in the autumn, and also in Cypress Valley in which many different varieties of Lawson cypress were planted in 1926

The Cypress Grove, Bedgebury Pinetum

and are now approaching maturity. The tallest tree here is an Intertexta which is now over 20 metres high.

Though Bedgebury is a cold spot (temperatures as low as −22°C have been registered) some fairly tender species have survived in sheltered places, including several species of podocarpus, *Dacrydium franklinii* and *D. bidwillii* and *Phyllocladus alpinus*. Some trees have grown very fast, one *Abies grandis* planted since the national pinetum was started now being over 31 metres in height. All trees in an avenue of Leyland Cypress planted in 1935 now exceed 24 metres. Probably the tallest tree in the pinetum is an *Abies grandis* in Cypress Valley which was 44 metres in 1970, but this is pre-national pinetum planting, as is the big *Araucaria araucana* in Dallimore Avenue close to the lake.

Of interest to garden owners is a well arranged planting of 180 varieties of dwarf conifers.

BENMORE, *Dunoon, Strathclyde. From Dunoon follow A885 or A815. The entrance to the garden is a little over a mile north of the junction of these two roads. Peak season May–June. Dept. of Agriculture and Fisheries for Scotland. Open daily from April to September.*

The official title of this garden is the Younger Botanic Garden, in memory of Mr Harry George Younger, who left it to the nation in 1928, but everyone

Wellingtonia avenue, Benmore

knows it as Benmore, its original name. The 100 acre garden is now administered by the Department of Agriculture and Fisheries for Scotland and used as an annexe of the Royal Botanic Garden, Edinburgh, especially for rhododendrons, conifers and other trees and shrubs which thrive in the moister, milder climate of the west coast.

Benmore is in fact a woodland garden and one that has been long in the making, since some planting is known to have been done as early as 1820. The avenue of *Sequoiadendron giganteum*, the wellingtonia or big tree, leading from entrance to house is probably the finest in the British Isles. One tree was 44·5 metres high in 1970 and another 40·5 metres. There are also many other outstandingly fine conifers including large specimens of *Abies alba*, *A. concolor* and its variety *lowiana*, *A. procera*, *A. veitchii*, *Cryptomeria japonica*, *Pseudotsuga menziesii*

and *Tsuga heterophylla*. One *Araucaria araucana* was 19·5 metres high in 1970 and a feature of all the Benmore monkey puzzles is the way they retain their lower branches, so producing splendid looking specimens, green virtually to ground level.

The collection of rhododendron species is one of the most extensive in the British Isles and the setting, partly on a mountain side, partly on level ground beside the River Eachaig, is wildly beautiful. In such a garden one does not expect many obviously man-made features, but there is, in fact, one of a striking nature at Benmore, a great rectangle of lawn, enclosed on three sides by walls, but open on the fourth to the mountainside and overlooked by a handsome pavilion. This garden is bisected by twin borders filled with a fascinating collection of dwarf conifers.

BERKELEY CASTLE, *Berkeley, Gloucestershire. In Berkeley on B4509. No peak season. Privately owned. Open frequently from spring to mid-autumn.*

This twelfth century castle is so romantically beautiful that any garden could only play a minor supporting role. But the battlements at several levels, extending like narrow terraces around the south and east sides of the castle overlooking the water meadows of the Doverte Brook, do provide opportunity for skilful planting combined with plenty of shelter for climbers or slightly tender shrubs. Excellent use has been made of these facilities and the garden, almost entirely made this century, is most attractive. It takes in an old bowling alley and terminates in a rectangular pool, apparently intended for swimming, but now pleasantly stocked with water lilies.

Planting on the battlements, Berkeley Castle

BICTON GARDEN, *Colaton Raleigh, Devon. On A375, 7 miles north-east of Exmouth.*
No peak season. Clinton Devon Estates. Open daily from spring to autumn.

The complete story of Bicton has yet to be written and there are several unexplained mysteries about this very fine garden. It is, for example, one of the best examples remaining in Britain of what may be termed the French grand manner, yet apparently work did not start on garden making at Bicton until 1735, by which time the style had ceased to be fashionable in England, most new gardens being then made in the new landscape manner. The designs are said to be by André Le Nôtre, but he had then been dead for thirty-five years so if Le Nôtre's plans were used they can hardly have been made for Bicton. Then there is the puzzle that the gardens are not made around the house, as would be customary with a formal design of this kind, but have as their focal point a temple and flanking conservatories. This was a fortunate choice for present day visitors since garden and house are no longer even under the same ownership, one being run as an amenity park owned by a private company, the other having become an agricultural and horticultural institute.

There are really several distinct gardens at Bicton, the formal garden consisting of terraces, canal-like pools and a straight vista through trees to an obelisk on the skyline; a picturesque garden, known as the American garden because it was created primarily for the cultivation of American plants, which is centred on the church; a large and botanically important pinetum; and beyond this, on the perimeter of the estate, a pool and rock bank backed by a romantic looking single-storey garden house known as the Hermitage.

By far the most important of these from the design standpoint is the formal garden; a fine creation by any standards, well placed, well proportioned

and well ornamented. The centre-piece is a large rectangular pool surrounded on three sides by a narrow, canal-like pool. All are displayed on a simple grass parterre decorated with charming lead figures on pedestals, with a tall fountain in the centre of the big pool consisting of several basins of diminishing size one above the other. Between the temple and this final parterre there is a big natural drop in the land which then rises equally steeply to the obelisk on the top of the ridge. There are two big cedar trees below the temple which help to frame the view.

The American garden is laid out in island beds and is unremarkable, but at one end is an extraordinary rockery and a shell house; the first looking more like a model for Stonehenge or a dog's cemetery, the latter circular and built of rustic stone. They appear to be Victorian additions.

The pinetum began to be planted in 1830 and contains some very fine trees. The araucaria avenue was planted in 1844 and some trees now exceed 25 metres in height. Particularly notable specimens here and elsewhere in the garden are *Abies cephalonica, A. concolor lowiana, A. numidica, A. pinsapo, A. squamata* a species rare in Britain, *Athrotaxis*

Formal pools and terraces, Bicton

cupressoides, Carya cordiformis, Cedrus deo-dara grown from the original importation of seed, *Corylus colurna, Cryptomeria japonica, Cunninghamia lanceolata, Fitzroya cupressoides, Libocedrus decurrens, Picea orientalis, Pinus ayacahuite, P. montezumae, P. ponderosa, P. wallichiana, Pseudotsuga menziesii* and *Quercus robur fastigiata* the cypress oak.

The rock garden by the Hermitage was made by W. E. Th. Ingwersen in 1928.

See also illustration on page 27.

BIRR CASTLE, *Birr, Co. Offaly, Eire. In Birr on L32, 11 miles north of junction with T5 at Roscrea. No peak season. Privately owned. Open all the year.*

This mediaeval castle was largely re-fashioned in 1620, but still retains the aspect of a building made for defence. It stands on a little eminence with the little River Camcor beneath it and an extensive park stretching more than a mile to the north-east. There is a very large lake in the middle distance, a well stocked arboretum beyond this and as an impressive and intriguing object in the foreground, the castellated walls on which the huge reflecting telescope of the 3rd Earl of Rosse, a notable astronomer, swung for three quarters of a century after its completion in 1845.

The park, as one might guess from its appearance, is eighteenth century, but considerably altered by later planting and the addition of the arboretum in the succeeding centuries. Interesting conifers include *Abies cephalonica, A. squamata, Cupressus lusitanica* 23 metres high in 1966 and grown from seed collected by T. Coulter in Mexico in 1837, *C. macnabiana, Libocedrus chilensis, Picea maximowiczii, P. wilsonii, Pseudotsuga menziesii* and *Taxodium distichum*. Good broad-leaved trees include *Pterocarya fraxinifolia, P. stenoptera* and *P. rehderiana* (the hybrid between them), *Fagus englerana, F. sie-*

The riverside garden, Birr Castle

boldii, Populus maximowiczii, P. lasiocarpa and numerous species of oak. The common beeches at Birr are also uncommonly fine, and there is a good specimen of the Chinese walnut, *Juglans cathayensis*.

Interest of a different character is to be found in two relatively new gardens, one beside the river close to the castle, the other within part of the old walled kitchen garden to the north across the park. The former is a plantsman's garden full of good material put together with great skill, the second a formal pattern of beds outlined in box and with walks lined by pleached hornbeams. In some of the beds lilacs are trained as standards and there are many other ideas borrowed from a bygone age but charmingly adapted to the requirements and preferences of present day gardeners.

Visitors who have also been to Nymans may see a resemblance in both these gardens at Birr to features in that lovely Sussex garden, which is not surprising since they were designed by the present Countess of Rosse, whose childhood home Nymans was, and who still spends much of her time there. Birr however has limestone soil, while that of Nymans is sandstone and slightly acid, so the range of plants used is different.

BLENHEIM PALACE, *Woodstock, Oxfordshire. On A34, 7 miles north-west of Oxford. No peak season. Privately owned. Open very frequently during spring and summer.*

Blenheim was the nation's gift of gratitude to the Duke of Marlborough after his victory over the French, and Vanbrugh, the most daring and imaginative architect of the day, was engaged to design it. He produced a palace and, aided by London and Wise, the famous Kensington nurserymen, he made a

The water parterre and landscape lake, Blenheim Palace

palatial garden to display it. There were terraces with elaborate parterres and, in the valley to the north, Vanbrugh made a canal and an elaborate stone bridge to cross it, built high with rooms below the carriageway. Then half a century later, in the 1760s, 'Capability' Brown was called in to lay out a landscape, and in the process he destroyed all the garden that was already there. By damming the River Glynne he converted Vanbrugh's canal into a large lake, at the same time partly submerging the bridge so that it lost half its height. The parterres were removed, smooth grass swept up to the palace walls and the whole landscape was altered and cunningly shaped with the typical Brownian clumps and belts of trees. Many consider this his finest work, and it is certainly an impressive landscape, though whether wholly in character with Vanbrugh's elaborate architecture may be open to doubt.

This, at any rate, was the opinion of the 9th Duke of Marlborough, who in the first decade of the present century decided to restore a formal setting in the immediate vicinity of the palace. To this end he engaged a Frenchman, Achille Duchêne, a specialist in this kind of work, to design first a new and very elaborate parterre for the east front, bounded by the orangery on the north side, and later, in the 1920s, a highly original water parterre for the west front, overlooking part of Brown's lake. Duchêne's work is of such imagination and beauty that it bears this close comparison with the master landscaper's work and seems a perfect foil for Vanbrugh's architecture. It is certainly a favourite feature with visitors today. There were plans to replace the Great Parterre to the south, the largest made by Vanbrugh and Wise, but these never materialized and this remains open lawn with a distant view of Bladon Church where Sir Winston Churchill is buried.

The park contains some fine trees including big Lebanon cedars.

BLICKLING **H**ALL, *Aylsham, Norfolk. On B1354, 1½ miles north-west of Aylsham. National Trust. Peak season May to August. Open very frequently from spring to autumn.*

Blickling Hall is a lovely Jacobean mansion, one of the finest of its kind in the country, built from about 1616 onwards, but in a romantic style that was more characteristic of Elizabethan times. The approach, up a wide, straight drive flanked by long rectangular lawns, could scarcely be simpler or better calculated to allow the elaborate facade with its slender towers, elegant gables and high mullioned windows to make their full impact on the newly arrived visitor.

Meanwhile the main gardens remain concealed by the house itself and long wings extending at right angles from it. When they are revealed they prove to be as visually exciting as the house itself.

To the east is a large formal design, first a big rectangular parterre partly enclosed by raised terraces, then a wide grass walk leading through woodland to a temple. Closer inspection reveals that the woodland is itself criss-crossed with a pattern of straight alleys in the manner so fashionable in the seventeenth century, but in fact this garden seems to be a late example of the style made, perhaps, in the early years of the eighteenth century with the temple added fifty or sixty years later as a kind of landscape feature.

On the north and west of the building is a very large, roughly crescent-shaped lake, backed by parkland and, a long way off, a pyramidal mausoleum, all of

Blickling Hall from the terrace

which are undoubtedly eighteenth century landscape additions, though no one seems certain who designed them. They are sometimes attributed to Humphry Repton, but there is no proof and the lake was certainly there in 1770, which is before Repton set up in business as a garden designer.

So at Blickling the styles of two centuries seem to have been mixed together in one, even the handsome orangery, rather oddly placed on the edge of the woodland out of sight of the house, not having been constructed until 1781. What is certain is that the parterre by the house, used in Victorian times as a place for bedding out in many small beds, was completely redesigned about 1930 by Norah Lindsay on much simpler but bolder lines, with four very large rectangular beds, symmetrically placed and permanently planted with herbaceous perennials – an adaptation of the island bed idea for a completely formal purpose.

There is some very good modern planting in the dry moat around the house, including *Buddleia farreri*, *Hydrangea villosa* and *Trachelospermum jasminoides variegatum*. In rough grass to the west and also on the terrace above the parterre are some exceptionally fine colonies of *Cyclamen neapolitanum*. Trees include a very large oriental plane and Turkey oak.

BODNANT, *Tal-y-cafn, Gwynedd. The public entrance is in the lane to Eglwysbach, just north of Tal-y-cafn, off the A496 from Llandudno Junction to Betws-y-coed. Peak season May to September. National Trust. Open frequently from April to October.*

This is one of the greatest gardens in the British Isles and one which combines large scale design with plant collection in a remarkable way. The house overlooks the valley of the River Conwy, with magnificent views of Snowdonia to the south-west, but the garden itself is spread across a glen through which the River Hirathlyn (really no more than a stream except where it has been dammed for a mill pool) flows to the Conwy.

Garden making began over a century ago, but the really big development

91

The view of Snowdonia from Bodnant

began about 1900 when the second Baron Aberconway was given control of the garden by his mother. He immediately began to plant on an extended scale and about 1905 started to terrace the slope in front of the house. For these terraces he adopted the Italian style which had become popular in the preceding century and for which the site was well suited. He was his own architect, designing the terraces in all their detail on graph paper, and he was also his own master builder, directing the constructional work of the estate employees. The result, considered purely as an architectural achievement, is impressive, with five terraces each different in depth, width and ornament and engineered to take in two large blue Atlas cedars that had been growing there since 1875. Between these trees he placed a large formal pool (this is known as the Lily Terrace) and on another, lower down, he made a long narrow canal pool with an open air stage at one end and, as a later addition, an elegant pavilion at the other. The stage is framed in clipped yew and the pavilion was brought from the Cotswold village of Woodchester where it had originally been built in the late eighteenth century as a gazebo, but had later been used for the manufacture of pins, for which reason it is still known as the Pin Mill. It was dismantled stone by stone and re-erected in 1938.

The beautiful glen has been developed as a woodland garden full of choice trees and shrubs. There is a large rock garden behind the Pin Mill, most of it made by the process of exposing the native rock, and containing a fine selection of evergreen azaleas. On the more level ground beside the house where lawns had already been made, extensive beds have been cut to permit an ever growing collection of plants to be established. Some of these are new species introduced as a result of plant hunting expeditions which Lord Aberconway supported financially, some, especially the rhododendrons of which there are now thousands, are hybrids made at Bodnant.

The climate is mild, the rainfall fairly heavy and the soil acid, conditions well suited for many Asiatic and American plants. Bodnant is particularly famed for its rhododendrons, camellias, magnolias, embothriums and euchryphias, but the range of plants grown is vast and to be compared with that in many botanic gardens. Notable conifers, all planted before 1903, include *Abies bracteata, A.* *cephalonica, A. concolor lowiana, A. grandis, A. homolepis, A. pinsapo, Chamaecyparis lawsoniana erecta* (a whole row near the entrance), *Cryptomeria japonica, Pinus ayacahuite, P. monticola, P. muricata, P. ponderosa, Sciadopitys verticillata, Sequoia sempervirens, Sequoiadendron giganteum* and var. *pendulum*, and *Tsuga heterophylla.* A spectacular feature in late May and early June is a covered walk of laburnum, which at that season is a golden tunnel of bloom. An exceptionally fine specimen of *Arbutus andrachnoides*, planted in 1905, is splendidly displayed on the highest terrace in front of the house. In the circular bed around the dolphin fountain there is a fine collection of daphnes. There is an excellent guide book which should be obtained. *See also* Colour Plate 10 opposite page 77.

BORDE HILL, *Haywards Heath, West Sussex. On by-road to Haywards Heath 3 miles south of its junction with B2036 at Balcombe. Peak season May–June. Privately owned. Open fairly frequently from spring to late summer.*

Borde Hill is one of the fine Sussex gardens made at the turn of the century. It was created by Col. Stevenson Clarke in what had previously been well wooded parkland, the new planting beginning in 1893. Col. Clarke was a plant collector with a special interest in trees and shrubs, including rhododendrons and azaleas. He was also interested in plant breeding and raised many rhododendrons and azaleas at Borde Hill as well as a new race of alstroemerias and many hybrid nerines.

In disposing his ever growing collection of plants Col. Clarke made full use of features already there including the cover provided by mature trees and the shelter of two little dells which may be the result of excavations in earlier times.

Because of the constantly changing contours provided by these and the naturally undulating land and also by

Rhododendrons in the woodland at Borde Hill

the use of paths which wind in and out among the trees, the garden has been made to appear much larger than it is. In fact Col. Clarke's rhododendrons increased so rapidly from seed that they soon outgrew the garden proper and further plantations were made in the surrounding woods, but it has not been possible to maintain these so well.

A pool in one of the dells has permitted the cultivation of a number of moisture-loving plants and here will be found a good drift of the ostrich plume fern, *Pteritis struthiopteris*.

There is also a big collection of conifers at Borde Hill, some in a pinetum, some in adjacent woodlands, including Warren Wood, where many of the overflow rhododendrons are, and some

scattered around the garden. Notable trees include *Abies pinsapo* and *A. veitchii* (both planted in 1890), *A. magnifica*, *Clethra delavayi, Cupressus lusitanica, Fagus englerana, Fitzroya cupressoides, Fraxinus spaethiana* (rare in British gardens), the largest recorded specimen of *Magnolia campbellii alba* (in an area known as the Tolls), *Picea brewerana, Pinus balfouriana, P. thunbergii, P. wallichiana, P. jeffreyi* and *Podocarpus salignus*. There is also an exceptionally good collection of maples.

Though this fascinating garden remains in private ownership it is now endowed by a trust and managed by a council comprised of members of the Clarke family, the Royal Botanic Gardens of both Kew and Edinburgh, and the Royal Horticultural Society.

B O W O O D, *Studley, Wiltshire. On A4 between Calne and Chippenham. No peak season. Privately owned. Open regularly spring to autumn.*

Bowood possesses one of the best preserved of all the Brown landscapes and also one of the most beautiful. He worked there from 1761 onwards, following his usual system of placing a dam across a valley below the house to form a lake, filling in the background with trees and planting more trees in clumps to channel the views. He only made one small temple to humanize his landscape, but it is beautifully placed on a little promontary on the far side of the lake where it fulfils its purpose perfectly. In 1785 a ten metre high cascade was built to take the outward flow of water, but this was designed by John Whitehurst and, since it is cut off from the main landscape by trees along the edge of the dam, it really makes a romantic feature of its own.

Then in 1841 Italianate terraces were built around the house, designed by George Kennedy, whose name is also associated with Drummond Castle, but

about whom very little appears to be known. The terraces at Bowood are simple and effective and do not obtrude offensively on Brown's landscape.

Over the years many more trees have been added as single specimens and small groups, giving parts of the park somewhat the character of a well designed arboretum, but nearly all this late planting is outside the landscape as seen from the house and terraces and so increases the arboricultural interest without spoiling the pictorial effect. When in 1955, for the sake of economy, it became necessary to demolish a large part of the mansion, part of the lower terrace was raised and the east terrace was extended over the site of the demolished building, thus preserving a satisfactory balance for the beautiful Adam range which remains.

Among the fine trees in the park are *Abies alba, A. grandis, Araucaria araucana, Cedrus atlantica* (40 metres in 1968 and

Cascade and grotto below the Bowood lake

described by Alan Mitchell as a 're-markable tree'), *C. atlantica glauca, C. deodara, C. libani, Chamaecyparis lawsoniana erecta, Cryptomeria japonica, Pinus ponderosa* (one specimen planted in 1829 and 36·5 metres in 1968), *Pseudotsuga menziesii, Sequoia sempervirens, Sequoiadendron giganteum* and *Taxodium distichum*. *See* back jacket.

BRAMHAM PARK, *Bramham, West Yorkshire. Off A1 at Bramham, 1½ miles north of its junction with A64 from Leeds. No peak season. Privately owned. Spring to early autumn, usually on Sundays.*

Bramham Park was the finest example of the seventeenth century formal French style of gardening in Britain until in 1962 a freak gale destroyed many of the trees which provided the boskage framing the long, radiating, criss-crossing avenues that are a feature of this style of gardening. The architectural features to which these avenues led – formal pools, a stone pavilion, various urns and other ornaments – remained, but looked strangely bare

and inappropriate without the formal setting that gave them meaning.

For some years after this disaster the garden declined still further, but then money was made available for its restoration as a work of art and Bramham Park is beginning to take shape again. It is fascinating to see the pattern emerging once more, and, because the trees are still young, to be able to view it much as its creators must have seen it in the early eighteenth century when it was being made.

Statue at intersection of allées, Bramham Park

BRANKLYN, *Perth, Tayside. Off A85 on the outskirts of Perth. Peak season April to June. National Trust for Scotland. Open on weekdays from spring to early autumn.*

Branklyn is unique, a small bungalow garden that eventually grew to two acres because of the passion of its owners for plants. It is unique also in its design, an almost complete tapestry of plants in which the main open spaces are provided by scree beds and grass is used chiefly as a surface for winding paths.

Unlike many plant collections it has very definite form, due in part to the partial segregation of plants of a particular type to certain areas – here rock plants, there herbaceous plants, elsewhere trees, ferns and so on. But it is much more than this and it has to be conceded that John and Dorothy Renton, who made it little by little between 1922 and the time of her death in 1966, had quite uncommon skill in the arrangement of plants.

They started apparently without any knowledge except that Mrs Renton was interested in botany and Mr Renton in design. It was a gardening partnership that worked perfectly and many would regard Branklyn as the most perfect example of the Robinsonian ideal of 'natural' planting to be found anywhere in the British Isles. It is also full of good plants, some of them rare and difficult, including lilies, notholirions, meconopses, cassiopes, rhododendrons (especially the smaller species), daphnes, snowdrops from many countries, snowflakes (leucojum) and trilliums. There are fine trees and shrubs, too, even in this small space, including betulas, eucryphias, desfontainia, *Genista aetnensis* and maples. Because of this variety it is a garden that can be visited time and time again with fresh delight.

See Colour Plate 11 opposite page 77.

BRESSINGHAM HALL, *near Diss, Norfolk. On A1066, 2½ miles west of Diss. Peak season May to September. Privately owned: Open about twice weekly in summer and early autumn.*

Some people think that Alan Bloom invented the island bed method of displaying plants. In fact it was in use much earlier than that, but in the 1950s he publicized it more effectively than anyone else and in his own garden at Bressingham Hall laid out what is certainly one of the finest examples of the style to be found anywhere in the country. The garden is large and might be described as an irregular and shallow bowl, an ideal setting for this kind of design.

A pool occupies the lowest level with plenty of grass around and the beds, themselves irregular in shape and size, fit logically the contours of the land. So often island bed gardens look as if someone had scattered the ground with jigsaw pieces and simply cut round them where they lay. The result is chaotic, whereas at Bressingham everything seems inevitable.

Mr Bloom has also been a great collector of hardy plants, including rock plants which take their place quite naturally in this setting. He has reintroduced many species that were nearly lost and has also raised new varieties himself and introduced good new varieties from other countries. As a result the Bressingham beds are unusually well stocked yet the plants are always well associated and there is none of the random clutter that so often mars large collections of plants.

A relatively new feature is an annexe to the main garden almost entirely planted with heathers, and beyond this, across a lane, Alan's son, Adrian Bloom, has laid out with great artistry around his own bungalow, heather beds and a mini-pinetum of dwarf conifers.

Island beds at Bressingham Hall

BRISTOL ZOOLOGICAL GARDEN, *Bristol, Avon. In Downs Road on east side of Durdham Downs. Peak season summer. Bristol, Clifton and West of England Zoological Society. Open all the year.*

Summer bedding in Bristol Zoo

The garden of Bristol Zoo has always been an attraction in its own right, known particularly for its brilliant sub-tropical summer bedding and for its numerous fine trees. It was laid out in 1836 by a Mr Forrest of Acton, about whom little seems to be known. Presumably he also planted many of the trees which have now grown to great size. They include all three cedars, Lebanon, Atlas and Deodar, wellingtonia, redwood, araucaria, gingko, liriodendron and *Ailanthus glandulosa*. There is also a fine specimen of fern-leaved beech. In recent years a rock garden has been made and is well planted, also a mini-pinetum of dwarf conifers. There is a good tropical house. The summer bedding continues the Victorian tradition and is some of the best of its kind in the country.

BRODICK CASTLE, *Isle of Arran, Strathclyde. 1½ miles north of Brodick, reached by steam ferry from the mainland (Ardrossan, Fairlie etc.). Peak season March to June. National Trust for Scotland. Open all the year.*

The Isle of Arran is a largish island (approximately 20 by 10 miles) dominated by a mountain, Goat Fell, 2866 feet high, and lying snugly in the Firth of Clyde with the long arm of Kintyre protecting it to the west and the mainland 14 miles or so away to the east. Brodick Castle is on the east side of this island at the foot of Goat Fell, facing south across Brodick Bay. It is, therefore, a very sheltered spot, protected from Atlantic gales yet with the warm Gulf Stream lapping at its feet.

Some parts of the castle are 600 years old, though additions have been made right up to the present century and most of the garden which has made it famous has been planted from 1923 onwards. There is, however, one older feature of

importance, a big rectangular area enclosed by a high wall, originally the kitchen garden, but now used for ornamental plants including roses, herbaceous perennials and an outstandingly good collection of fuchsias, which is planned in a formal way.

The rest of the garden follows the natural contours of the land and makes good use of every natural feature, including rock, stream and woodland. Rainfall is high, the atmosphere humid and frosts rare. Rhododendrons thrive so well that thousands of seedlings can be seen germinating on some of the moist, moss-covered rocks. In a particularly sheltered dell near the sea are some of the finest specimens of the large leaved rhododendrons to be seen anywhere in the British Isles. These include such species as *R. arizelum, falconeri, giganteum, macabeanum; magnificum* and *sinogrande*.

Brodick Castle now belongs to the National Trust for Scotland, who also own the plants, but not the garden, at Achamore House on the Isle of Gigha. So the Trust has for some years been propagating the best Gigha plants and bringing them to Brodick Castle to form a Horlick collection in memory of Sir James Horlick who made the garden on Gigha.

In the damper spots Asiatic primulas of many kinds have become naturalized and by the pond the rare and difficult Chatham Island forget-me-not, *Myosotidium hortensia*, thrives. There are many more plants from other parts of the world, callistemons, leptospermums and tree ferns from New Zealand, acacias from Australia, crinodendrons, desfontainias, eucryphias and lapagerias from South America, watsonias from South Africa, pieris species from the Far East, a notable *Clethra arborea* from Madeira, and so on.

See also Colour Plate 12 opposite page 102.

BURFORD HOUSE, *Tenbury Wells, Salop. On A456, 4 miles east of its junction with A49. Privately owned. Open daily from late spring to mid-autumn.*

The red brick house was built in 1728 and is severely beautiful. The garden that surrounds it today is completely modern, laid out since 1954 by the owner, John Treasure, and displaying probably better than any other garden in the country the virtues of the island bed system when used with skill and planted with the eye of an artist. Only in one feature does the garden reflect the prim rectangularity of the house, and that is a canal pool on the north side. But even here the formality is instantly subdued by irregular beds around winding stream-like pools on each side.

There is water in plenty at Burford House since two small rivers converge beside it and though they are at too low a level to contribute much themselves to the garden views they do provide an inexhaustible supply of water which is pumped up to feed the numerous streams and pools in the garden.

At Burford House island beds are used to create long vistas, some of them carrying the eye well beyond the limits of the garden. There is also a frequent intermingling of freehand with geometric shapes, noted already in the north garden and reappearing in other places.

On paper this might seem incongruous; in practice it seems to work out very well.

Another characteristic touch is the use of a dipping line in many of the beds, with the tallest plants at each end and the shortest in the middle. This opens up cross vistas between one grass walk and another or occasionally almost across the whole width of the garden.

But what no doubt most greatly

Galtonia candicans **and** *Festuca ovata glauca* **at Burford House**

impresses visitors to Burford House is the artistry of the planting, in which plants of all kinds, annual and perennial, herbaceous and woody; are interwoven to create colour and foliage associations which are always delightful and often highly original. *See* Colour Plate 13 opposite page 103.

BURNBY HALL, *Pocklington, Humberside. In Pocklington on B1247. Peak season July and August. Stewart's Burnby Hall Gardens and Museum Trust. Open daily from April to September.*

What is almost certainly the largest collection of water lilies in the British Isles was made here by Major P. M. Stewart in two concrete-lined lakes linked by a

rock garden. They are known respectively as the Upper Water and the Lower Water, the former 187 metres long and 60 metres wide, the latter 100 by 27 metres with a three metre drop between them. Work commenced on the Upper Water in 1910, but the planting of water lilies was mainly from 1918 onwards and was not completed until about 1950. In all about 58 species and varieties were established, many in large colonies. Numerous others were tried but found unsatisfactory. When Major Stewart died he left his house and garden to the Pocklington Rural District Council which now uses the house as offices, has built a museum for Major Stewart's big game shooting and fishing trophies, and maintains the gardens as a park.

Burnby Hall seen across the Upper Water

BUSCOT PARK, *Buscot, Berkshire. On A417, 2 miles east of Lechlade. No peak season. National Trust. Open about once a week from April to September.*

The major gardening interest here is in the formal walk to a large lake at some distance from the house as this is one of the few readily accessible examples of the work of Harold Peto. This walk, which contains many architectural adornments and for much of its length has a narrow rill or canal running down the centre, is described in some detail on page 55. There are other more recent additions including several tree avenues, also with statues, urns and other

ornaments, but these lack the dramatic impact of Peto's work.

100

The walk to the lake, Buscot Park

CAMBRIDGE BOTANIC GARDEN, *Cambridge. Entrance in Bateman Street off Trumpington Road on the south side of Cambridge. No special peak season, but rock garden best in May – June. Cambridge University. Open all the year.*

This is primarily a teaching garden run by the Department of Botany, Cambridge University, but it is also a delightful place even for those with no knowledge of plants, let alone botany. The present forty acre site, purchased in 1831, has never been completely used, but thanks to a generous endowment, considerable improvements in design as well as extensions of the garden have been made since about 1950, including the planting of new avenues of trees and the inclusion of an intriguing multi-jet fountain at a central junction of paths. There are many fine trees including cedars, gingkos and balsam poplars, but the most unique features are the two rock gardens, one of limestone and the other of sandstone. These make it possible to grow an exceptionally wide range of plants under ideal conditions, the limestone garden in particular having been constructed with all the peculiarities of rock formation that occur naturally in limestone formations. In general the plants are segregated according to the country or the continent in which they are native, a feature of special interest to the student of ecology.

Of considerable interest to students of plant relationships is the way in which the systematic beds are arranged. These are the beds in which plants of the same

The limestone rock garden, Cambridge Botanic Garden

family are grown together, and at Cambridge the beds themselves are grouped to illustrate the manner in which the different families are themselves believed to be related. There are also good collections of tulip and rose species.

A good range of glasshouses is arranged like the teeth of a rake, so forming sheltered bays in which many plants can be grown which might be considered too tender for this relatively cold part of England. The greenhouses are themselves well stocked with an extensive range of plants.

CASTLE DROGO, *Drewsteignton, Devon. On by-road to Drewsteignton off A30, 7 miles east of Oakhampton. No peak season. National Trust. Open daily from spring to autumn.*

Castle Drogo has been described as the very last country house to be built in England. It is also one of the most extraordinary, built of granite in the style of a mediaeval castle and standing on an exposed bluff on the northern edge of Dartmoor. It was designed by Sir Edwin

Lutyens between 1910 and 1920, and he also planned the garden with terraces at three levels retained by granite blocks and linked by granite steps. He had hoped that Gertrude Jekyll would determine the planting, but for some reason this did not happen and the planting

101

A terrace at Castle Drogo

plans were made by George Dilliston. The garden is almost as remarkable as the house, severe in its formality and the bleakness of its situation, the angularity of its walls emphasized by rectangles of clipped yews containing weeping elms. There are also flower beds, but the plants are mainly short so that they do not soften the lines much, as Miss Jekyll's planting almost certainly would have done. It remains a remarkable composition, unique in Britain.

CASTLE HOWARD, *Coneysthorpe, North Yorkshire. On branch road to Slingsby, 4 miles north of its junction with A64 at Barton Hill. No peak season. Privately owned. Open very frequently from spring to autumn.*

The landscape movement really got into its stride at Castle Howard, and what started about 1705 as a formal garden, with the architect Vanbrugh and the nursery firm of London and Wise principally concerned, developed into what has been described as the masterpiece of the heroic age of English landscape architecture. The genius of this transformation was the owner himself, Charles Howard, 3rd Earl of Carlisle, who by the time of his death in 1738 had completed the grand design which the visitor sees today and in the process had invented many of the features which were to become the stock in trade of later landscape gardeners.

In every way Carlisle was an innovator. He was the first to perceive and use the architectural talent of the actor

12. Candelabra primulas and gunnera, Brodick Castle (*see* page 98)

13. Contemporary use of plants, Burford House (*see* page 99)

John Vanbrugh who designed for him an immense, exciting mansion to occupy the summit of an east-west ridge of the Howardian Hills, commanding extensive views both north and south across the Vale of York. While London and Wise were still engaged in laying out elaborate gardens around this building, Carlisle was already embarking on a quite new conception which would bring the whole southern landscape into a Claude-like composition of a pictorial and evocative nature. With this end in view he placed classical buildings at key points on the ridge to the east of the house; first the graceful Temple of the Four Winds by Vanbrugh on a bluff reached by a broad walk, and then, much further away, a huge domed temple designed by Hawksmoor which was to serve not only as the distant focal point of the view but also as Carlisle's burial place. The broad walk provided a constantly changing panoramic view both of these buildings and of the country to the south, and was itself punctuated with classical statues. Below in the vale he made a serpentine river and a lake. The large stone bridge which now spans the river, perfectly completing this part of the picture, was not built until shortly after his death, though it seems probable that it had already been planned by him. An early object in the landscape was a pyramid placed beyond the London and Wise parterre, and serving as an eye catcher.

Later, after Carlisle's death, the parterre was removed but a new one was designed by Nesfield in 1850, less elaborate than the original but restoring the kind of solid, stable foreground for a great building which was then considered essential. The huge central fountain which decorates this had been designed for the Great Exhibition of 1851.

Castle Howard – the Temple of the Four Winds, mausoleum and bridge

CASTLEWELLAN, *near Newcastle, Co. Down, Northern Ireland. At Castlewellan on A25 close to junction with A50. Peak season May–June. Ministry of Agriculture, Forestry Division. Open daily.*

The walled gardens around the mansion are not open to the public, but the Annesley Arboretum, itself contained within a large walled rectangle on the side of a hill, and also the park with its big lake and the backing woodlands

103

The Annesley Arboretum, Castlewellan

Charlecote Park – the lead shepherdess is probably by John Van Nost

with lovely carpet of bluebells in May are open. They not only contain a very fine collection of trees, which commenced to be planted by the 5th Earl of Annesley in the 1870s, but also a great many shrubs including rhododendrons and azaleas which make a spectacular display in late spring and early summer. A good deal of new landscaping behind the arboretum has also been carried out by the present owners, the Forestry Division of the Ministry of Agriculture. In the arboretum itself are a great many eucryphias, including *E. cordifolia* and *E. glutinosa*, hoherias, tricuspidarias, some very large pittosporums, including *P.*

eugenoides variegata, drimys, sophoras, embothriums and rhododendrons. The climate is also sufficiently mild for *Cordyline indivisa* to grow well.

Conifers include a good *Dacrydium franklinii*, *Athrotaxis selaginoides*, *Abies georgei* with the pale grey of the undersurface of the needles showing up against the dark green of the upper surface, and a *Picea smithiana* about 22 metres high. Other notable specimens are *Cupressus lusitanica pendula glauca*, *Fitzroya cupressoides*, *Picea brewerana*, *P. jezoensis,* several species of podocarpus and *Torreya californica*.

CHARLECOTE PARK, *Charlecote, Warwickshire. On a by-road off B4086, 4 miles east of Stratford-upon-Avon. No peak season. National Trust. Open almost daily from spring to autumn.*

Though Capability Brown worked here in the 1760s he was not given an entirely free hand and so the result is not typical of his work. Nor, perhaps, did the landscape here require much improvement since it is naturally beautiful and the River Avon flows past the mansion. This is not Elizabethan, as it appears, but mainly nineteenth century in the then fashionable neo-Jacobean manner. The lovely gatehouse is, however, genuine sixteenth century and around it are some splendid cedars and other trees, well made terraces and an orangery.

CHARLESTON MANOR, *Westdean, East Sussex. Off A259, 2 miles east of Seaford on by-road to Litlington. Peak season May to July. Privately owned. Open frequently from about mid-May to September.*

A modern garden created around a very old flintstone house and dovecot and a large tithe barn. It is of great interest for the wealth of plants, including roses and irises, grown on thin chalkland soil. The design is firm and regular, with terraces emphasized by walls and yew hedges, but the planting is generous and in the Jekyll manner.

The old dovecot, Charleston Manor

CHATSWORTH, *Edensor, Derbyshire. On B6012, 2½ miles north of its junction with A6 at Rowsley. No peak season. Privately owned. Open daily from spring to early autumn.*

Garden making has been going on almost continuously at Chatsworth for nearly four centuries and often it has been a leader in gardening fashion. The first formal garden was designed for the first Duke of Devonshire by the famous Brompton Road nurserymen London and Wise, and although much of it has disappeared their magnificent Cascade, a water staircase leaping down the hillside behind the house, the elaborate Sea Horse Fountain below it and the huge canal pool to the south which so splendidly fits its setting remain as examples of the style of that day. In the eighteenth century 'Capability' Brown worked at Chatsworth, widening the River Derwent which flows in front of the mansion and improving the park. Then in the nineteenth century came Joseph Paxton, full of invention as engineer and architect as well as gardener, to build a gigantic conservatory, flower the giant Royal Water Lily (*Victoria amazonica*) for the first time in the British Isles, add a fountain of suitably majestic size and simplicity to the Canal, and construct the great rock features which still astonish visitors.

Even today innovation continues. Paxton's conservatory regrettably had to be demolished as unsafe, but a new plant house of the most modern kind has been built, its weight largely suspended from outside on gantries and cables so that glass panes of exceptional size can be used and the interior space left entirely unobstructed by pillars, so making any style of ornamental planting or display possible. It is heated and ventilated by the most up to date automatically controlled systems and in it the great Amazon lily flowers again at Chatsworth. The greenhouse was

designed by G. A. Pearce, who also made the new plant houses at Edinburgh Botanic Garden.

These are architectural and design features and there are many more of them, such as Paxton's wall cases (a kind of lean-to greenhouse originally designed for the cultivation of fruit), the orangery, Flora's Temple, the formal rose garden and the handsome greenhouse which backs it, and the strange willow tree fountain, its branches made of copper pipes which spurt water in all directions.

But there are also splendid plants at Chatsworth, all there thanks to man's intervention, since this was virtually bare Derbyshire dale before garden making began. Even the dense woodland on the hillside behind the house had to be planted in the first place, though many of the trees are now self-generating. The walks seem endless, with encouraging milestones to tell you how far you have gone, and there are plenty of individual specimens to maintain the interest of specialists. The pinetum contains many good specimens, including trees of *Abies procera* from the original importation of seed by Douglas in 1831, and *Pseudotsuga menziesii*, brought, it is said, by Paxton in 1829 as a seedling carried in his hat.

The cascade, Chatsworth

CHESTER ZOOLOGICAL GARDEN, *Chester, Cheshire. On A51 at Upton-by-Chester. Peak season spring and summer. The North of England Zoological Society. Open all the year.*

Considerable pains are being taken to develop the grounds of this relatively new zoo as an attraction in themselves. Particularly good use is made of spring and summer bedding out with some spectacular displays of violas, polyanthus, tulips, pelargoniums etc. A considerable amount of permanent planting of trees and shrubs has also been undertaken and there is a good rose garden mainly planted with free flowering floribunda varieties; so each year this zoological garden becomes increasingly worth visiting for its horticultural interest.

Spring bedding at Chester Zoo

CHILHAM CASTLE, *Chilham, Kent. On A252, ½ mile west of its junction with A28. No peak season. Privately owned. Open frequently from Easter to October.*

The contrasting styles of many centuries meet here. There is an extensive landscape created in the valley of the Great Stour by 'Capability' Brown from 1777 onwards, and below the house, which overlooks this landscape from the north, formal terraces which clearly belong to an earlier period, though the guide books attribute them to Brown. They

Brown's landscape seen from the terraces of Chilham Castle

are a fine piece of work in themselves, ornamented with gigantic topiary shapes cut in yew. They are connected by handsome flights of steps and provide an ideal setting for the Jacobean house as well as a perfect viewpoint for the Brownian landscape. They could well have been made when the house was completed in 1616, but no one seems to know their history for certain. On the upper terrace there is a mammoth holm oak

(*Quercus ilex*), its many trunks held together by chains, and there is also a mulberry which is reputed to be very old. To one side is a grove enclosing a female statue, which is old in character if not in actuality. It could well be a Victorian addition, as almost certainly are many of the fine cedars planted around the terraces.

At a lower level, between terraces and landscape, is a rock garden completely overrun by conifers; no doubt an early twentieth century addition made with the mistaken idea that these were genuinely dwarf, and not merely rather slow growing, varieties.

Classical ornaments beneath cedars at Chiswick House

CHISWICK HOUSE, *Chiswick, Greater London. In Burlington Lane, Chiswick. No peak season. Department of the Environment. Open all the year.*

Chiswick House still stands exactly as it was when the Earl of Burlington had finished building it early in the eighteenth century. Unhappily little remains of the garden which had so powerful an influence on the fashion of the period, yet there is enough, and it has been sufficiently well restored to give some idea of what it was all about. Perhaps the greatest difficulty for modern eyes is to detect the dawning informality amid so much that appears extremely formal. There are also nineteenth century additions which must be discounted, like the big conservatory and the parterre with beds for gay flowers in season which accompanies it. But many of William Kent's temples and other buildings remain to indicate the classical passion which inspired so much eighteenth century building and landscaping, and there is Charles Bridgeman's straight canal magically changed into a river

apparently meandering through meadows, though suburbia presses in closely on all sides. There are also remnants of the older, French style of gardening, including radiating alleys through close plantations of trees and an exedra of clipped yew, a semi-circular hedge against which statues of Roman emperors are displayed.

The cedars of Lebanon are very fine. There is also a very tall maidenhair tree (*Ginkgo biloba*), a good stone pine (*Pinus pinea*), and one of the largest narrow-leaved ash trees (*Fraxinus angustifolia*) in the country.

King's College Chapel seen from the Fellow's Garden, Clare College

108

CLARE COLLEGE, *Cambridge. In Cambridge, across the River Cam, behind Clare College. Peak season June to September. University of Cambridge. Open Monday to Friday afternoons all the year.*

Within a rectangle, little more than two acres in extent, a delightful garden has been created which portrays many of the ideas that have dominated twentieth century English gardening. There is a strong element of design, a readiness to divide even this relatively small area into several subdivisions, some of which could pass as complete gardens in their own right, recognition of the importance of plants as individuals as well as in the mass and appreciation of the effect colour can have in heightening perspective and creating mood. In this garden both straight borders and curving borders are used effectively and, with carefully placed trees, create vistas which make full use of the beautiful Cambridge architecture, including Clare Bridge, Clare College and King's College Chapel (*see* previous page). One border is planted almost entirely with white flowers, another in shades of blue and yellow, yet another is mainly red.

Though the peak season is undoubtedly in summer when the herbaceous and bedding plants are at their best, this is a garden that has been planned for all year use and even in winter flowers will be found as well as the colour of evergreens and various barks.

Good trees include a very fine metasequoia (which races neck and neck for size with another similar tree at nearby Emmanuel), a swamp cypress (*Taxodium distichum*) appropriately placed at the river side and 23·5 metres high in 1969, a handkerchief tree (*Davidia involucrata*) which usually flowers well and a fine silver-leaved lime (*Tilia petiolaris*).

CLAREMONT WOODS, *Esher, Surrey. On A3 about 1 mile south of Esher. No peak season. National Trust. Open all the year.*

Claremont was one of the great eighteenth century houses and its garden had the distinction of being successively designed by Vanbrugh, Kent and Brown. Only the landscape lake and surrounding woodland with temple and belvedere remain much as Brown left them, except for later additions of exotic trees, rhododendrons and other shrubs. It is this portion that now belongs to the National Trust and is being restored. The house is now a girls' school, the property of Claremont School Trust Ltd., and is occasionally open. The rest is covered by the southward spread of Esher. Notable trees at Claremont include *Cunninghamia lanceolata* planted in 1819 only fifteen years after its introduction from China; *Pterocarya caucasica*, a massive Lebanon cedar and a good *Sequoia sempervirens*.

The lake, Claremont Woods

CLAVERTON MANOR, *Claverton, near Bath, Avon. On by-road to Coombe Down off A36, 2 miles east of Bath. Peak season summer. The American Museum in Britain. Open frequently from spring to autumn.*

The house is old but the garden has been almost entirely remade since 1960. It is of interest for its accurate reproduction of the formal flower garden which George Washington made at Mount Vernon, Virginia, and also for some clever planting below the house terrace by Lanning Roper.

CLIVEDEN, *Cookham, Buckinghamshire. On B476, 3 miles north of its junction with A4 on the eastern edge of Maidenhead. No peak season. National Trust. Open frequently from spring to autumn.*

So many mansions have stood on the terrace at Cliveden overlooking the Thames, so many changes and additions have been made to its surroundings that the history of this place is complex and confused. There is complexity, too, in its gardens, but they follow an orderly progression and contain, or frame, a great amount of beauty.

What always impresses the visitor seeing Cliveden for the first time is the enormous parterre below the house to the south. It is this huge level expanse of grass, bow-shaped at its extremity so that it seems to jut out like the blunt prow of a barge, that forms the foreground of the great panorama of woodland, river and meadow, laid out in the valley of the Thames below. Much of that scenery is man-made but from this vantage point it appears completely natural, as if that is the way it was before man appeared on the scene. The foreground with its firm yet simple pattern of beds lined with box is clearly an artefact and it is the contrast between the two that so greatly heightens the impact of each. At the house end this terrace is terminated by a marvellous stone and brick balustrade created in the early seventeenth century for the garden of the Villa Borghese in Rome and purchased by Lord Astor for Cliveden.

The cockleshell fountain at Cliveden

The rest of the garden is far more complex and is only revealed by exploration. Much of it is woodland, underplanted with rhododendrons and other shrubs, but constantly the visitor discovers new and previously unsuspected features. There is a chapel hidden among the trees; an open air theatre in which Frederick, Prince of Wales, who rented Cliveden for a time, listened to the first performance of 'Rule Britannia'. Not far from this, in the extreme north-west corner of the garden, is the Blenheim pavilion in memory of the Duke of Marlborough, and from here a long formal garden with box scrolls and topiary leads back to the main avenue and an immense fountain in the form of a Sienna marble cockleshell, female figures and water basin.

At the house end of this avenue, to the north of the forecourts, are sarcophagi which will serve as a further reminder that William Waldorf Astor was here before he moved on to Hever Castle, leaving Cliveden to his son and American-born, politically minded daughter-in-law to become the centre of the influential 'Cliveden set'. Beautiful new flower borders have been added recently in this area, and in the forecourt itself there is a fine old mulberry tree.

But if instead of going south the visitor elects to continue eastwards from the fountain, beyond the car park, he will discover a Japanese garden around a kidney-shaped lake containing an island with a little pagoda, which was first displayed at the Great Exhibition in Hyde Park in 1851. From this point it is only a short walk to the exit or one can return to the house by way of the rhododendron valley.

CLYNE CASTLE, *Swansea, West Glamorgan. On A4067 between Swansea and Mumbles. Peak season April to June. Swansea Corporation. Open all the year.*

In this large park and woodland, overlooking Swansea Bay, Admiral Sir Vyvyan Heneage Vyvyan made a notable collection of rhododendrons and other exotic shrubs, trees and herbaceous plants. The climate is mild, the land well contoured with a stream flowing through it, and so conditions are ideal for this kind of garden making. After the admiral's death the park was acquired by Swansea Corporation and some changes made to render it suitable for use as a public park. The general effect of these has been to give the whole place a more obviously man-made appearance, with wide, well paved paths in place of rough tracks, but it remains a fine example of a collector's garden.

A walk through the woods, Clyne Castle

COATES MANOR, *Fittleworth, West Sussex. On road to Coates, off B2138, 2 miles north of its junction with A29. Privately owned. Occasionally open.*

This is a small manor house, really not much more than an exceptionally lovely farm house, built of local stone towards the end of the sixteenth century. Its garden is entirely new, made since 1960 by Mrs G. H. Thorpe, who until then had no experience of garden making, though she had a great deal of experience as a flower arranger. So the garden she made is of particular interest as revealing the skills of the florist applied to the arrangement of living plants. Every plant is chosen and placed with the greatest care, and if, after a time, it proves to be not quite right for the effect intended, it is removed and replaced with something else. Form is as important as colour and Mrs Thorpe takes great delight in concealing hard edges with the encroaching growth of plants. Nowhere is this better displayed than in a little walled courtyard behind the house, which when she arrived was almost completely covered with concrete. By knocking a few holes in this, building up the surrounding borders so

The courtyard garden, Coates Manor

that they were level with the concrete and then planting the whole with carefully chosen shrubs, climbers and herbaceous perennials, she converted this unpromising spot into one of the most delightful little courtyard gardens it would be possible to imagine.

COMPTON ACRES, *Poole, Dorset. In Canford Cliffs Road, Poole, between Bournemouth and Poole. Peak season summer. Privately owned. Open daily from spring to autumn.*

The idea of Thomas William Simpson who made this garden between the two world wars was to create a series of linked but separate gardens representing different styles and periods. They are arranged almost in a circle below the house itself which stands in an English garden with lawns, rose beds, flower borders and splendid views over Poole harbour. There are eight other sections, one of the most spectacular being an Italian garden, with a canal pool, terraces, classical statues, a little temple and well stocked flower borders.

The Italian garden, Compton Acres

Also very popular with visitors is the Japanese garden, which has all the romantic trappings of this style as interpreted by English garden makers, including a red tea-house, a temple, a statue of Buddha and plenty of cherries, maples and azaleas.

Among the other gardens, one is a small enclosure said to represent a Roman garden, another a palm court with more classical statuary; a third a big heather dell which contains rhododendrons and azaleas as well as heathers; in addition, in other parts of the circuit, are a garden of memory designed as a memorial to the present owner's son, a rock and water garden and herbaceous borders.

COMPTON WYNYATES, *Tysoe, Warwickshire. Between A422 and B4035, 8 miles west of Banbury. No peak season. Privately owned. Frequently open from spring to early autumn.*

Compton Wynyates is a Tudor house built, at least in part, with brick and stone from Fulbroke Castle near Warwick, a semi-ruin which in 1509 was given to Sir Henry Compton by Henry VIII to whom he had been page, gentleman attendant and soldier. When Compton Wynyates was built Henry VIII came several times to stay with his trusted friend and later Queen Elizabeth I visited it. It remains much as it must have been then, a delightfully romantic building partly surrounded by a moat, standing in a hollow so that it can be viewed from above. This is, in fact, the first view that visitors approaching from B4035 will get.

And it is one of the most delightful for it reveals not only the whole of the building but also the garden in which it stands. On the south side this garden is almost entirely filled with large topiary specimens cut in yew and box and these look so right for the house that it is quite hard to believe they are a relatively recent addition. They were planted in

The topiary garden, Compton Wynyates

1885 partly to simplify maintenance of the garden, partly to give it a more convincing period character.

Since the topiary garden was made there has been considerable planting of ornamental trees on the slopes of the dell, good climbers have been trained on the walls of the house and a formal garden has been made in a small area enclosed by the moat.

CORSHAM COURT, *Corsham, Wiltshire. On A4 between Chippenham and Bath. No peak season. Privately owned. Frequently open from spring to autumn.*

In 1760 'Capability' Brown began to lay out the park at Corsham Court. In the succeeding years he made the large lake in the middle distance, planted many of the trees, including some cedars of Lebanon, and built a Bath House, partly as an ornamental building in the landscape, partly (as its name implies) as a kind of cold plunge with a deep rectangular basin.

Then in 1799, after Brown's death, Humphry Repton was brought in and the landscape acquired a new look. The lake was enlarged, tree clumps were replaced by isolated trees, a great avenue of elms was planted running northwards across the Bath-Chippenham road, and Brown's little classical building acquired a gothic facade with crocketted pinnacles apparently with the help of John Nash.

In the mid-nineteenth century came more changes and additions, including an extraordinary serpentine wall, built of stones from Chippenham Abbey, to screen the stables from the houses newly built opposite. The wall is twenty metres high and is made to look like part of a ruin with genuine gothic windows and chimneys. Later a flower garden was made behind the Bath House with herbaceous borders, rose beds, etc.

It is perhaps not surprising that with so many diverse styles of garden making and garden improvement the total effect should appear a little disjointed, yet there are fine scenes and splendid trees at Corsham Court. The visitor is greeted

The bath house, Corsham Court

by a very tall *Ginkgo biloba* and a spreading cedar in the forecourt, and behind the house there is a mammoth oriental plane (*Platanus orientalis*) the branches of which have layered themselves all round the main trunk so that it now sprawls over a large circle. Nearby is a very big black walnut (*Juglans nigra*) now approaching 24 metres in height, and a purple beech that is about 28 metres high.

The dovecote at the head of the glen, Cotehele House

COTEHELE HOUSE, *near Tavistock, Devon. From A390 turn south at St. Ann's Chapel on to the St. Dominick road. Entrance to garden is about 1 mile from this junction. Peak season May–June. National Trust. Open daily from spring to autumn.*

Cotehele House is one of those ancient buildings that have grown little by little through the centuries so that it is impossible to give a precise date. 'Late mediaeval' perhaps best describes what meets the eye today, and it is an exceedingly romantic sight, a high gabled, crenellated building of grey granite perched at the summit of a steep, heavily wooded glen, at the foot of which the River Tamar can be glimpsed. There are stone retained terraces immediately below the house to give it a suitably firm foundation and to one side there are lawns and flower beds, a little formal garden around a pool and an area of

rough cut grass in which daffodils, bluebells and other flowering plants are naturalized and a few ornamental trees are planted.

But from the gardener's point of view the real glory of Cotehele is the glen itself which has been developed as a picturesque landscape. Here everything was in the designer's favour and little had to be done except to colour with flowers and embellish with beautiful leaves the lovely landscape that already existed. A beehive-shaped dovecote built of the same grey granite provides exactly the right architectural interest in the foreground, a natural stream has been made to cascade into a man-made pool and the native trees enriched with exotic species and flowering shrubs including many rhododendrons and azaleas. Among them are many good specimens, but it is for the beauty of the picture as a whole rather than for the quality of its separate ingredients that this lovely garden is to be savoured.

CRAGSIDE GROUNDS, *Rothbury, Northumberland. On B6341, ½ mile east of Rothbury. Peak season May and June. Privately owned. Open daily from Easter to September.*

This is not so much a garden as a rhododendron and azalea drive – or hike if one is prepared for several miles of quite tough going. Cragside is, in fact, a remarkable example of *Rhododendron ponticum* and *R. luteum*, the common yellow azalea, taking complete charge of miles of craggy moorland so that only the perimeter road and the areas of bare rock are not covered. This is nature in control, with man's intervention kept to a minimum. There are other rhododendrons and shrubs around the house, and also some good trees, including tall specimens of *Abies concolor* and *A. magnifica*.

Cragside embedded in trees and rhododendrons

CRANBORNE, *Dorset. At Cranborne on B3078, 7 miles west of its junction with A338 at Fordingbridge. Privately owned. Open occasionally from spring to autumn.*

Cranborne is one of the oldest and most beautiful houses in England, some parts of it pre-Tudor, but acquiring its lovely stone loggias later, in the sixteenth century. It came into the possession of the powerful Cecil family in the early seventeenth century, shortly before Robert Cecil was created Earl of Salisbury and acquired Hatfield House. So the earl was making two gardens at once, and not unnaturally paid greater attention to Hatfield which was his own creation, a new and fashionable house close to London and the Court. Cranborne acquired the framework of a garden divided into several courts and with an orchard, kitchen garden and mount, which may well have been made earlier. But thereafter it remained neglected and virtually unused for over 200 years until the beauty of the place was rediscovered in 1863 by the 2nd Marquis of Salisbury and his family. It became their favourite residence, the old courts were cleared and replanted and Cranborne began to live again.

117

Then almost a century later, the 6th Marquis and his wife, while still Viscount and Viscountess Cranborne, decided to replant the garden once again in the style that had proved so successful at Hidcote and Sissinghurst. At Cranborne the formal framework and subdivision into separate 'rooms' already existed as genuine relics of the past. All that was required was to provide them with a suitable rich clothing of plants, not chosen, as Victorian gardeners so often did, primarily for their brilliance or rarity, but because by colour or form they would contribute to carefully considered compositions.

The north court, enclosed by walls and the house, has become a white garden, full of roses, pinks and other sweet smelling flowers. The south court is largely paved, but the paving is broken up into elaborate patterns with panels of coloured pebbles to contrast with the stone slabs. There are also panels of grass and wide flower borders with more plants clothing the walls and a profusion of roses draping the beautiful gate houses.

What was once the mount is now laid out in a pattern of large beds edged with box and filled with an almost cottage-like medley of plants. There is a streamside garden that seems completely natural and a walk to the church in which flowers mingle with fruit trees in an almost mediaeval manner.

Even more mediaeval is the herb garden at some distance from the house, a secret place, totally enclosed by walls and only reached through two other enclosures. This garden, a simple rectangle, is laid out in an orderly, pattern of beds edged with lavender cotton, chives and other small plants and filled with a profusion of aromatic and sweet smelling plants, including honeysuckles trained as standards. It is a delightful spot, expressing perhaps better than any other small plot in the country the effort made by twentieth century gardeners to understand and reinterpret the ideas of the sixteenth century.

See front jacket.

The gate houses, Cranborne

Lysichitums flowering beside a quiet backwater, Crarae Lodge

CRARAE LODGE, *Crarae, Strathclyde. On A83, between Inveraray and Lochgilphead. Peak season April to June. Privately owned. Open daily from spring to autumn.*

This is probably the finest example of a truly 'natural' garden to be found anywhere in the British Isles. It is made around a little stream and gorge on the shores of Loch Fyne. The climate and soil are right for many exotic trees and shrubs, including rhododendrons, azaleas, eucalyptus, nothofagus and sorbus species, embothriums and eucryphias. The site is so beautiful that it required no improvement when in the early 1930s the late Sir George Campbell began to develop it as a garden. At that time his main horticultural interest was conifers, but some exotic trees, including *Eucalyptus urnigera*, had already been planted by his mother, and rhododendron seeds came to Sir George through his membership of the Rhododendron Group of the Royal Horticultural Society. They germinated and grew so well that they soon became a major feature, though never a completely dominating one. Moreover the rhododendron collection itself is catholic and well balanced, so that it is impossible to single out any one group as better than the rest. Big-leaved and small-leaved, hardy and not so hardy, are all to be found in good condition. But the most spectacular time for bloom is undoubtedly late May and early June when the deciduous azaleas are at their peak. Eucalyptus species include *E. archeri, coccifera, gunnii, johnstonii, niphophila, perriniana, simmondsii, stellulata* and moisture-loving *viminalis*. Notable conifers are *Abies magnifica, A. veitchii, Cunninghamia lanceolata, Cupressus lusitanica glauca, Picea jezoensis, Saxegothaea conspicua* and *Sciadopytis verticillata*. A specimen bush of *Camellia reticulata flore pleno* is one of the largest in Scotland.

CRATHES CASTLE, *Banchory, Grampian. On A93, about 2 miles east of Banchory. Peak season May to September. National Trust for Scotland. Open all the year.*

Though the castle – really a dwelling house in the Scottish baronial manner and never designed for war – was built mainly in the sixteenth century and much of the present garden has been made in the twentieth century, the two fit together perfectly, since the style chosen was the modern version of the mediaeval method of dividing a garden into a series of more or less rectangular sections rather like open air rooms. The designer of these gardens was the late Lady Burnett, wife of Sir James Burnett, who gave the property to the National Trust for Scotland. She began work in 1932 and her skill in the selection and cultivation of plants, and most of all in their association to obtain the most delightful effects, quickly made the garden one of the finest of its kind in the British Isles.

The garden falls quite steeply from the house, but the land had been terraced long before Lady Burnett started to plant and the terrace walls provided shelter for many of the more tender species she decided to grow. It is astonishing how well many of these have succeeded in what would appear to be a relatively cold part of Britain, without the sea and the warm Gulf Stream to ameliorate its climate. The list includes *Buddleia colvilei, Carpenteria californica, Cornus nuttalli, Hoheria lyalli, H. populnea, H. ribifolia, H. sexstylosa, Eucryphia glutinosa, Illicium anisatum, Koelreuteria paniculata, Feijoa sellowiana, Mutisia oligodon, Paulownia imperialis* and *Umbellularia californica.* The giant lily, *Cardiocrinum giganteum,* thrives at Crathes and in summer the 2·4 metre high spikes of white trumpet flowers are very impressive, especially when seen against the background of the romantically turreted castle and its massive surrounding hedges of yew, planted in 1702.

It is, in fact, for these pictorial effects so carefully contrived and for the subtle blending of flower and foliage colours that these gardens will be chiefly remembered and loved by most visitors. Near the house there is a little formal garden with rectangles of clipped yew round a rectangular pool and beds all planted in shades of purple, red and

Giant lilies at Crathes Castle

yellow. Below there is a larger 'blue' garden, two of the most massive herbaceous and shrub borders are also in shades of blue and purple, while mixed herbaceous and shrub borders which cross them are in white and grey. A recent addition, made by the National Trust for Scotland, which now owns Crathes Castle, is a yellow garden in which the range of shrubs and herbaceous plants is from lime green to orange.

There are well stocked greenhouses which contain among other things some spectacular passion flowers (passiflora). A fine specimen of *Prunus serrula*, with shining mahogany coloured bark, forms the central feature of the garden in front of these greenhouses.

See Colour Plate 14 opposite page 136.

CRITTENDEN HOUSE, *Matfield, Kent. Off B2160 at Matfield on by-road leading to B2015. Peak season April to June. Privately owned. Open occasionally from April to July.*

Crittenden House at apple blossom time

This is a modern garden made amid orchards and containing some old apple trees which were once part of an orchard. It is, therefore, closely integrated with the countryside, and has been cleverly developed, partly with island beds and mixed planting of shrubs and herbaceous perennials, partly with more formal design filled with plants in a luxuriant cottage garden style. There are two large pools,

one probably an old cattle pond, the other made in an old iron working, and both attractively planted.

The bole of an ancient sweet chestnut, Croft Castle

CROFT CASTLE, *near Leominster, Hereford and Worcester. On B4362, 2½ miles west of junction with B4361. No peak season. National Trust. Open frequently from spring to autumn.*

Garden interest here centres in the very old avenue of sweet chestnut and the magnificent oaks and other trees, many of them planted in the seventeenth century long before the British landscape style was developed. There are, however, later additions including the Fishpool Valley with pools and mixed planting of trees and shrubs, an example of the late eighteenth century picturesque style, also a collection of old-fashioned plants made by the Hon. Mrs Uhlman, who now lives at Croft and is a descendant of the Crofts who originally built the castle.

See illustration on previous page.

CULZEAN CASTLE, *Maybole, Strathclyde. On A719, 3 miles west of Maybole. No peak season. National Trust for Scotland. Open all the year.*

There are several distinct gardens here, one a formal garden below the mansion (it was never a castle despite its name), another an old walled garden some distance away, and a distinctly wild woodland garden. Some of the best plants are in the formal garden and especially in the sheltered borders and against the walls of the terraces that link it with the house. Here are many exotic shrubs and climbers though nothing like the variety or rarity to be found at some other Scottish west coast gardens such as Logan and Brodick Castle. In the old walled garden is a grotto and on the way to it a camellia house, both probably made in the nineteenth century. The park has been developed as a recreation centre, with nature trails.

A rustic archway and rockery, Culzean Castle

DARTINGTON HALL, *near Totnes, Devon. Off A384 about 3 miles south of its junction with A38 at Buckfastleigh. No peak season. Privately owned. Open all the year.*

The garden is famous for its lovely vistas, its good design and its fine collection of plants. The beautiful, stone house is very old, some parts of it built in the fourteenth century, but the garden as seen today has been almost entirely made since 1926. Various well-known people have given advice at one time or another, but the two principal designers have been Beatrix Farrand, an American who worked at Dartington Hall before the Second World War, and Percy Cane who continued to develop the garden from 1946 onwards.

There is a charming garden in the Quadrangle formed by the buildings,

(*above*) Henry Moore's reclining woman at Dartington Hall; (*below*) Terraces above the tiltyard, Dartington Hall

but the main garden centres around an ancient tiltyard a little distance away. This is in a natural depression, shaped to make an open air amphitheatre with a balustraded walk on one side and the land moulded into a series of gigantic tiers on the other. Mr Cane designed stone steps and terraces to lead down into the tiltyard from one end and out of it at the other and another, much wider, longer flight of steps up the steep bank just outside the tiltyard to a level grass area where he constructed a belvedere and placed one of Henry Moore's figures of a reclining woman. From the belvedere one can look outwards across park-like country to a stream and it had been part of Percy Cane's scheme that this should be dammed to form a lake in the middle distance, but this was never done. Nevertheless the views are very fine, one of the most dramatic being across the valley towards the house, with twelve large Irish yews standing in line on the far side of the tiltyard. They are said to have been planted in the mid-nineteenth century and are therefore not so ancient as their great size might suggest. There is a fine *Davidia involucrata* and some Lucombe oaks, so characteristic of gardens in Devon.

See also page 64.

D A W Y C K, *Stobo, Borders. On B712, 7 miles south-west of Peebles. Peak season April to July. Privately owned. Frequently open from spring to early autumn.*

The owners of Dawyck have been foresters for centuries and experimental tree planting has been carried out there for a very long time. Some of the larches near the house are said to have been planted in 1725 which is very early indeed, for, though the larch may have been known in England a century before that, it was not widely distributed nor was it thought of as a forest tree. Even earlier is a silver fir (*Abies alba*) said to have been planted in 1680. The fastigiate form of the common beech actually originated at Dawyck some time in the mid-nineteenth century, but was not brought to general notice until F. R. S. Balfour purchased the property in 1897 and distributed scions to Kew and other gardens. The original tree still grows at Dawyck and in 1966 was 25 metres high but only 2·5 metres in diameter.

So until near the end of the nineteenth century Dawyck could be described as an arboretum rather than a garden. From that time onwards it changed rapidly. The lawn was enclosed with ornamental stone balustrading and similar decorations were used in walks through the woodland and for the stone steps which connected them. A hump bridge in the Dutch style was built to cross the little burn that comes tumbling down the glen and the parapets of this bridge were also attractively capped with stone. Thus almost at a stroke a semi-wild woodland was converted into an obviously man-made woodland garden.

At the same time the planting was greatly increased. Many new trees were

The Dutch bridge, Dawyck

added including what is now a particularly fine weeping elm, and hundreds of rhododendrons, azaleas and other shrubs were planted beneath the trees. Meconopsis species, primulas and other herbaceous plants were introduced and huge quantities of daffodils were planted in the open valley and also in the wide ride up the hillside facing the house. So today Dawyck retains its old place as a trial ground for potentially useful forest trees, but has developed into a beautiful semi-formal woodland and garden which all can appreciate without any specialist knowledge.

For the tree lover a few special specimens to look for in addition to those already mentioned are an exceptionally narrow form of the cypress oak (*Quercus robur fastigiata*), a very well formed *Picea brewerana* also some early plantings such as *Abies procera* (1850), two trees of *Pseudotsuga menziesii* planted in 1835, *Pinus ponderosa* (1838), *Sequoiadendron giganteum* (1856) and *Tsuga heterophylla* (1860). A specimen of *Abies fargesii* is, according to *Trees and Shrubs Hardy in the British Isles*, the only one of its kind recorded in the country, and two other very rare firs are *Abies squamata* and *A. sutchuenensis*. A tree of *Kalopanax pictus* about 24 metres high appears to be the largest recorded in Britain. A feature of the garden is the excellent naming of the trees often coupled with height and girth.

DERREEN, *Lauragh, Kenmare River, Co. Kerry, Eire. Off L62 at Lauragh on by-road to Bunaw. No peak season. Privately owned. Open occasionally.*

Derreen occupies a tiny peninsula, almost an island, jutting out into Limackillague Harbour, one of the numerous deep inlets on the south side of the Kenmare River. It is a sheltered spot with high rainfall and mild winter temperatures, natural advantages which were appreciated as early as 1870 by the 5th Marquis of Landsdowne who commenced to make a collection of exotic plants, mainly trees and shrubs, which has been maintained and enlarged ever since.

The style of planting is natural, in line with the surroundings, a mixture of woodland and glade with one long undulating lawn leading to a wide grass walk and an enormous dome-like outcrop of rock in front of the house which somewhat impedes its view but must add considerably to its shelter.

To the garden lover Derreen is interesting for its many fine plants and particularly for its tree ferns (*Dicksonia antarctica*), originally planted about 1900, which so enjoy the conditions that they have virtually taken control of some parts of the garden, spreading by self-distributed spores which seem to grow best of all in the drainage channels dug in the dark peaty soil.

There are other good plants at Derreen including many fine bushes of *Rhododendron fragrantissimum*, a 7·6 metre tall specimen of *R. sinogrande*, some big *R. arboreum* and numerous bushes of *R. delavayi*. What is said to be the biggest *Cryptomeria japonica elegans* in

Tree ferns naturalized at Derreen

the British Isles grows here. Unhappily this has been partly blown over by a gale and now leans at a perilous angle supported by heavy timber props and almost blocking one of the paths through the woodland. It was 21·3 metres high in 1966.

Hedges throughout are of *Gaultheria shallon*, and *Pernettya mucronata* is virtually a weed, seedlings appearing all over the place even in quite long grass.

There are some of the tallest western red cedars (*Thuya plicata*) I have seen anywhere in the British Isles, some planted as early as 1880 and one specimen 25 metres high in 1966. Other notable trees, with planting dates, are *Abies nordmanniana* (1880), *Cupressus macrocarpa* (1856) and *Pinus radiata* (1880). According to *Trees and Shrubs Hardy in the British Isles* three specimens of *Eucalyptus globulus*, about 29 metres high, are among the largest recorded in the British Isles.

DODINGTON HOUSE, *Chipping Sodbury, Avon. On A46 just north of junction with M4. No peak season. Privately owned. Open daily from spring to early autumn.*

The landscape here is by 'Capability' Brown who started work in 1764 and made two lakes by damming the River Frome which actually rises in the park. Despite the apparent suitability of the site it does not appear now as one of Brown's best efforts, perhaps because it was designed for another, Elizabethan, house. The present massive mansion was designed by James Wyatt and built between 1796 and 1816. It appears to stand too close to the landscape and overpower it, and it may well be that insensitive later planting and insufficient care to restrain natural growth have helped to blur Brown's intentions. He carried water from one lake to another in a curious serpentine aqueduct which discharges over an even more curious gothic cascade. Perhaps of greatest interest to the garden-loving visitor is the curved conservatory which Wyatt built beside the house. Not only is the shape unusual but it has a high gallery at the back from which the plants can be viewed.

Dodington House conservatory with viewing gallery

DRUMMOND CASTLE, *Crieff, Tayside. On A822, about 1 mile south of Crieff. No peak season. Privately owned. Open about twice weekly from April to mid-August.*

The great parterre of Drummond Castle is one of the most impressive garden spectacles to be seen anywhere in the British Isles and its impact is increased by the dramatic way in which it is revealed. This is because it is made on the roughly levelled floor of a valley below buildings of dark grey stone which screen it from the approach drive. One of these buildings is an elaborately turretted and gabled dwelling house, the other a keep, all that remains of a fifteenth century castle that was sacked three times in wars. The two are

The descent from the keep, Drummond Castle

The great parterre, Drummond Castle

separated by a stone paved courtyard. Visitors enter through the keep and it is only after they have crossed this courtyard and reached its boundary wall that the garden is seen at all. Then suddenly the whole is revealed at the foot of a great stone staircase down the valley side, which is very steep at this point.

The parterre is about thirteen acres in extent, laid out in the form of a St. Andrew's cross, but with many elaborations in the form of beds, topiary specimens, trees, buildings and statues.

Right in the middle stands a tall sundial, rather like an obelisk in shape, with something like fifty separate faces and gnomons. It bears the date 1630 and is said to have been made by John Mylne, Master Mason to Charles I, for John Drummond, 2nd Earl of Perth. Some say that since then it has always stood in this place, but it seems more probable that it was brought there in the nineteenth century when the parterre was made, probably between 1820 and 1840. On the far side of the valley there is a stream, the Drummond Burn, and beyond that, on a more gentle slope, woodland bisected by a wide grass ride centred on the stone stairway and the multiplex sundial. In the parterre itself is a copper beech planted by Queen Victoria in 1842, perhaps the date when this great garden was complete and ready for a royal visit.

127

DUNCOMBE PARK, *Helmsley, North Yorkshire. In Helmsley on A170. No peak season. Privately owned. Open occasionally.*

Duncombe Park is important in the history of English gardens as one of the links in the progression from the formalities of seventeenth century garden making to the pursuit of idealized landscape in the following century. The house, designed for Thomas Duncombe, stands on the northern edge of a plateau with the land falling away quite steeply to north and west, and even more sharply, though at a greater distance from the building, to the east to the River Rye. Work started on both house and garden in 1713, the garden occupying the more or less level area to the east. In the main it followed conventional lines with a green parterre in front of the house framed by blocks of trees on each side, with one wide ride parallel with the house and some more winding paths, in the character of a 'wilderness', leading to a little secret garden to the south-east. It is in the treatment of the edge of the escarpment that the originality occurs. Here a great grass terrace was made, banked on its outer edge like a fortification, and decorated with one

large statue of Father Time observing a sundial, and two temples, one in the Ionic, the other in the Tuscan manner. To the east the terrace, nearly half a mile long, is curved to follow the natural contour of the land, whereas to the south it is quite straight.

Today tall trees, growing densely on the slopes below these terraces, obscure the view, which can be best appreciated from the Ionic temple at the extreme northern end. But it is clear that when they were made the view would have been open and it seems an inescapable conclusion that the terraces were made to take advantage of it. This may be compared with what was happening at about the same time at nearby Castle Howard and also with what appears to be a similar tentative approach to landscape a few years earlier in the park at Levens Hall.

The purpose of the Duncombe Terraces must also be compared with those of the related Rievaulx Terrace made about 1758 by the third Thomas Duncombe. This is discussed on page 201–2.

East terrace and Ionic temple, Duncombe Park

Dundock Wood in early June

DUNDOCK WOOD (The Hirsel), *Coldstream, Borders. On A697 2 miles west of Coldstream. Peak season May–June. Privately owned. Open all the year. This woodland garden can be entered by a wicket gate beside the main road from Coldstream to Edinburgh.*

A rhododendron and azalea wood in which planting started in the nineteenth century. *Rhododendron ponticum* and its hybrids and the common yellow azalea (*Rhododendron luteum*) preponderate, but there are also other kinds and together they make a wonderful display as spring gives way to summer.

DUNROBIN CASTLE, *Golspie, Highland. On A9 just north of Golspie. Peak season July to September. Privately owned. Open daily from mid-May to mid-September.*

This is another of Scotland's remarkable houses and formal gardens, the latter a series of parterres which are revealed almost as dramatically as the great parterre at Drummond Castle. Parts of Dunrobin Castle, including the keep, were built at the beginning of the fifteenth century or even earlier, but later building has enclosed much of the former castle. Sir Charles Barry completely redesigned the place between 1835 and 1850 in the Scottish baronial manner, with many gables and cone-topped turrets and then, after this building had been gutted by fire in 1915, it was restored and improved by Sir Robert Lorimer.

The house stands on an eminence overlooking the sea, only a few hundred yards away, and the garden below it, invisible until one comes round the house to look down on it from the terrace.

There are three parterres, probably laid out by Barry when he made his alterations to the house, one circular, the other two rectangular, separated by a belt of trees and shrubs and a large bed of azaleas. Originally the parterre patterns would have been picked out with bedding plants in season, but nowadays to save labour and expense they are permanently planted with floribunda roses. There are also good mixed flower borders and many fuchsias which thrive well despite the fact that this is the most

The circular parterre, Dunrobin Castle

northerly garden of fame in the British Isles. The parterres make a wonderful sight in summer whether seen from the top terrace with the sea as a background or from below overtopped by the fairy-tale castle.

129

Dyrham from the pool

DYRHAM PARK, *Dyrham, Avon. On by-road off A46, 6 miles north of Bath. No peak season. National Trust. Open frequently from April to September.*

In the late seventeenth century, when the Bath stone mansion was built, a great formal cascade in the manner of that of Chatsworth occupied the hillside before the east front, its water plunging into a conduit which took it beneath the building to reappear in the west garden and fill the pool there. Now the pool is all that remains of that noble scene, the cascade having been removed a century after it was constructed to make way for Reptonian landscaping. It seems rather a pity for we have plenty of landscapes and few cascades in the grand Italian manner, but Dyrham is nevertheless a charming place, perfectly situated in rolling, well wooded country. It has an exceptionally handsome orangery built as an extension of the house. Good modern use has been made of the high terrace wall below the church which overlooks the west garden by clothing it with shrubs and climbers.

EASTNOR CASTLE, *Ledbury, Hereford and Worcester. On A438, 1 mile east of junction with A449. No peak season. Privately owned. Occasionally open from spring to autumn.*

This is one of the great nineteenth century pinetums made mainly between about 1840 and 1880 by the 2nd and 3rd Earl Somers, though some planting was done at least twenty-five years before that by the 1st Earl. The castle, in mediaeval style, was built from 1812 onwards. The site is hilly and well wooded, ideal for this kind of 'natural' planting. *Abies bracteata* was grown from the original importation of seed in 1854;

130

Incense cedars at Eastnor Castle

A. grandis was planted in 1861 and is now very tall. Numerous specimens of *Cedrus atlantica glauca* were grown from seed collected by the 2nd Earl in 1845. There are good redwoods, wellingtonias and incense cedars (libocedrus). According to *Trees and Shrubs Hardy in the British Isles* a specimen of the American beech, *Fagus grandifolia*, is the only example recorded in the country, and *Acer lobelii* is another uncommon broadleaved tree.

THE ROYAL BOTANIC GARDEN, EDINBURGH, *Lothian. On the north side of Edinburgh, entrance from either Inverleith Row or Arboretum Road. No peak season. Dept. of Agriculture and Fisheries for Scotland. Open all the year.*

Once inside this remarkable garden it is difficult to realize that it is little more than sixty acres in extent, is almost square and completely enclosed by city streets. The irregularities of both contour and design combine to create an impression of much greater size and fine trees so screen the neighbouring houses that Edinburgh only appears, and then most dramatically, when the visitor ascends the little hill to the tea room and gallery of modern art or follows the winding paths to the highest point of the rock garden in the south-west corner of the garden.

This rock garden is one of the glories of Edinburgh Botanic Garden and is unsurpassed, in some respects unequalled, by any other in the British Isles. It is an early example of the natural style, made between 1908 and 1914 under the direction of Professor Bayley Balfour, but so well was the work done that little alteration has been necessary, though a peat garden has been added to permit an even wider range of plants to be grown. The gentians, primulas and meconopsis species are particularly good.

The arboretum, also started at about this time, contains many rare specimens and there is also an outstandingly good collection of rhododendrons, though since the acquisition of Benmore some of the more difficult kinds are grown there.

Edinburgh has long been famous for its greenhouses, including two hand-

Peat beds in the Edinburgh Botanic Garden

some Victorian palm houses. In 1967 these acquired a worthy companion, an exhibition plant house made in an entirely new way, the weight of the structure almost completely suspended from outside by steel cables so that the interior space is unimpeded. The only other greenhouse using this form of construction is at Chatsworth and the Edinburgh house is many times larger, divided into six sections with different temperatures and humidities and including a large tank for tropical aquatics

131

which can be viewed from below so that the growth of the plants under water can be observed. Two notable plants in this tank are *Victoria amazonica* and *Euryale ferox*. This remarkable plant house was designed by George A. Pearce, an architect employed by the Ministry of Public Building and Works. (*See* illustration on page 27 and Colour Plate 15 opposite page 136.)

One section of this botanic garden is reserved for demonstration plots in which hedge plants, grasses, herbaceous perennials and other plants suitable for particular garden purposes are compared.

EDZELL CASTLE, *Edzell, Tayside. One mile west of Edzell (B966) on the road to Witton. Secretary of State for Scotland. Open all the year.*

This is almost certainly the oldest complete garden remaining in the British Isles, almost mediaeval in its compactness and enclosure yet astonishingly elaborate in its design. It was made by Sir David Lindsay in 1604 and is completely shut off from the outside world by high walls on three sides and the ruined castle on the fourth, all built

The walled garden of Edzell Castle

of the same red sandstone. This rectangular space is overlooked by a stone pavilion or gardenhouse in one corner and by the windows of the castle, and is laid out in a pattern executed in closely trimmed box. When the garden was placed under the custody of H.M. Office of Works in 1932 no trace remained of the original pattern and a new one was designed in the manner of the period. But what did remain, surprisingly intact seeing that the place had been a ruin for over 150 years, were the walls which are remarkable for their craftmanship and decoration. The walls are divided into panels, forty-three of them in all, and these are alternately decorated with a chequer pattern of niches dished to receive flower boxes, and with sculptured symbolical figures, some copied from German engravings made in 1528, with a single large recess for flowers below. There are nesting holes for birds (some say for bees) above the panels and along the top of the wall are more large niches apparently intended for busts, but no attempt has been made to replace these.
See also page 4.

EXETER UNIVERSITY, *Exeter, Devon. On the west side of Exeter within the area bounded by Pennsylvania Road and Cowley Bridge Road. Exeter University.*

As the old University College of the South West of England expanded, until in 1955 it became the University of Exeter, it became necessary to acquire

Victorian pinetum at Exeter University

more and more land to accommodate the new buildings. This involved purchasing a number of old houses with their own gardens and estates, some of them already well stocked with fine trees and shrubs. The site lies round the curve of a hillside overlooking the town and to walk right around it involves a journey of at least four miles. So clearly landscaping of the new campus with its many new buildings was of great importance and the work has been undertaken with energy and enthusiasm.

From the outset the aims have been clear; to maintain a good skyline, to blend new buildings into the landscape, to preserve the best plants that were already there and to introduce new ones in character with the site, its soil, climate and surroundings, bearing in mind that for at least a century it has been Exeter policy to exploit the relatively high winter temperature to give the city a slightly sub-tropical look.

One of the most centrally placed houses acquired in the expansion had a mature arboretum much of which had been planted about 1866 by Robert Veitch and Sons of Exeter, who were active in introducing new species from America and other parts of the world. Other gardens acquired had some of the earliest Lucombe oaks (hybrids between the Turkey oak, *Quercus cerris*, and the cork oak, *Q. suber*) raised about 1762 by another Exeter nurseryman.

So here lay the key to the whole problem; to develop the campus as a kind of loosely extended arboretum with specimen trees and denser plantings, but around the buildings themselves to break into purely decorative planting, using in the main woody plants of a permanent character and being ready to take advantage of every specially sheltered spot to introduce the more tender species that might be expected to survive.

The scheme has prospered amazingly, growth has been so rapid that many of the plantations are already in need of thinning, and the range of plants grown exceeds that in many botanic gardens. There are now 600 species and varieties of trees and shrubs, including 150 conifers, besides many herbaceous plants. There is a comprehensive collection of eucalyptus and acacias, as well as many unusual trees and shrubs, including three species of zelkova, many magnolias, azaras, leptospermums, eucryphias, rose species etc. *Cassia corymbosa* is used as a wall covering for some buildings, *Tibouchina semidecandra* survives in sheltered places outdoors, and yuccas, phormiums, cordylines and various palms add to the sub-tropical appearance of the campus, while such rarities as *Vallea stipularis, Vestia lycioides, Lobelia tupa* and at least one aristea are also to be found. These are mostly young plants. Among the older conifers notable specimens are *Abies bracteata,*

133

Cedrus atlantica glauca, Chamaecyparis lawsoniana vars. *filiformis* and *wisselii, Cupressus sempervirens, C. torulosa, Picea engelmannii glauca, Pinus ponderosa,* *Sequoiadendron giganteum* (one tree 32·5 metres high in 1970), *Torreya californica* and *Tsuga diversifolia.*

FALKLAND PALACE, *Falkland, Fife. In Falkland. Peak season June to September. H.M. The Queen, National Trust for Scotland. Open daily from April to mid-October.*

This is one of the most ancient buildings in Scotland, once a hunting palace of the Stuarts, now partly a ruin, but in part still used as a residence. There are records of a garden here as early as 1464, when Mary of Gilderland lived in Falkland Palace after the death of her husband, James II of Scotland, but when garden restoration began in 1946 there was no trace remaining either of this garden or of any later gardens since the whole area had been turned over to the cultivation of vegetables during the war. So Percy Cane was called in to design an entirely new garden which would be modern in idiom yet would be in keeping with the character of the place and would enhance the beauty of the buildings both ruined and intact. This he succeeded in doing brilliantly by grouping a number of beds, mostly irregular in shape, around a large central area of lawn and disposing them so that the

vistas they created centred upon key features of the palace. This is a fine example of the island bed and garden glade system applied to a practical problem of display. The planting is mainly with trees, shrubs and hardy perennials and right down one side of the garden, against the high wall which separates it from the road, is a very large herbaceous border backed by clematis, roses and other climbers.

In some places restricted colour schemes are used to add further to the pictorial effect, and among the ruins several smaller 'gardens' have been made, one devoted to roses (not Cane's work) and another of heathers around the foundations of a bastion.

A few years later Percy Cane designed a courtyard beyond the main garden and screened from it by a hedge. This is outside the Royal Tennis Court, said to be the only indoor court to remain in

Falkland Palace – planting to highlight a lovely building

Scotland from Stuart times, and is appropriately formal with two raised rectangular water basins planted with white water lilies, surrounded by flower borders and a few Irish junipers symmetrically placed like topiary columns.

FISHBOURNE ROMAN PALACE, *Chichester, West Sussex. In Salthill Road, Fishbourne, off A27, 1½ miles west of Chichester. No peak season. The Sussex Archaeological Trust. Open all the year.*

Britain's largest Roman residence, believed to have been the palace of King Tiberius Claudius Cogidubnus. It has been possible to reconstruct the garden in what is believed to be a realistic manner. *See* page 1.

Davidia involucrata **in bloom at Fota House**

FOTA HOUSE, *Foaty Island, Cobh, Co. Cork, Eire. On T12a, 2 miles south of junction with T12. No peak season. Seen by appointment with University College, Cork, the present owners.*

Planting in this small but very fine arboretum covering about 15 acres began in the 1820s and has continued to the present day so that young trees are now growing up to replace the old. The climate is sufficiently mild to enable many rather tender species to be grown. There is, for example, a *Juniperus bermudiana* over 14 metres high, a very beautiful specimen of the weeping *Dacrydium franklinii* planted in 1854 and a very big specimen of the hybrid between *Pinus montezumae* and *P. patula*. Several species of podocarpus grow well, there are banks of embothriums and the beautiful Chilean evergreen *Gevuina avellana* has attained tree-like proportions. Other good trees include davidias, sophoras, fern leaved beech and oriental plane. This fine collection, made entirely by private owners, is now used by the agricultural department of the University College, Cork, but the arboretum is being preserved and cared for. An intesting feature is an outdoor Victorian fernery in which tree ferns (*Dicksonia*

A hybrid pine in the arboretum at Fota House

antarctica) grow freely and there are also some woodwardias.

FRAMPTON COURT, *Frampton-on-Severn, Gloucestershire. In Frampton-on-Severn, off A38, 8 miles south of Gloucester. No peak season. Privately owned. Open occasionally.*

Here will be found one of the few eighteenth century canal pools which were once a common feature of gardens in this part of England. This one is particularly delightful since it is centred on an elegant two-storey pavilion in the Strawberry Hill gothic style.

The canal and gothic pavilion, Frampton House

14. Herbaceous borders at Crathes Castle (*see* page 120)

15. *Victoria amazonica* in the new plant house, Edinburgh Botanic Garden (*see* page 131)

16. Colour scheme with rhododendrons, The Garden House (*see* page 137 opposite)

17. Permant planting in the parterre, Hatfield House (*see* page 148)

FURZEY, *Minstead, near Lyndhurst, Hampshire. On by-road south from A31, 1½ miles south-west of Cadnam. Peak season spring and summer. Privately owned. Open all the year.*

Furzey is in the New Forest, but in a relatively open spot on high ground with extensive views. It is a plantsman's garden of the present century, laid out in the main in large island beds with grass walks and some larger areas of lawn. A considerable area in front of the picturesque old cottage is filled with heathers, including tree varieties which thrive here. There are also many shrubs including embothriums, eucryphias, rhododendrons and a tree-like specimen of *Corylopsis platypetala* over 6 metres high. Ground cover is used freely to give a complete carpet of growth in keeping with the New Forest landscape with which this fascinating garden merges admirably despite its high content of exotic species.

Hardy heathers at Furzey

The Garden House

THE GARDEN HOUSE, *Buckland Monachorum, Devon. In Buckland Monachorum off A386, 10 miles north of Plymouth. Peak season April to July. Privately owned. Open about once weekly from spring to early autumn.*

The house overlooks steep terraces believed to have been made centuries ago for the cultivation of vines. The garden has been entirely remade since 1948 and contains an outstandingly good collection of rhododendrons, azaleas, camellias, magnolias, cherries and other trees and shrubs and herbaceous perennials arranged with exceptional care in colour association. Though the soil is naturally acid the lower terraces are alkaline through long cultivation and this soil diversity increases the range of plants that can be grown.

See Colour Plate 16 opposite.

137

GARINISH ISLAND, *Glangariff, Co. Cork, Eire. By ferry from Glengariff, on T65 between Kenmare and Bantry. No peak season. Government of Eire. Open all the year.*

Garinish Island, also known as Ilnacullin, is a tiny islet in Bantry Bay in the extreme south-west of Ireland. The islet is close to the shore in an inlet known as Glengariff Harbour, with high mountains to west and north so that it is a little sheltered from the Atlantic gales that can roar into Bantry Bay itself. Yet it is a wild spot and until 1910 nothing grew there except rough grass, thrift and gorse clinging to the thin acid soil. The only sign that man had ever attempted to make any use of it was a stumpy Martello tower crowning the little eminence which terminates the island at its eastern end, but even this had been abandoned for generations. The story of the transformation of this unpromising site by Harold Peto into a series of interlocked gardens with a strong Italian flavour has already been told on pages 55–6.

To attempt such a sophisticated design in such an untamed setting might have seemed crazy. In fact it proved a triumphal success, though only the garden was ever made and became Peto's masterpiece. Work on the mansion was constantly delayed, by business difficulties, war, ill health and finally death. So the little Martello tower still stands solitary guard over this Italian garden filled with exotic plants, amidst some of the most rugged scenery of the Irish west coast. It is, of course, the contrast that increases the tension and so makes this garden bewitching. There is nothing like it anywhere else in the British Isles and possibly nowhere else in the world.

Quite apart from its setting and its design Garinish Island would merit

The Italian garden, Garinish Island

fame for its plants. Many tender things thrive. There are good plants of many uncommon rhododendrons, among them *R. iteophyllum*, *R. fragrantissimum* and *R. tsangpoense*. *Desfontainia spinosa* grows and flowers freely as do lepto-spermums, *Vestia lycioides*, various gre-villeas, abutilons, *Drimys aromatica* and *D. colorata*, *Corokia cotoneaster*, many callistemons, eucryphias and myrtles, embothriums, *Coprosma acerosa, Psoralia*

pinnata, azaras, dicksonias, beschor-nerias and watsonias. There are some notable trees too, including *Agathis australis*, *Athrotaxis laxifolia*, *Chamaecyparis formosensis*, *Dacrydium cupressinum*, *Fitzroya cupressoides*, *Pyllocladus glaucus*, *Podocarpus cunninghamii*, *Taiwania cryptomerioides*, *Torreya californica*, *Clethra arborea*, eucalyptus species, and an *Acacia melanoxylon* over 16 metres high.

See illustration on page 55.

GLASGOW BOTANIC GARDEN, *Glasgow, Strathclyde. In Great Western Road, Glasgow. No peak season. Glasgow Corporation. Open all the year.*

Nowadays this is more of a public park than a botanic garden, but it retains its Victorian greenhouses, including a large circular fernery as fine as any in the country. There are many marble statues among the ferns, which suit the atmosphere well and make this a most attractive period piece. The palm house is also good and there is a small but quite representative collection of orchids, and a succulent house with some big specimen plants.

GLASNEVIN BOTANIC GARDEN, *Dublin, Eire. Off Botanic Road, Glasnevin, on north side of Dublin. No peak season. Department of Agriculture and Fisheries, Government of Eire. Open daily except Christmas Day.*

This exceptionally well stocked botanic garden occupies 48 acres on undulating ground beside the River Tolka which has been cleverly used as a landscape feature. The garden has been con-tinuously developed since 1795 and has some very early and beautifully con-structed glasshouses, including a quite elaborate range divided into warm and intermediate sections which was erected in 1843. The very high palm house is flanked by other, lower wings one of which is devoted entirely to orchids. In other houses there are good collections of cacti, ferns and house plants.

Though the purpose of this garden is primarily educational, considerable effort has been made to interest ordinary gardeners by demonstrating matters of practical interest such as the different

swards produced by individual species of grass, the various garden types of nar-cissus, representative collections of veg-etables and herbs and other similar

Tropical water lilies, Glasnevin Botanic Garden

features. There is a large rock garden, a long scree bed, a peat garden on a steep north facing slope, a river-like water garden, a well stocked arboretum, herbaceous borders and many other features of interest to gardeners, all very attractively assembled and well maintained.

The water garden at Glasnevin

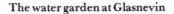

GLENAPP CASTLE, *Ballantrae, Strathclyde. On A77, 1½ miles south of Ballantrae. Peak season May to July. Privately owned. Open very frequently from May to September.*

The 'castle' is, in fact, a mansion built in the Scottish baronial manner and it is surrounded by a park and fine woodlands and a garden made largely in the late nineteenth and early twentieth centuries. Gertrude Jekyll was consulted and sent suggestions for many details, including steps, arches, lookouts, paved areas and a water lily pond, but just how much of her advice was taken is not clear.

To meet present day needs this garden has been simplified, the more elaborate beds eliminated and many shrubs planted, including some fine drifts of deciduous azaleas around a small lake below the house. There is a large walled kitchen garden bisected by herbaceous borders, a frequent characteristic of Scottish gardens, and there are also many fine trees and shrubs, including a notably large *Enkianthus campanulatus* close to the walled garden. Conifers of note include tall specimens of *Abies alba*, *A. cilicica*, *A. grandis*, *A. procera*, *A. veitchii*, *Araucaria araucana*, *Cryptomeria japonica*, *Larix kaempferi*, *Picea jezoensis*, *P. sitchensis* and *Sequoia sempervirens*, the last said to have been planted in 1851 and therefore one of the early plantings since the redwood was not introduced to Britain until 1843.

The pool, Glenapp Castle

Gunnera manicata and spring flowering shrubs, Glendurgan

GLENDURGAN, *Mawnan Smith, Cornwall. 4 miles south of Falmouth on the road from Mawnan Smith to Constantine. Peak season April to June. National Trust. Open fairly frequently, April to September.*

This is one of the first gardens in which the mild Cornish climate was exploited for the cultivation of the new, and often slightly tender, trees and shrubs that were arriving in Britain from Asia, North and South America and Australasia. It is a particularly sheltered place, lying across a narrow valley which runs southwards to the Helford River almost at the extreme south-westerly tip of England. Here planting probably began in the 1820s and the large maze formed with laurel, which is such an unexpected feature of a semi-wild garden such as this, is said to have been planted in 1833. It is placed on the steep valley side so that from the opposite side it is possible to see the maze pattern almost in plan.

Glendurgan is notable for many fine trees and shrubs. There are rhododendrons in plenty, camellias, hydrangeas, eucryphias, magnolias, various species of cornus and some very tall specimens of the handsome South American evergreen, *Drimys winteri*. A rare and beautiful conifer here is the weeping form of the Mexican cypress, *Cupressus lusitanica glauca pendula*. *Agave americana* grows well and has flowered. A tulip tree (*Liriodendron tulipifera*) planted in 1832 was 24 metres high when measured in 1965.

141

The grotto, Goldney House

GOLDNEY, *Bristol, Avon. In Constitution Hill, Bristol. No peak season. Bristol University. Open very occasionally, mainly in the summer vacation.*

Here is a rare opportunity to see an eighteenth century town garden much as its owner made it, but Goldney is chiefly famous for its grotto, probably the most elaborate and best preserved of its kind in the British Isles. This grotto was made by the third Thomas Goldney, a prosperous Bristol banker and industrialist and work started on it in 1737. It was in part excavated, in part covered by a raised terrace of soil which Goldney made right across the end of his pleasure garden, so providing himself with a magnificent platform from which to view Bristol and the River Avon laid out like a map below him. At one end of this terrace he built a bastion and towards the other he erected a round tower, though this was not until 1764. Its purpose was not simply to increase his view still more, but also to house a steam engine that he had designed to pump water for fountains in a canal pool that he had made down one side of the garden.

The terrace served yet another purpose for on the far side its high retaining wall protected a narrow strip used as a kitchen garden and probably also for the florist flowers, auriculas, ranunculus, hyacinths etc., in which Goldney had become interested.

All these features remain and are fascinating, but it is the grotto which is the culminating glory of this garden. From the garden one enters a main chamber, with domed roof, from which a long tunnel leads to an exit on the terrace. There are side chambers to be viewed but not entered, the whole completely covered in shells, ammonites, Bristol 'diamonds' and many other ornamental rocks, fossils and petrifications. The place is still in mint condition; the shells, many of them probably brought back by privateers and adventurers (his father had assisted financially the voyage of the *Duke and Duchess* which discovered Alexander Selkirk, whose strange story was immortalized by

142

Defoe in *Robinson Crusoe*), glittering like jewels in the discreet lighting that has been installed by the university authorities. This is a dazzling subterranean goblin palace calculated to convert the most inveterate grotto hater.

GRAVETYE MANOR, *Sharpthorne, East Grinstead, West Sussex. On the road from B2110, ½ mile from its junction with B2028 at Selsfield Common. Peak season May–June. Gravetye Manor Hotel and Country Club.*

In this lovely Elizabethan manor-house William Robinson lived for many years and put into practice his own highly individual ideas about garden making. Much of it is woodland with trees and shrubs disposed in a fairly natural manner, either among the native trees or in open glades or more obviously man-made plantations. But immediately around the house he preserved a considerable degree of formality, making a terrace and a parterre, but planting both more or less permanently with woody and herbaceous plants. After his death in 1935 the estate passed into the hands of the Forestry Commission and the garden was for a time neglected or considerably changed, but later the mansion became a hotel and country club and considerable pains have been taken to restore the garden to something like its condition in Robinson's day. It is a charming garden made on a hillside overlooking beautiful country and it contains many good trees including a couple of large davidias and big nyssas.

The parterre planted with azaleas and heathers, Gravetye Manor

GREAT DIXTER, *Northiam, East Sussex. Off A28, ½ mile north of Northiam. Peak season April to September. Privately owned. Open very frequently from spring to autumn.*

The romantic half-timbered house was originally a fifteenth century farm, but in the early years of the present century it was enlarged and renovated by the architect, Edwin Lutyens, for Nathaniel Lloyd. Lutyens also designed some of the garden features and though Gertrude Jekyll does not seem to have worked professionally there she was undoubtedly consulted about the planting. The property remains in the Lloyd family and has been constantly well maintained and improved. Like many gardens of its period it is divided into

143

The mixed border at Great Dixter

sections, a sunken garden with an octagonal lily pool, a little courtyard completely enclosed by high walls, a topiary garden, a rose garden, a splendidly large border of shrubs, climbers, perennials and bedding plants, and a little orchard underplanted with bulbs including fritillaries. Many of these features are basically architectural, but the planting is so generous that the sharp line of masonry is seldom revealed in its entirety and the effect, so characteristic of Miss Jekyll's ideas, is of a complete partnership between stones and plants. Another of Miss Jekyll's preoccupations is to be seen in the carefully considered use of colour and of foliage shapes. This is a garden which contains many rare and unusual plants, but always they are used to enhance the overall effect and are not simply displayed as botanical specimens.

See frontispiece.

HADDON HALL, *Rowsley, Derbyshire. On A6, 6 miles north-west of Matlock. Peak season late spring and summer. Privately owned. Open very frequently from spring to early autumn.*

Haddon Hall is very old, some parts of it built in the twelfth century, and looking like a square-towered castle with a more homely Elizabethan wing. This impression of a building originally intended for defence is enhanced by its position, perched high on a bluff overlooking the picturesque valley of the River Wye. Garden making has only been made possible here by terracing, and some of the terraces are very high, the lowest supported by massive buttresses which in spring are covered with aubrieta. Roses feature prominently in much of the terrace planting, but there are also many flowering shrubs and herbaceous plants. This is an excellent example of modern planting (work started in 1928) making the best possible use of an old site. The terraces are very lovely, especially at rose time, but no attempt has been made to create a period effect, either in design or in the choice of plants.

144

Hardy plants and roses, Haddon Hall

HAMPTON COURT PALACE, *East Molesey, Greater London. On A308 at junction with A309. No peak season. Department of the Environment. Open all the year.*

One of the first great gardens in England was made here by Cardinal Wolsey in the early sixteenth century, but, though Wolsey's palace remains, all trace of his garden has been obliterated by later developments. Charles I made an artificial water course, the Longford River, to bring water to the garden all the way from the River Colne eight miles away although the Thames flows beside Hampton Court. But the water in the Thames is below the level of the garden and it was presumably easier to bring water by gravity flow from the Colne than to lift it by machinery from the Thames.

But the really great changes at Hampton Court which remain to impress the visitor today were made in the late seventeenth century when William and Mary reigned and employed Sir Christopher Wren to enlarge the palace, and the famous nurserymen, London and Wise, to redesign the garden. This was done in the grand French manner with formal parterres, radiating avenues, a great canal pool stretching into the distance, statues, clipped trees and shrubs, beautiful wrought iron screens and gates and, indeed, all the fashionable features of the time. Most remain though some have been altered and some additions have been made. The maze was added by Queen Anne and modern taste has required bedding out in season and the creation of great flower borders and of a fine rose garden in the old tiltyard. The huge vine in the vinery was planted in 1769. Yet despite the passage of time Hampton Court remains primarily an example of the formal, architectural style of gardening which dominated Britain at the opening of the eighteenth century yet was soon to be swept away by the landscape revolution.

See also Colour Plate 1 opposite page 16.

HARDWICK HALL, *Ault Hucknall, Derbyshire. On by-road south from Glapwell (A617), 1½ miles east of M1, exit 29. No peak season. National Trust. Open daily from April to October.*

This great Elizabethan mansion has not retained its Elizabethan garden but what exists today, partly made in late Victorian times, partly between the two world wars, and partly since the National Trust took possession in 1959, is simple and in suitable style. The main garden area to the south of the mansion is divided into four rectangles by two wide alleys, one running north and south of yew, the other running east and west of hornbeam. Two of these rectangles are planted as orchards, that to the south-east ringed with rose borders, a third is mainly grass and a fourth is a herb garden and nuttery, well designed

The gatehouse, Hardwick Hall

Capability Brown's landscape at Harewood House

in a formal manner with culinary and medicinal herbs planted in large blocks and tripods for hops and other climbers. Elsewhere there are wide flower borders well planted with a mixture of shrubs, herbaceous plants and bulbs. The park is extensive and the views, mainly to the west, are fine.

HAREWOOD HOUSE, *Harewood, West Yorkshire. On A61 between Leeds and Harrogate. No peak season. Privately owned. Open daily from Easter to September.*

The landscape garden here was made by 'Capability' Brown in the ten years following 1772, and is unusual in being in a considerably more hilly situation than those in which he commonly worked. So here one looks down on the Brown lake from a height and this feeling of having a picture laid out at one's feet is enhanced by the nineteenth century addition of formal terraces beside the house which provide a perfect viewing point. These terraces, with their handsome ornamentation and balustrades, were designed by Sir Charles Barry.

146

HARLOW CAR, *Harrogate, West Yorkshire. Off A59, 1 mile south-west of Harrogate. Peak season spring and summer. The Northern Horticultural Society. Open all the year.*

So mature does this garden appear that it is hard to believe that none of it is more than twenty-five years old. It was started as a demonstration garden for members of the Northern Horticultural Society, a kind of Wisley of the north, and it has expanded rapidly to include all the elements that are important in twentieth century garden making. There are large shrub borders, two rock gardens, one of which includes scree beds, a rose garden and also borders of shrub and old-fashioned roses, a big border for annuals, trial beds for various plants and an extensive woodland garden. But perhaps the most effective feature of all and one that almost puts Harlow Car in a class of its own, is the streamside garden in the bottom of the valley across which the garden is made. This stream is one of those that once supplied medicinal water similar to that of the spa in Harrogate, and what was once a pump house has now become one of the Society's buildings, housing its offices and its library and containing a rest room for its members.

Standing beside the stream or on one of the bridges that cross it one can often detect the smell of the chemicals it contains and one might suppose that this would adversely affect the plants that grow in or beside it. In fact the reverse appears to be true for everything grows with great vigour including some plants, such as white daisy-flowered *Senecio smi-*

View from the stream garden, Harlow Car

thii, not often seen elsewhere. The Asiatic primulas are superb in June, there are great drifts of astilbes, mimulus, and many other moisture-loving plants which so completely fill the banks that in places the water can scarcely be seen.

Harlow Car is of particular interest to gardeners in cold climates since this is a cold part of Britain, high, exposed and about as far from the ameliorating influence of the sea as it is possible to get.

See page 48 and Colour Plate 7.

HASCOMBE COURT, *Hascombe, near Godalming, Surrey. On B2130, 3½ miles south-east of Godalming. Peak season spring to autumn. Privately owned. Open occasionally in spring and summer.*

This is entirely a garden of the twentieth century and one which exhibits many of the dominant themes of the period. Massive twin herbaceous borders separated by wide paths are centred on both fronts of the house; to the east terminated by a stone built summer-house, to the west open to the delightfully wooded and hilly Surrey countryside. The house itself stands high and on the steep slope to the south there is a big rock garden ending in a water garden with Japanese features. Gertrude Jekyll supplied plans in the early days of the making of this fine garden, and later Percy Cane added a good deal of stonework in his characteristic style.

HATFIELD HOUSE, *Hatfield, Hertfordshire. Garden entrance is in Hatfield on A1000. Peak season May to August. Privately owned. Open daily from spring to autumn.*

There are two buildings here, one a nobleman's mansion built by Robert Cecil, 1st Earl of Salisbury, between 1609 and 1611, the other the sole surviving wing of a much older building, the Royal Palace of Hatfield, built in 1497, in which Queen Elizabeth I lived as a girl. It is a little distance away to the west and at a lower level. Formal terraces link the two buildings and it is on these that the main new planting has been carried out in the present century. The principal parterre on the west side is enclosed by yew hedges and laid out in a geometric pattern of beds around a central water basin and fountain. However nowadays these beds are not filled with bedding plants in season as doubtless they originally were during Victorian times, but are permanently filled with a medley of shrubs, roses and herbaceous perennials which make a very gay display throughout the summer. A smaller parterre in front of the royal palace is used for roses, including the lovely old French variety, Gallica Complicata, and there are many climbing roses on walls. On the east side of the mansion is yet another large parterre dominated by a maze, but this is only open about once a week.

There is also an extensive park with long tree avenues extending both to the north and south of Hatfield House and on the south side there is a modern woodland garden with good groups of rhododendrons, azaleas and other appropriate shrubs. The present park at Hatfield resulted from the union in the nineteenth century of two parks that had existed since the thirteenth century. *See* Colour Plate 17 opposite page 137.

HEASELANDS, *Haywards Heath, West Sussex. On A273, 1½ miles south-west of Haywards Heath. Peak season May to July. Privately owned. Open occasionally May to July.*

This is a fine example of a modern landscape in which exotic plants play an important part. It has been created entirely by its owner, Ernest Kleinwort, and spreads across a wide, shallow valley through which a small stream flows. This has been cleverly dammed at several points to give the illusion of a continuous river-like lake. On the house side there are lawns and flower beds flanked by trees and shrubs so that there is a transition from a semi-formal to a

148

A large tree of *Acer griseum* **at Hergest Croft**

park-like style, but on the far side there is an extensive woodland garden under-planted with rhododendrons, azaleas and other shrubs that enjoy tree cover.

Lutyens architecture and Jekyll planting at Hestercombe

HERGEST CROFT, *Kington, Hereford and Worcester. On A44 on the outskirts of King-ton. Peak season May and June. Privately owned. Open frequently from mid-May to mid-June.*

There are two quite separate gardens at Hergest Croft, one around the house, the other half a mile away in a wood. Both have been made in this century, primarily as collections. The house garden is laid out around a lawn and in a semi-wild setting and contains a wide selection of trees and shrubs, many of them from Asia and introduced in the last 100 years or so. There are numerous good forms of Lawson cypress and other conifers and also birches and maples. The woodland garden, in a coomb

known as Park Wood, is primarily for rhododendrons and azaleas and is in-tentionally maintained in a semi-wild condition.

A few of the most notable trees are *Abies bracteata, A. squamata* (rare in Britain), *A. sutchuenensis* (also a rare species), *Acer griseum* (a tree of quite exceptional size and beauty), *A. nikoense, Athrotaxis cupressoides, Betula papyrifera, Carya cordiformis, Fraxinus pennsylvanica, Juglans cathayensis* (15 metres high in 1963 and, according to *Trees and Shrubs*

149

Hardy in the British Isles, the finest recorded in the British Isles), *Kalopanax pictus, Koelreuteria paniculata, Picea brew-* *erana, Pinus pungens glauca* (planted 1897) and *Torreya californica* and its variegated variety.

HESTERCOMBE, *Cheddon Fitzpaine, Somerset. On a by-road north from A361 at Taunton. Peak season May to September. Somerset County Council. View by request only.*

When the garden at Hestercombe was completed in 1910 there were many who regarded it as the finest collaboration between the architect, Edwin Lutyens, and the garden designer, Gertrude Jekyll. Basically it consists of a large sunken parterre or plat surrounded by terraces and raised walks with a very substantial stone pillared pergola across its southern boundary and some fairly elaborate terraces on the north linking it with an eighteenth century terrace in front of the house. As a quite separate extension to the east, but linked with this main garden by a rotunda which acts like the joint between body and limb, is an orangery leading to a formal rose garden in the Dutch style.

What gave Hestercombe its distinction were the many typical Lutyens touches, the straight, narrow rills of water broken by circular pools or tanks on the flanking terraces, the cunningly contrasted curves of masonry and the bold overall pattern softened and beautified by Miss Jekyll's planting.

By the 1960s Hestercombe was in decay and it seemed likely to be lost like many another Lutyens/Jekyll garden. Fortunately by then it had become the property of the Crown Estate Commissioners who had leased it to Somerset County Council, for use as headquarters for the Fire Brigade, and by 1970 plans were afoot for its restoration. At the time of writing this work is by no means complete, but it does seem that the twentieth century garden at Hestercombe is destined to live again. There is also an eighteenth century landscape in the coombes behind the house, but this is completely overgrown and there are no immediate plans for its restoration. *See* pages 51 and 149.

HEVER CASTLE, *Hever, Kent. Follow signposted lanes to Hever from the south end of Edenbridge on B2026. No peak season. Privately owned. Open about twice a week from Easter to September.*

Anne Boleyn was born in Hever Castle and there is still a path there known as Anne Boleyn's walk. But this tiny castle with its drawbridge and moat had to wait four more centuries for a real garden and then, in some parts, in a style almost totally at variance with its own character.

In 1903 the property was purchased by William Waldorf Astor, an American millionaire who had been American Ambassador in Rome and later adopted British nationality and was created 1st Viscount Astor of Hever. While in Rome he had acquired a considerable collection of antiquities and he required a garden in which these could be displayed. Also the castle not only required complete renovation but was too small for his needs, so he decided to build a little 'village' in Tudor style behind the castle for his staff.

In most of the work that followed it would appear that Lord Astor provided the main ideas, leaving it to specialists to put them into effect. An architect, F. L. Pearson of Pangbourne, designed the village and helped with the garden. J. Cheal and Sons of Crawley planted avenues and a series of small gardens (Lord Astor called them the Anne Boleyn gardens) between the old moat and a new outer moat conceived as a formal water feature. For one of these little gardens Cheals prepared a set of topiary chessmen, shaped in yew, from drawings in the British Museum of chessmen used in the time of Henry VIII. Cheals also planted a maze here, importing 2-metre high yews from Holland for the purpose. Mr. Pearson planned a series of formal gardens in the Italian renaissance style at a little distance from the castle for the antiquities, and Cheals made for this a gallery of fountains, based on those at the Villa d'Este in Tivoli, which Joseph Cheal was despatched to study, sketch and photograph. Much later, about 1938, Cheals made a further fountain and pool to the design of Geoffrey Jellicoe.

Beyond the Italian gardens engineers made a lake 35 acres in extent, fed by the River Eden which flows close to the castle, and the terminal feature of the Italian garden was a colonnaded piazza overlooking the lake and decorated with a huge marble fountain flanked by female figures, carved by Frith.

So the garden grew and acquired its unique characteristics. There are many other fine features. The herbaceous border is of exceptional size and is very boldly planted. An equally bold rock garden made of massive blocks of local sandstone links it with the Italian garden. Everywhere there are good plants, cleverly placed and well grown, so that the plant lover is kept constantly alert. There are also numerous views and vistas, some of them so carefully concealed until one is right on them that they come with the added delight of complete surprise. And everywhere in the Italian garden are statues, busts, sarcophagi – all the miscellanea that Lord Astor acquired – some beautiful, some interesting, some merely strange, but all framed in plants. It is the nicest possible way to see a collection of this kind.

HIDCOTE MANOR, *Hidcote Bartrim, Gloucestershire. Approached by a lane from Mickleton, midway between Broadway and Stratford-upon-Avon, on A46. No peak season. National Trust. Open frequently from spring to autumn.*

This garden, made by Major Lawrence Johnston from 1905 onwards, has almost certainly had a greater influence on the subsequent design and planting of small to medium size gardens in Britain than any others. Only since the garden was given to the National Trust in 1948 has this been a direct influence, since Major Johnston himself was something of a recluse and did not invite the public into his garden. But he had many influential admirers, including Vita Sackville West who was later to create a similar garden at Sissinghurst Castle,

Statues in the Italian Garden, Hever Castle

and his ideas, which were very similar to those of Gertrude Jekyll, were frequently copied and written about.

Lawrence Johnston's particular problem was to cope with a bare and wind-swept site high up on the western edge of the Cotswold Hills. He did this by planting a cross pattern of hedges, formed mainly of beech and holly, and then subdividing the areas so formed into still smaller sections, some of them almost totally enclosed, others more open, and treating each in a highly individual manner. The largest area, leaving out of count the kitchen garden which is a completely separate unit on the other side of the house, is a Theatre Lawn, a long rectangle of lawn surrounded by

Dutch style topiary at Hidcote Manor

centuries-old beech trees and a thick yew hedge, but otherwise almost undecorated by plants.

Parallel with it is a central alley to which all the other sections are related, so that it somewhat resembles the long gallery or corridor of a house. It is itself divided into several sections, the first

dominated by a cedar, the next planted mainly in pinks, blues and white, a third circular and simple, a fourth planted mainly in reds, oranges and shades of copper or bronze leading to some stone steps flanked by little pavilions and then two rows of close-trimmed hornbeams on bare trunks, like hedges on stilts (it is known as the Stilt Garden). Beyond this handsome wrought iron gates lead to the hillside and extensive views.

Beside this central axis are other small gardens, one a white garden, another a fuchsia garden, yet another almost completely filled by an immense stone basin for bathing; an annexe to this for use as a dressing room and enclosed in high yew hedges; a streamside garden that is quite natural in style and hard by a highly sophisticated little garden planted in shades of green, lime, lemon, yellow and bronze. Another section suggests the tumbling plants of a cottage garden were it not for the formality of rows of yews trimmed into columns. There is also a semi-wild garden, an area devoted to shrubs and ground cover plants and in the kitchen garden there are borders of old roses.

Since any one of these sections, and even many bits of the larger areas, would make complete gardens on their own, Hidcote is full of lessons and ideas for gardeners whatever the size or character of their gardens. It is also a great collection of plants, full of uncommon as well as familiar flowers and with innumerable happy plant associations which are themselves worthy of the closest study. Even some of the hedges are made of several different shrubs to give a tapestry effect or are spangled with the vivid colour of *Tropaeolum speciosum*. No wonder it is a favourite with other garden owners.

See Colour Plate 8 opposite page 43.

On a hillside a little below Hidcote is Kiftsgate Court, and visitors to one should certainly try to see the other.

HIGHDOWN, *Goring-by-Sea, West Sussex. On A269, 2 miles west of Worthing. Peak season April to June. Worthing Corporation. Open frequently all the year.*

At Highdown Colonel Frederick Stern, who was later knighted for his services to horticulture, set himself the problem of making a garden on a chalk down and in a disused chalk quarry. It is said that when he showed the place to Anthony Waterer, the nurseryman, and asked him what would grow there the reply was 'Nothing'. That was in 1909. By the time of Sir Frederick's death in 1967 Highdown had become world famous and even the chalk sides of the old quarry were densely covered with growth.

The design at Highdown might be described as a mixture of Robinsonian 'natural' and plain convenience. Around the chalk quarry there are pools, irregular areas of grass, trees planted in an irregular manner and lots of underplanting. It is astonishing to see the almost jungle-like profusion of growth which has been coaxed out of this once nearly barren soil. The chalk is still there for all to see, only in a few isolated places has any attempt been made to alter the alkalinity of the soil and the success is due to choosing the right plants and seeing that they are properly looked after.

In one place *Anemone blanda* has become so firmly established that it makes a great sheet of blue each spring. Crocuses of all kinds do well and so do daffodils, snowdrops and hardy cyclamen, all genera of which Sir Frederick Stern was especially fond. In this part of the garden there are many interesting trees including *Aesculus indica, Davidia involucrata* and specimens of *Magnolia highdownensis,* a seedling raised at Caerhays Castle and sent to Highdown in 1927 which proved particularly successful on chalk. It is usually described as a

Daffodils in the chalk quarry, Highdown

hybrid between *M. sinensis* and *M. wilsonii*, but some authorities regard it as a form of *M. wilsonii*. *Acer griseum*, planted in 1912, has grown well and produced good seed from which seedlings have been reared; *Euonymus grandiflorus* has grown to great size; and other notable successes are *Arbutus andrachnoides*, *Cornus capitata*, *Carpinus turczaninowii* (from seed collected by Farrer in 1914) and *Juniperus cedrus*.

On the slope of the down outside the quarry the design is more utilitarian with many long borders separated by straight grass paths. Here it was that Col. Sir Frederick Stern grew the many plants he hybridized, including great beds of eremurus, many peonies, pulsatillas, irises and lilies. Those gardeners who regard lilies as mainly lime-hating will be astonished to find how many kinds do succeed in this thin soil over solid chalk. But then Highdown always has been full of surprises. One wonders what Anthony Waterer would say if he could see it today.

HODNET HALL, *Hodnet, Salop. In Hodnet on A442 between Wellington and Whitchurch. Peak season May to July. Privately owned. Open daily from April to September.*

The garden here is modern, planned and made from 1922 onwards by Brigadier Heber Percy and centred upon a chain of lakes made by damming a stream at various points. In consequence it has some of the characteristics of an eighteenth century landscape, and it is appropriate to find two 'eye-catchers', one a brick dovecote, the other a huge glacial boulder on the far side of the shallow valley in which the ponds have been made. But Hodnet Hall is totally unlike a classical landscape in the density and variety of its planting and the mass of colour which this sustains in spring and summer. There are roses and rhododendrons, irises, primulas, astilbes, lupins and many more in large beds or extensive drifts.

Around the house there are some formal features, but in the main this is a 'natural' garden in the sense that the lines of design are flowing, the grouping of plants irregular and intermingling. But there is nothing 'wild' about this garden, except in its outer reaches where the care of the gardener and the artistry of the arrangement are less obvious, and the garden merges gradually into the surrounding countryside. This is a large garden and, considered either as a spectacle or as a plant collection, is one of the best made since the First World War.

See page 61 and Colour Plate 18.

HOLKER HALL, *Cark in Cartmel, Cumbria. On B5278, 3½ miles west of Grange over Sands. No peak season. Privately owned. Open almost daily from spring to summer.*

For those who think of Victorian gardens as over-elaborate places for the display of bedding out plants, Holker Hall may serve as a useful reminder that there was much more to the period than this. For the garden here is really a Victorian park designed for the good cultivation and display of a wide variety of plants, woody and hardy herbaceous as well as half-hardy. There are generous plantations of rhododendrons and azaleas, well grown magnolias and other flowering trees as well as conifers and other foliage trees planted as specimens

Holker Hall – firm design and generous planting

or in groups. Formal features intermingle in these more informal features as no doubt they did in many Victorian gardens and this gives no sense of incongruity since even the 'wildest' areas, as those in which daffodils are naturalized, are so clearly part of a well ordered, man-made scene. This is a big garden, well maintained and always with something of interest to show.

A classical temple at Holkham Hall

HOLKHAM HALL, *Holkham, Norfolk. At Holkham on A149, 14 miles east of Hunstanton. No peak season. Privately owned. Open about twice weekly from June to September.*

This is one of the great eighteenth century landscapes with lake, tree clumps and belts, and various architectural features including a strategically placed obelisk. Many famous names have been connected with the landscape since work started on it soon after 1718. William Kent designed some of the buildings, 'Capability' Brown altered some of the contours and supervised the making of the great lawn between 1762–4, and later

Hopetoun House – the semi-formal landscape with exhibition of sculpture

Humphry Repton created features which have now disappeared. Further alterations were made in the succeeding centuries, including formal terraces around the house by Sir Charles Barry, but the park remains an impressive spectacle of great interest both to historians and to those who simply appreciate well composed landscape design for its own sake.

HOPETOUN HOUSE, *South Queensferry, Lothian. Off A904, 3 miles west of junction with A90 on by-road to Abercorn. No peak season. Privately owned. Open frequently from May to September.*

Scotland escaped most of the eighteenth century landscape revolution, but some echoes of it are to be seen at a few places, including Hopetoun House. Here is a formal, but very simple, design, really a huge lozenge, shaped in paths and grass banks, with a circular pool at one end to emphasize the pattern of regular curves. The very long house straddles across the middle of this lozenge, dividing it into two roughly equal areas. The whole is nearly surrounded by trees, which on the western (pool) side, are grouped in an irregular way so as to create vistas in various directions. It is this that gives the garden its naturalistic, landscape style, setting. Quite separate from this main design, hidden away in a walled enclosure, is a very attractive little rose garden. *See* illustration on previous page.

HOWICK HALL, *Howick, Northumberland. On B1339, 5 miles north-east of Alnwick. Peak season May to July. Privately owned. Open daily from April to September.*

Here is a fine example of the Robinsonian style of wild gardening applied to an exceptionally suitable site. Quite close to the house are woods and, by judicious thinning to make paths and glades, it has been possible to provide congenial conditions for a wide range of exotic trees, shrubs and herbaceous perennials. Rhododendrons, azaleas, magnolias, hydrangeas, meconopsis, primulas, peonies and many other plants seem to be growing so naturally that they almost appear to be naturalized as, indeed, the daffodils and colchicums undoubtedly are. On the terraces in front of the house the plan is formal, but the planting is not. Agapanthus grows freely and some particularly deeply coloured and hardy varieties have been raised in the garden. There are raised beds for alpine plants, many small shrubs are established in pockets of soil or are trained against the walls and space is found for many other plants. This is a collector's garden, but one made with uncommonly good taste.

Howick Hall from the wild garden

HYDE HALL, *Rettenden, Essex. Off Buckhatch Lane from East Hanningfield road, from A130. 5 miles south of Chelmsford. Peak season April to September. Privately owned. Open occasionally in spring and summer, or by appointment.*

This is the garden of a collector and specialist in roses, unusual trees and shrubs and greenhouse plants. It is a relatively new garden on an exposed site not far from the Essex coast and on good, rather heavy farm land. It is astonishing how many plants, normally considered tender except in the mildest parts of Britain, thrive here. There are numerous species of eucalyptus, acacias, solanums and other plants from warm climates as well as more obviously suitable things such as extensive collections of malus, sorbus and crataegus. There are peat beds for such plants as *Cornus canadensis* and the large-leaved rhododendrons, and greenhouses filled with lapagerias, passifloras, cassias and other handsome plants. The rose beds are extensive and exceptionally well stocked and there is a good iris collection.

INVERESK LODGE, *Inveresk, Lothian. In Inveresk village on A6124, ½ mile south of Musselburgh. Peak season May to July. National Trust for Scotland. Open all the year.*

The whole of the seventeenth century village of Inveresk now belongs to the National Trust for Scotland and the garden of Inveresk Lodge, its largest house, has been completely re-made. There has been no direct attempt to make a period garden, but instead it has been given the kind of treatment which educated modern taste so often applies to old houses such as this. The design is firm without being over formal, there are plenty of flower beds, including one border reserved for old-fashioned and shrub roses and good use has been made of the several high walls which retain the terraces on what is a quite steeply sloping site. One section has been devoted to peat beds, so that an even greater diversity of plants and garden styles can be exhibited to visitors.

INVEREWE, *Poolewe, Highland. At Poolewe on A832. Peak season May to July. National Trust for Scotland. Open all the year.*

It is strange that this stormy site in the north of Scotland should have been one of the very first in which the potential of the west coast for the cultivation of rather tender and difficult plants should have been revealed. Yet so it was, and Osgood Mackenzie had such foresight that in 1862 he purchased the bare rocky peninsula on which was to be established one of the greatest collections of exotic plants to be found anywhere in the British Isles.

157

Old-fashioned roses at Inveresk Lodge

The rock bank with large eucalyptus, Inverewe

It took a very long time to make this garden for there was little soil on the site and more had to be transported there, in the early days carried bit by bit in creels. A shelter belt, mainly of Scots fir and Corsican pine, also had to be planted and given time to grow sufficiently high to protect more delicate plants from fierce, salt-laden gales.

But eventually it was done, woodland began to cover most of the little peninsula jutting out into Loch Ewe and all manner of shrubs and herbaceous plants were established within its protection. Only the house and the lawn and rock banks immediately in front of it remained open to the loch and the magnificent mountain scenery beyond.

Today a list of plants grown at Inverewe reads like the catalogue of a botanic garden. Rhododendrons, celmisias, primulas and meconopses are specialities grown here as well as (in some cases better than) in any other garden in the British Isles. But there are so many other good things that it is useless even to attempt to list them in a brief guide such as this. The National Trust for Scotland, which has owned Inverewe since 1952 and has constantly improved and developed it ever since, issues an excellent illustrated guide with a good list of the most interesting plants.

This is in the main a woodland garden with few open spaces and many walks through the trees. Though not very large the paths are so complex and twisting that it is easy to lose all sense of direction and get hopelessly lost, so that in itself is sufficient reason to purchase the guide and follow its map and suggested route. Only in front of the house is the style quite different, more regular, with flower borders, a good rock wall full of rare alpines and a larger rock bank beneath it.

Because of the mild winters there are always some plants in bloom, but it is in late spring and early summer that this garden bursts into full colour and this is the most popular season for visitors to come to savour the whole scene in its wonderful, wild setting, rather than to search for particular specialities.

See Colour Plates 3, 4 and 5 opposite page 17.

Isabella Plantation at azalea time

159

ISABELLA PLANTATION, *Richmond Park, Greater London. Off A3, to north of the carriageway leading from the Robin Hood to the Kingston Gates in Richmond Park. Peak season May–June. Department of the Environment. Open all the year.*

In 1950, shortly after J. W. Fisher began to lay out the Waterhouse Plantations in Bushey Park, he embarked on a similar development in an area of about forty-two acres of woodland in Richmond Park. This woodland, known as the Isabella Plantation, was originally planted in 1840 and contains a stream and two small lakes. Mr. Fisher ceased to be responsible for Richmond Park in 1951, from which time development was supervised by George Thompson, and so the Waterhouse Plantations and the Isabella Plantation, though both fine examples of twentieth century woodland gardening, have acquired distinctive characteristics of their own. The overall plan for the Isabella Plantation is less complex than in the Waterhouse Plantations and there are more long, open vistas through the trees.

In the early years there was a greater emphasis on species rhododendrons in the Isabella Plantation, though on the whole these did not succeed as well as the hybrids, probably because of the slightly polluted atmosphere. Many of the best rhododendrons are planted as individual specimens. By contrast evergreen azaleas of the Kurume type were planted very freely in huge colonies and these have done so well that late May – early June is the favourite time for visiting this garden. There is also a fine collection of camellias, started by Mr. Thompson. There are now two streams, a second having been dug and supplied with water pumped from the Thames, and this has given more scope for planting of moisture-loving species, including primulas, calthas, astilbes, irises, hostas and ferns. *See* illustration on previous page.

JAPANESE GARDEN, *Tully House, Kildare, Co. Kildare, Eire. On the southern outskirts of Kildare which is on T5. No peak season. The Irish National Stud. Open daily from Easter to the end of October.*

This is one of the most elaborate gardens in the Japanese manner remaining in the British Isles and it is maintained in superb condition. It was made by a Japanese specialist, Tassa Eida, who worked on it for four years between 1906

Two views of the Japanese Garden at Kildare

and 1910. The site, narrow at the entrance, widens out at the far end where there is a Tea House, pool, cascade and lawn. Apparently it was Tassa's idea to use the garden to symbolize the life of man from birth to death, emerging from a dark tunnel representing birth and the ignorance of childhood, through various paths which cross streams or actually follow their course on stepping stones, up hills of learning and of ambition to arrive eventually at a garden of contentment and the gateway to eternity. It is likely that much of this will seem obscure to visitors, who will instead be charmed, as no doubt Lord Wavertree who ordered its construction was, by its romanticism and constantly changing vistas cleverly intertwined in a relatively small space.

JERMYNS ARBORETUM, *Ampfield, Hampshire. In Jermyns Lane, off A31, 1 mile east of Romsey. No peak season. Hampshire County Council. Open all the year.*

This is one of Britain's youngest arboretums and is fast becoming one of its most interesting because of its very rapid extension and the great variety of genera included in it. At Jermyns an area of 311 acres was acquired by the nursery firm of Hillier and Sons early in the 1950s, mainly as a propagating unit for conifers, camellias and other trees and shrubs. Some of it is still used for this purpose, but from 1961 onwards Harold Hillier, well known throughout the world for his vast knowledge of woody plants, decided to use some of the land as a nucleus for a tree collection and this has rapidly grown in extent and variety during the intervening years, now occupying about 108 acres.

The development has been largely on 'natural' lines with trees and shrubs well spaced but sited primarily where they are likely to find conditions most congenial rather than to create a preconceived landscape. However the nature of the land, lying in part across a valley with some water at the lower levels, and extensive views, mainly to the north, ensures that the arboretum has considerable beauty as well as botanical interest and this effect is increased by several more obviously designed features.

There are, for example, very large twin borders cutting through the original plantation of trees and used for mixed planting of herbaceous peren-

Jermyns Arboretum: *(left)* **an almost jungle-like profusion of growth.** *(right)* **Gravel-covered beds in a damp depression.**

nials, roses and shrubs. Near the head of the valley extensive peat beds and a bog garden have been made for acid soil and moisture-loving plants, and to the south of Mr. Hillier's house, on gently rising ground, there is a series of what appear to be scree beds, though in fact the fine gravel covering is quite thin, serving mainly to deter weeds and keep the soil cool and moist, rather than to provide a growing medium of its own. Some of these beds are used for dwarf conifers, some for alpines and one, following the line of a damp depression, looks like the bed of a dry stream and is planted with grasses, including *Stipa gigantea*, yuccas, phormium and other interesting foliage plants.

Across Jermyns Lane is the rhododendron collection and at the edge of this, in a disused sand pit, Harold Hillier has started to make what he describes as a sub-tropical garden for really tender things.

THE ROYAL BOTANIC GARDENS, KEW, *Greater London. Entrances at Kew on A307. No peak season. Ministry of Agriculture, Fisheries and Food. Open all the year.*

It is correct to refer to these famous botanic gardens in the plural for there were originally two gardens here, both connected with royalty, but separately designed by rival garden makers in the eighteenth century. Both the houses connected with these gardens have disappeared, Richmond Lodge to the west, at one time a country residence of George III and Queen Caroline, and Kew House to the east, occupied for a while by Prince Frederick, son of George III, and his wife Augusta. Both employed famous garden designers, 'Capability' Brown working at Richmond Lodge and producing, amongst other changes, the Long Lake and the dell now used for rhododendrons; and Sir William Chambers working at Kew House and erecting a number of buildings there, including several temples, the orangery and the famous 'Chinese' pagoda. It was Augusta who commenced to make a botanical collection at Kew House and it was George III who amalgamated the two gardens, but it was not until 1840 that Kew was given to the nation and the Royal Botanic Gardens were established under the directorship of Sir Joseph Hooker.

From that time the gardens prospered exceedingly. New glasshouses were built, the great Palm House, designed by Decimus Burton, creating a record for size and advanced design and remaining after more than a century and a quarter one of the most beautiful glasshouses in the British Isles. W. A. Nesfield redesigned the main walk and its surroundings, designed the arboretum and planted new avenues including the Syon Vista of ilex from the Palm House towards Syon House on the far bank of the Thames. In the process he succeeded in giving the whole garden a greater unity than might have appeared possible from its diverse origin. As a result Kew has become a magnificent spectacle giving pleasure to millions who have little or no expert knowledge of plants.

Nevertheless it was for its ever increasing collection of plants, its herbarium, library and educational and research work that Kew became most highly esteemed throughout the world, and that pre-eminence has continued to the present day. New greenhouses have been added, some for specialist purposes, such as the Sherman Hoyt cactus house, succulent houses, alpine house, ferneries and Australia house; a great rock garden has been made; a fine heather garden near the pagoda and, as

18. A chain of lakes at Hodnet Hall (*see* page 154

19. Meconopses and primulas, Logan (*see* page 175)

20. The Italian garden, Mount Stewart (*see* page 181)

21. Herbaceous borders at Nymans
(*see* page 188)

22. The Royal National Rose Society's
garden at St Albans (*see* page 204)

a recent addition, the Queen's Garden. This is a little garden in the seventeenth century style behind Kew Palace, the only old dwelling house remaining in the Royal Botanic Garden. The Queen's Garden includes a formal parterre, a mount topped by a wrought iron pavilion overlooking the river, a gazebo copied from one at Packwood House, and a sunken garden planted with herbs and flowers that were popular when Kew Palace was built (1631) and surrounded on three sides by a covered alley of laburnum. Made in 1960, it is not an actual reproduction of any particular garden, though it is based on a French garden plan of the period.

Though Kew has something to offer throughout the year it is especially lovely in spring when daffodils, magnolias and cherries are in bloom, to be followed shortly by great beds of tulips and many species and varieties of malus. In May, too, the azaleas are in bloom, particularly around King William's temple and the Japanese Gateway on Mosque Hill.

There is a *Ginkgo biloba* that was planted in 1762 and was 22 metres high in 1970 and also an *Arbutus andrachnoides*, 11 metres high in 1967, which may well be one of the tallest in the country, though the soil at Kew is poor and so trees do not in general grow to record proportions. One of my favourites is an enormous weeping beech beside the Broad Walk. An excellent guide plan is available.

(*above*) **King William's Temple surmounts a heather-covered bank at Kew;** (*below*) **The Queen's Garden.**

KIFTSGATE COURT, *Mickleton, Gloucestershire. On by-road to Hidcote Bartrim off A46 at Mickleton. Peak season summer. Privately owned. Open about twice weekly from spring to early autumn.*

This delightful modern garden is on a hillside a little below Hidcote and visitors to one should certainly try to see the other. There are similarities between them in their combination of formal design with informal planting and in their intelligent use of plant colour and form. There is less variety of treatment

163

at Kiftsgate, but rather more exuberance in plant growth, particularly in the use of roses which are grown here in great numbers. It is mainly the shrub and old-fashioned varieties that are grown, together with climbers, one of which, apparently an extra vigorous form of *Rosa filipes*, originated here and is named Kiftsgate.

KILLERTON, *Broad Clyst, Devon. Off A38, 5 miles north-east of Exeter. No peak season. National Trust. Open all the year.*

This is one of the very early tree collections started around 1800 by Sir Thomas Acland, assisted by John Veitch, who later founded the Veitch nursery in Exeter. Successive generations of Aclands continued to enlarge the arboretum which became National Trust property in 1944.

The site is on the south face of a ridge and a relatively narrow strip of the gently sloping land at its foot. The house stands at this lower level with a considerable expanse of lawn to the west dotted with specimen trees and a long rectangular terrace beside the southern boundary. This is the only formal feature in the whole garden, laid out in a regular pattern of beds planted with perennials and shrubs, mainly with blue, pink and cream flowers. Handsome urns add to the sophistication of this charming feature which not only makes a striking contrast to the almost complete informality of the arboretum itself but also provides the best view point of it.

The arboretum extends up and over the hillside, traversed by zig-zagging

Killerton arboretum seen from the terrace garden

paths, with an avenue of beeches said to oe 200 years old beside part of the main path. But apart from this and a few open places left to provide views over the low land through which the Rivers Exe and Clyst flow, there is little evidence of design, the trees being disposed at a more or less even density and only occasionally grouped according to their families. It is nevertheless a fine spectacle, the wellingtonias towards the top being especially impressive. There are also some very tall Lawson cypresses in a good selection of cultivars which make a fine contrast of colour and form when viewed from a distance. Among the biggest are *Chamaecyparis lawsoniana* itself, one specimen over 31 metres high and vars. Lutea, Triomh de Boskoop and Wisselii all over 15 metres. There are also very tall specimens of *Chamaecyparis obtusa* and *C. pisifera*. On the way up the hill the visitor may note good specimens of *Saxegothaea conspicua*, *Fitzroya cupres-*

soides planted in 1864, *Keteleeria fortunei*, *Cunninghamia lanceolata*, *Sciadopitys verticillata* the umbrella pine, and *Picea brewerana* wonderfully placed where its dark curtain of growth can be seen silhouetted against the sky. *Pinus leucodermis*, at the top of the hill, is one of the two best in Britain.

It is not only conifers that are remarkable at Killerton. There are many fine broad-leaved trees as well, including numerous maples, oaks including the cork and Lucombe oaks *Betula maximowicziana* and *Arbutus menziesii*. Magnolias with rhododendrons and azaleas make a display of colour in spring. Outside the garden, by the chapel, are more good trees, including the rare hop hornbeam, *Ostrya carpinifolia*.

A good guide book is available which includes a map and a fairly comprehensive list of notable species.

See also illustration on page 23.

KILORAN, *Isle of Colonsay, Strathclyde. On A871, 1½ miles north of Scalasaig. By ferry from Oban. Peak season April to June. Privately owned. Open frequently all year.*

The Isle of Colonsay lies right out in the Atlantic, west of Isla and Jura. It is a small island without any hills above 500 feet so it escapes a good deal of the cloud and rain which are characteristic of Scottish west coast gardens, though it does share with them the warm waters of the Gulf Stream. It is therefore possible to grow here a great many semi-tender trees and shrubs and it has in fact been a collector's paradise for several generations. A stream flows through the garden and there is also adjacent woodland to give shelter to those shrubs, most notably rhododendrons, that require it. The garden is particularly famous for its large-leaved rhododendrons, but there are also many other species and hybrids.

Other notable plants include embothriums, desfontainia, myrtles, lomatias, tricuspidarias and grevillias.

Azalea bank at Kiloran

(*above*) **The purple and grey parterre, Knightshayes Court;** (*below*) **The woodland from the pool enclosure.**

KNIGHTSHAYES COURT, *Tiverton, Devon. On A396, 1½ miles north of Tiverton. Peak season April to October. Knightshayes Trust and National Trust. Open daily from spring to autumn.*

This is really a very young garden, in its present form made entirely since the last war by Sir John Heathcoat-Amory and his wife. The garden owes its appearance of age partly to the fact that there were already a great many mature trees, including Turkey oaks and Douglas firs, in the parkland to the south and the woodland to the north-east, and also big yew hedges surrounding formal enclosures on the terrace on the east side of the house. These hedges, and also many of the trees, had been planted from about 1865 onwards when the house itself was built on a site that slopes to the south.

In a few years Sir John and Lady Heathcoat-Amory had completely transformed this scene and made it one of the most charming gardens created in the last quarter century.

First they simplified the formal gardens, retaining their best features including the topiary fox hunt that decorates the top of one of the yew hedges, and cut in the 1920s. Another yew enclosure was made into an almost completely green parterre ornamented with a large, stone-edged circular pool with one white statue set in a yew alcove and a well placed silver grey willow-leaved pear (*Pyrus salicifolia pendula*). Yet another enclosure was permanently planted by Graham Thomas in shades of purple, mauve, grey and silver, and a

scree bed was made below the terrace wall.

Some of the trees in the park to the south were thinned and under-planted with good rhododendrons and a little dell with pool to the west, which was formerly filled with yellow azaleas and bluebells, was made into a willow collection.

But the biggest change of all was made in the woodland behind the formal gardens. Here long island beds follow the natural contours of the land. They are separated by wide grass paths and are frequently built up at the edges with peat blocks to enable an even greater variety of plants to be grown.

It is, in fact, in this variety, and in particular in the number of small herbaceous species which thrive here, that Knightshayes Court scores over many other woodland gardens. Here will be found not only the usual rhododendrons, azaleas, pieris species etc., but also all manner of charming trilliums, erythroniums, hellebores, hostas, dicentras, violets, daphnes, lilies and other plants, making an almost complete ground cover and associated with great skill. This woodland garden was still being extended when the National Trust joined the Knightshayes Trust after Sir John Heathcoat-Amory's death in 1972.

LANHYDROCK, *Trebyan, Cornwall. On B3268, 2½ miles south of Bodmin. Peak season April to June. National Trust. Open all the year.*

This is the most highly organized of all the Cornish gardens and the one with the longest history, since tree planting began here early in the seventeenth century. The house, built about 1640 of

Cornish granite around a quadrangle, had its east wing removed in 1780, presumably to open it to the fine park which had by then been created on that side. In 1881 it was gutted by fire, but was so

167

skilfully restored that no one looking at it today could guess that such a disaster had occured. It is a severely lovely building rendered even more beautiful by the church that stands beside it and the elaborate two-storey gatehouse that stands some distance in front of it. From this a great avenue of sycamore extends right through the park, but since this was first planted about 1648 many trees are coming to the end of their life and are being gradually replaced by beech.

Formal terraces were made in 1857 in the area bounded by house, church and gatehouse. They are enclosed by a low balustraded wall decorated with finials and are variously laid out, some as simple lawns, some with a pattern of beds edged with box. There are also some handsome bronze urns, said to be the work of Louis Ballin, goldsmith to Louis XIV. Lines of clipped yew add to the orderly formality of this section which is in complete contrast to the woodland planting on the hillside which forms a background to the whole scene. Here and also in the more open parkland to the north, planting is in the more typical informal Cornish style. It consists of choice exotics, including rhododendrons, azaleas, magnolias, camellias, hydrangeas, Japanese maples and many other trees and shrubs. Much of the planting here dates from 1930 onwards, so that the gardening tastes of many generations mingle in this delightful place.

Trees of special note include a Douglas fir (*Pseudotsuga menziesii*) planted in 1880, a fine Sitka spruce (*Picea sitchensis*) which was 37 metres high in 1971, a big wellingtonia (*Sequoiadendron giganteum*), several large specimens of *Thujopsis dolobrata*, including one variegated form planted in 1889, and a good *Magnolia veitchii*. One Irish yew was 15 metres high in 1971 and must be one of the tallest in England.

LEITH HALL, *Kennethmont, Grampian. On A927, 7 miles south of Huntley (junction of A96 with A97). Peak season June to August. National Trust for Scotland. Open daily from May to September.*

Like many gardens in Scotland this one is at a considerable distance from the house and is in no way planned as a setting for it. Its purpose is as a pleasant place full of flowers to be visited but not lived in. Some new planting nearer the house and on more modern lines has been done since the National Trust for Scotland took charge of the property, but it is the old garden and the old ways of doing things that are of greatest interest to the garden-minded visitor. It is almost entirely composed of flower borders and a large rock garden, the latter romantic rather than natural in conception. There are no lawns or open spaces within this section, just masses of flowers, mainly perennial, very well grown and making a tremendous display in summer. Even the rock garden is planted mainly with herbaceous perennials chosen for their ability to flower freely rather than for any particular association with mountains or rocky places.

The rock garden, Leith Hall

LEONARDSLEE, *Lower Beeding, West Sussex. On A281. 4½ miles south-east of Horsham. Peak seasons May and October. Privately owned. Occasionally open in late spring and autumn.*

Leonardslee is one of the great Sussex woodland gardens created by the Loder family and the only one to remain continuously under Loder care for nearly a century. It is a very large garden (over 100 acres) occupying virtually the whole of a south running valley in which there are several 'Hammer' ponds, the artificially made ponds which provided power for the hammers in the old Sussex iron works. There must always have been forest here and so it is a perfect site for a woodland garden which is precisely what Sir Edmund Loder set out to

create when he started planting in 1888. Within a few years he was raising new rhododendrons as well as buying existing ones. Many fine hybrids were produced by Sir Edmund and his successors, but none destined to have a greater impact on rhododendron breeding than *Rhododendron loderi*, the result of a Leonardslee cross between *R. fortunei* and *R. griffithianum*. It is first referred to in 1907 and the cross must have been made long before that. Some of the original plants, now of tree-like proportions, still grow at Leonardslee.

169

Lanhydrock – the gatehouse and terraces with woodland garden as background

One of the hammer ponds, Leonardslee

It is for its rhododendrons and azaleas that this garden is most famous, but many other things are grown equally well if not in quite the same quantity. There is a comprehensive collection of camellias and two large glasshouses are devoted to those varieties that are better for protection. The hardy palm, *Trachycarpus fortunei*, has become almost a weed, seeding itself about so freely that many palms have to be felled. Their trunks are so durable that they are used as edgings for woodland paths.

There are also many maples and oaks, including the scarlet oak, *Quercus coccinea*, and these, with the azaleas, particularly the common yellow azalea (another 'weed' plant), contribute greatly to the autumn colour which is amongst the best in the country.

There are cherries, magnolias (including what is possibly the biggest *M. fraseri* in the country), halesias and, of course, many conifers including some quite rare species, such as *Athrotaxis cupressoides*, *Dacrydium franklinii*, *Keteleeria davidiana*, *Pinus montezumae*, *P. ponderosa*, *Saxegothaea conspicua* and *Sciadopitys verticillata*. There are redwoods and wellingtonias 35 metres or more in height and an *Abies concolor lowiana* which had reached over 37 metres in 1969. A tulip tree (*Liriodendron tulipifera*) about 34 metres high is one of the tallest in Britain, and there is also a good specimen of the uncommon Japanese birch, *Betula maximowicziana*.

No wonder that this remarkable and very beautiful garden has sometimes been used as a setting for jungle films.

LEVENS HALL, *Kendal, Cumbria. On A6 at junction with A590. No peak season. Privately owned. Open daily from May to September.*

At Levens Hall there are both a park and a garden, originally linked and related, but now so separated by the busy A6 road that most visitors to the garden probably remain completely ignorant of

the existence of the park. This is a pity because it is both beautiful and historically fascinating as an example of early stirrings towards a more natural, landscape orientated, style of garden

170

making. The park extends across the valley and gorge of the little River Kent, and trees in clumps and lines seem to have been planted expressly to beautify this naturally lovely piece of country, though the park appears to have been laid out very early in the eighteenth century before the landscape movement really got under way.

Historians may speculate as to the significance of all this. There can be no doubt about the historical importance of the garden around the house, formal in design, divided into numerous sections in the sixteenth and seventeenth century manner and in parts filled with topiary specimens cut in yew and box, some of fantastic form and size. Not all the topiary is ancient, for some was undoubtedly added in the early nineteenth century, yet sufficient of the original remains to convey a convincing impression of the manner of garden making in Stuart times. The size of individual specimens must, of course, be discounted as due solely to the passage of time and not at all to original intention, but there is no doubt that these huge solid shapes do add greatly to the romantic charm of this remarkable garden. The original architects of both garden and park were the owner of Levens Hall, Col. James Graham, and his head gardener, Guillaume Beaumont, a Frenchman trained by Le Nôtre at Versailles and then employed by James II before coming to Levens. The work appears to have been done between about 1690 and 1720.

See also page 11.

Giant topiary at Levens Hall

LINGHOLME, *Keswick, Cumbria. In Grange Road off A66 at Portinscale, 1 mile west of Keswick. Peak season May–June. Privately owned. Open frequently spring to autumn.*

This is a large garden, much of it woodland with rhododendrons, azaleas etc., beside Derwent Water and commanding some fine views of the lake. There are many fine trees, including *Abies grandis* and *Cedrus atlantica glauca*, and also a rather unusual rock garden and pool made in a little dell close to the house, which is entered through a wrought iron gate and is clearly intended as a romantic, not a realistic, feature.

The Derwent Fells from Lingholme

LIVERPOOL UNIVERSITY BOTANIC GARDEN, NESS, *Neston, Merseyside. In Neston Road, 1½ miles south of Neston, reached by B5136 from A540. No peak season. University of Liverpool. Open all the year.*

This garden is interesting for two quite different reasons, one as the home of a famous and idiosyncratic gardener of the past, A. K. Bulley, the other as the creation of a university anxious, as Mr Bulley was, to spread the love and knowledge of gardening among the public.

A. K. Bulley was a wealthy plant lover and a socialist. He helped to finance plant explorers, including George Forrest and F. Kingdon Ward, and early this century he founded a nursery, attached to his garden at Ness, expressly to grow the finest hardy plants and sell them very cheaply so that working people would be encouraged to grow them. He was also one of the first to open his garden regularly to the public, so that the plants he loved would become known and more widely planted.

Some years after Mr Bulley's death in 1942 the whole estate was given to the University of Liverpool on condition that a specified area should be open to

The heather bank, University of Liverpool Botanic Garden

the public. Some of the garden that Mr Bulley made has been preserved, including the large rock garden in a dell below the house, but much is new and in its present form the garden displays many of the popular features of gardens today. There is a very long rhododendron border backed by a pine wood, a rose garden, herbaceous garden and formal terrace overlooking the old rock garden.

But perhaps the most admired new feature is the very extensive heather garden made on the west slope of the hill overlooking the estuary of the River Dee and with views of the distant hills of Wales.

LOCHINCH AND CASTLE KENNEDY, *Stranraer, Dumfries and Galloway. On A75, 3 miles east of Stranraer. Peak season May to July. Privately owned. Open daily from April to September.*

Castle Kennedy was the original home of the Earls of Stair, but it was destroyed by fire in 1716 and was not replaced until 1864 when Lochinch Castle was built a mile away to the east. The ruins of Castle Kennedy still stand on a ridge between two large lakes, the Black Loch to the north and the White Loch to the south and the main garden has always been centred around Castle Kennedy, though Lochinch Castle has a separate and enclosed garden of its own.

The Castle Kennedy garden began in the early eighteenth century as a formal design, but with great terraces of soil taking the place of masonry. The 2nd Earl of Stair who made it had been an officer in Marlborough's army and later rose to the rank of Field Marshal. He appears to have used soldiers to dig the terraces and the circular pool below the castle as well as a canal that joins the two lakes, and some of these features certainly have a military look about them, as if the ideas had come, at least in part, from fortifications. No one knows how this garden was planted, or even if it was planted at all, but after a century of almost total neglect the 8th Earl of Stair began to restore the place. He planted trees and criss-crossed them with avenues and *allées*, very much in the French style of the seventeenth century.

It was into this slightly bizarre formal setting in an otherwise typically Scottish landscape that exotic plants, principally trees and shrubs, began to be introduced. Seeds were being sent to Britain

Rhododendrons around the circular pool, Lochinch

from many parts of the world and it was realized that west coast gardens such as Lochinch had exceptionally favourable conditions for growing many of them. Among the first to arrive was the monkey puzzle, *Araucaria araucana* and in

173

Castle Kennedy at azalea time

1849 the great avenue from the circular pool to Lochinch Castle was lined with them. It remains the finest araucaria avenue in the British Isles. Rhododendrons from Dr (later Sir) Joseph Hooker's expeditions to the Himalaya also came to Lochinch and the huge bushes (one could almost say trees) of *R. arboreum* are one of the spectacles of the garden in spring. The newly introduced conifers were also planted during the ensuing years and early specimens still growing at Lochinch include *Abies cephalonica* (1849), *A. cilicica* (1859), *A. grandis* (1877), *A. homolepis* (1872), *A. pindrow* (1876), *A. procera* (1851), *A. spectabilis* (1856), *Cryptomeria japonica* (1856), *Picea orientalis* (1886), *P. smithiana* (1851), *Pinus muricata* (1856), *P. nigra maritima* (1849), *P. radiata* (1849), *Pseudotsuga menziesii* (1856), *Sciadopitys verticillata* (1878) and *Sequoia sempervirens* (1856).

So the transformation continued until the whole of the Castle Kennedy area was changed from a formal to a picture garden, highly coloured at least in spring and early summer, instead of being mainly green as at the beginning. Yet the firm pattern still shows through and gives the garden the clear design which many modern plant collections lack. It is, in fact an outstandingly fine example of an old garden being used for a modern purpose and both gaining by the partnership.

The garden around the new house, Lochinch, is quite separate, shut off by walls and hedges from the main garden and landscape, and laid out on more conventional lines with lawns, flower beds and shrub borders. There are some good meconopses here as well as other unusual herbaceous plants, also a fine specimen of the Japanese cherry Shimidsu Sakura.

LOGAN, *Ardwell, Dumfries and Galloway. On B7065, ½ mile south of its junction with A716. Peak season April to June. Dept. of Agriculture and Fisheries for Scotland. Open daily (except Saturdays) from April to September.*

This is the most southerly garden in Scotland, almost at the tip of the Rhinns of Galloway, with sea close by to east, south and west, almost as if it were situated on a long narrow island. It enjoys, in consequence, an exceptionally mild climate and full advantage has been taken of this, as also of some old walled enclosures, to grow plants that would be far too tender to survive outdoors in most parts of Britain. The ancient walls, the almost sub-tropical vegetation and the frequent use of ornament give this garden a Mediterranean air unusual in British gardens.

For generations this was a private garden, but a few years ago it was acquired by the Royal Botanic Garden, Edinburgh, as an annexe for those plants that require the particularly favourable conditions that Logan can offer. This has necessitated some replanting, but many fine old plants remain, including large Chusan palms (*Trachycarpus fortunei*), cabbage palms (*Cordyline australis*) and four species of tree fern, *Cyathia dealbata, C. medullaris, Dicksonia fibrosa* and *D. antarctica*. Some plants of this last, Australian, species are about fifty years old and there are also young plants self-sown from the spores which they produce. An avenue of cabbage palms beside a rectangular pool was planted in 1913. There are many rare rhododendrons, including *R. nuttallii, R. taggianum* and *R. sinogrande*, a good collection of magnolias and camellias and also many meconopsis species,

Tree ferns and cabbage palms frame the water garden at Logan

lilies and notholirions. Several species of the daisy flowered climbing plants, mutisia, thrive at Logan, there are numerous watsonias and a colony of the difficult Chatham Island forget-me-not, *Myosotidium hortensia*. *Gunnera manicata* has escaped from the garden proper to colonize a damp woodland adjoining it and the primulas are so much at home that they seed themselves along the lane leading to the garden and at one time had to be removed from the car turn around as weeds. Spectacular in summer are the giant blue spires of *Echium pininana*. These are just a few of the hundreds of interesting and beautiful plants to be discovered in, and around, this fascinating garden.

See illustration on page 36 and Colour Plate 19 opposite page 162.

LONGLEAT, *Warminster, Wiltshire. On A362, 4 miles south of Frome. No peak season. Privately owned. Open all the year.*

Perhaps not many of the tens of thousands of visitors who come annually to admire this massive sixteenth century mansion or enjoy the thrills of its safari park realize that they are also seeing one of 'Capability' Brown's greatest creations. Yet so it is, for he worked here from 1757 to 1762 for the 3rd Viscount Weymouth, and planted so many of the recently introduced *Pinus strobus* that it acquired the popular name of Weymouth pine. Later, in 1803, Repton was employed at Longleat by the 2nd Marquis of Bath, and in our own time Russell Page has worked there, but it is still Brown's stamp that is most indelibly on the place. Yet in one respect it is not entirely typical of his work. He was not permitted to sweep away the formal terraces around the house, as was his wont, and they remain to this day. There are many fine trees added in the days when tree collection was in fashion, including some very tall specimens of wellingtonia, redwood, cryptomeria, *Pinus radiata*, *Abies pinsapo* and deodar (*Cedrus deodara*).

LUTON HOO, *Luton, Bedfordshire. Between A6 and B653 on the southern outskirts of Luton. Peak season summer. Privately owned. Open about once weekly from spring to early autumn.*

For garden lovers Luton Hoo has three special interests, two of them much publicized, the third scarcely ever mentioned. The famous ones are the great landscape park created by 'Capability' Brown between 1764 and 1770 and considered one of the finest examples of his work; and the three formal terraces, one a rose garden in the Italian manner, made by Romaine Walker in the first decade of the present century. The rose terrace, in particular, is typically Edwardian in its exuberance and grandeur and, so far as design is concerned,

176

The rose garden, Luton Hoo

is probably the best rose garden in Britain. The third and frequently overlooked feature is a rock garden concealed in a coppice at a little distance from the terraces. It was made in the 1920s by the garden staff at Luton Hoo, much of the placement of stone being supervised by a farm worker who exhibited a remarkable talent for this work. It is made in a dell with a pool and hump back bridge as a central feature, and is a fine example of the 'natural' style of the period, valued more for its picturesqueness than as a place in which to grow rock plants.

LYME PARK, *Disley, Greater Manchester. On A6 on the outskirts of Disley. No peak season. National Trust and Stockport Corporation. Open all the year.*

Originally this was a hunting park, something very different from the landscape parks of the eighteenth century. It is still immense and rather wild, horticultural interest centring on the formal garden in the Dutch style made in a rectangular area below the very high walls of the house terrace. Because of its unusual situation it is possible to look right down on the pattern of this little parterre from above. There is also an attractive stone built orangery made in the early nineteenth century.

MELBOURNE HALL, *Melbourne, Derbyshire. In Melbourne on A514, 7 miles south of Derby. No peak season. Privately owned. Open spring to early autumn, mainly at week-ends.*

For garden lovers Melbourne Hall is important as an example of the grand French seventeenth century style adapted to a relatively small garden in England. No doubt when it was made in the first decade of the eighteenth century, there were many other gardens of similar character, but few have survived. Melbourne Hall owes its preservation to lack of interest, since for at least a century and a half no one who owned the place was sufficiently concerned to alter it and bring it up to date. It must be admitted that this long neglect has made it a little difficult to see what the original designer really had in mind, for this was a London and Wise garden, an assemblage of parterres, alleys, geometrically shaped pools, pleached walks and all the other ingredients of a formal garden of the period. Through neglect the pleached walk has developed into a dense yew tunnel, the trees lining the alleys have grown too large and everywhere the trim lines of youth have been lost beneath the uncontrolled growth of age. So to modern eyes the place seems almost as much picturesque as formal, but for those with eyes to see – and particularly for those with a copy of the original plan to guide their eyes – the true character of the garden will still emerge.

Melbourne Hall from the Great Basin

It falls broadly into two parts, one a series of terraces to the east of the house, ending in a large, rather elaborately shaped pool, the Great Basin, that is almost as wide as the terraces themselves, and to the south, a pattern of radiating alleys with a smaller pool and some fine ornaments to mark their major intersections. There are further statues on and around the terrace. Some of these are cast in lead and are by Van Nost, the most important being a huge urn representing the four seasons and standing on a pedestal, and the most charming four groups of the young twins, Castor and Pollux, quarrelling, fighting and becoming reconciled.

But the decoration that most impresses visitors to Melbourne Hall is the Iron Arbour which stands beyond the Great Basin, centred on the axial line of the terraces and of the avenue through woodland that continues the vista to the skyline. This intricate piece of wrought iron work with domed top is the first known work of Robert Bakewell who later became something of a celebrity. He started work on the arbour in 1706. (*See* illustration on page 260.)

Also of interest, though probably added much later, is a grotto enclosing a mineral water well with a poetic inscription by C. Lamb. This could be Caroline Lamb, wife of the second Lord Melbourne (Prime Minister to Queen Victoria), which would make it Victorian. Lord Melbourne was a great-grandson of the garden's maker, Thomas Coke.

There are some fine taxodiums around the Great Basin.

MELLERSTAIN, *Gordon, Borders. On by-road off A6089, 2 miles south of Gordon. No peak season. Privately owned. Open almost daily from May to September.*

The garden at Mellerstain is probably the finest readily accessible example of the work of Sir Reginald Blomfield, who battled for so long with William Robinson over the rival merits of formal and natural styles of garden making. In fact Blomfield, like Robinson, could use both, so perhaps the argument was concerned more with degree than with absolute preference. For Mellerstain, itself an imposing mansion begun (but not completed) by William Adam, Blomfield designed suitably spacious and dignified terraces overlooking a lake and landscape worthy of Brown or Repton. It is a perfect union of the two supposedly opposed styles.

The lake and woodland from Blomfield's terraces at Mellerstain

MONTACUTE HOUSE, *Montacute, Somerset. In Montacute on A3088, 4 miles west of Yeovil. No peak season. National Trust. Open frequently from spring to autumn.*

This is one of the loveliest houses in Britain, a superb example of Elizabethan zest and craftsmanship and the stonework and pavilions which surround its forecourt are of equal quality and charm. But this forecourt, now a garden with lawn and flower borders, was originally the paved entrance to the house and what the character of the garden was in Elizabethan times or how it was disposed around the mansion nobody knows.

It is fortunate therefore that when the house was, as it were, turned around, the front entrance being made to the west and the old east court relegated to a back position, the work of remodelling, from about 1834 onwards, should have fallen to a lady and her gardener who appear to have been in complete sympathy with the place. She was Ellen Phelips, wife of the owner, and the gardener, Mr Pridham. Between them they made green parterres, planted yew hedges and generally produced a simple, sensible, unfussy design which leaves the bones of the original plan and the lovely stonework to make their own effect. The final touch came after the last war when the National Trust engaged Vita Sackville West, creator of the garden at Sissinghurst Castle, to design new planting for the borders. Her use of

The forecourt at Montacute House

shrubs, roses and perennials was as discreet as Mr Pridham's use of grass and yew, and the garden continues to be in perfect harmony with the house.

There are some fine blue Atlas cedars, as well as one of the tallest recorded Monterey cypresses, and a very tall Italian cypress.

MOTTISFONT ABBEY, *Mottisfont, Hampshire. On by-road off A3057 mid-way between Stockbridge and Romsey. Peak season June–July. National Trust. Open frequently from April to September.*

The house is Georgian, built on the site of a twelfth or early thirteenth century priory, some remnants of which are incorporated in the present building. It stands beside the River Test and is surrounded by extensive lawns and many fine specimen trees, including some immense planes, good beeches, holm oaks, a tulip tree (liriodendron) and catalpa and numerous blue Atlas cedars. Outside the garden proper, but visible from it, is an oak said to be eight

179

Mottisfont Abbey knot garden designed by Norah Lindsay.

hundred years old. On the north side the lawn takes the form of a level parterre closed in to the west at a slightly higher level by a fine avenue of pleached limes designed by Geoffrey Jellicoe.

The National Trust took possession in 1957 and a few years later its gardens adviser, Graham Thomas, laid out the large walled kitchen garden as a rose garden to contain all the old varieties gathered by him over a period of many years. There are also many herbaceous perennials in this new garden, some planted in borders with emphasis strongly on grey and silver foliage plants and pastel colours that associate well with the roses.

MOUNT STEWART, *Greyabbey, Co. Down, Northern Ireland. On A20, 5 miles south of Newtownards. Peak season April to July. National Trust. Open daily (except Tuesdays) from April to September.*

Garden making of two totally different kinds are to be seen at Mount Stewart, an eighteenth century green landscape with lake and at a little distance to the south, on a little knoll, an elegant two-storey pavilion, designed by James Stuart, about 1780, in Grecian style, known as the Temple of the Winds; and a modern garden divided into numerous sections, each with a distinctive character of its own and some lavishly planted. In front of the mansion is an Italian style terrace leading to a smaller formal garden with a Spanish flavour. Then there is a large rectangular sunken garden, a very curious topiary garden made in the form of a shamrock, a wild garden, a lily wood and a garden with beds formed in the pattern of a Tudor rose around a central fountain.

But what is far more important than the individual parts of the new garden is the manner of their decoration and planting which reflect the personality of their creator, the Marchioness of Londonderry, and is therefore unique. There is a rare sense of humour in this garden, exhibited in strange ornaments depicting dodos, rabbits, a dinosaur,

frogs and other animals, each, it is said, representing a member of the Ark Club which was started by Lady Londonderry early in the First World War. Originally intended for the entertainment of king's messengers on leave, it soon grew to include politicians, authors, sailors, soldiers, airmen and other people who were her friends. All were called by the names of animals, birds or fishes and some are here commemorated in appropriate statues made by a local craftsman, Thomas Beattie. The Italian terrace is also lined with stone pillars each bearing a different grinning or scowling mask and surmounted by a monkey with a large stone vase. These were also carved by Thomas Beattie and the masks are said to be caricatures of Lady Londonderry's friends. (*See* Colour Plate 20.)

Caricature again appears in the topiary garden, where the enclosing hedge of *Cupressus macrocarpa* is clipped into shapes depicting a hunt in which the stag is rescued by the devil. The idea was taken from Mary Tudor's psalter, but the figures represent Lady Londonderry's family. Within the

The topiary garden, Mount Stewart

garden are more strange shapes and on the paved floor the red hand of Ulster is set out in heather.

A fantasy of a more sombre character is the formal garden on the summit of the hill overlooking the estate and Strangford Lough as a burial place for the family and named Tir-N'an Oge, which means the Land of Eternal Youth.

But Lady Londonderry was a great plantswoman as well as a humorous and imaginative designer. The climate here is mild, many semi-tender plants thrive and the garden in consequence has an almost sub-tropical luxuriance. Banksian roses ascend the walls, cordylines grow to 4·5 metres and *Abelia floribunda* covers itself in trails of rose red bloom. The beds in the Italian terrace, once used for bedding plants in season, are now permanently planted with an astonishing variety of herbaceous perennials, roses and small shrubs and in the parkland behind the house many choice rhododendrons thrive.

MOUNT USHER, *Ashford, Co. Wicklow, Eire. On route 7, 3½ miles north-west of Wicklow. No peak season. Privately owned. Open daily except Sundays and Christmas week.*

Four generations of one family and over 100 years have gone into the making of this garden, but throughout that long period there has been no change of direction, no sweeping away of one generation's creation by the differing taste of another. Right from the outset in about 1860 the intention has been to make a collection of rare and beautiful plants. The site was favourable, in a shallow valley through which the little River Vartrey flows to the sea, only two miles away. The soil is lime free, the rainfall fairly heavy, the climate mild. Edmund Walpole started it, all his three sons took part in its development, a grandson succeeded them and now a great grandson, Robert Walpole, carries on the tradition. In the beginning the garden was only about an acre in extent; today it covers twenty acres and is probably complete.

The river has been dammed, both to widen it and to form a number of shallow cascades. Several bridges cross it, one of solid masonry, one almost a half moon in the Japanese fashion, and two very bouncy suspension bridges.

All this gives the garden form and character and so does the house, a pleasant two-storey building with jutting bow windows suggestive of short towers. Excellent use is also made of other design features of mainly 'natural' gardens such as this, namely good contrast between open spaces and dense plantings, and also between close mown and rough grass. In the latter daffodils, lilies, wood anemones, alliums, bluebells and many other bulbous or tuberous rooted plants are naturalized.

The collection of trees and shrubs is magnificent and some specimens are of gigantic size. Some of the eucalyptus trees must be well over 30 metres high. There are splendid specimens of *Lomatia ferruginea, Liriodendron chilensis,* nothofagus, tricuspidaria (one bush with many stems), *Cupressus cashmeriana, Cunninghamia lanceolata, Libocedrus decurreus, Pinus montezumae, Magnolia raffillii, Fitzroyia cupressoides, Dacrydium cupressinum, Picea brewerana, Sciadopytis verticillata, Podocarpus salignus, P. acutifolius* and many more too numerous to name. There is one grove of eucryphias, all very large, which includes *Eucryphia glutinosa, E. cordifolia, E. lucida* and hybrids between them. A *Libocedrus chilensis* is one of the finest examples of this species in the British Isles.

Maples are a great feature and one

Hardy palm and Brewer's spruce, Mount Usher

path is known as the Maple Walk. There are also good taxodiums, cercidiphyllums, liquidambars and other trees noted for their autumn colour. A specimen of *Telopaea truncata* must be about 7 metres high. There are also many rhododendrons and azaleas, including one, *Rhododendron vaseyi*, as good as any likely to be found in the British Isles.

The tree fern, *Dicksonia antarctica*, thrives at Mount Usher. A rarity that greets the visitor in a walled garden near the entrance is *Vestia lycioides* with hanging yellow tubular flowers, and here too is a very big plant of *Ceanothus arboreus* Trewithen Blue and another of *C. cyaneus*.

In short this is a garden which the plant lover will find it difficult to leave, yet everything is so charmingly set out and the little valley itself is so beautiful that Mount Usher equally delights visitors who do not know one plant from another.

MUCKROSS HOUSE, *Muckross, Co. Kerry, Eire. On T65, 3½ miles south of Killarney. Peak season May–June. The Trustees of Muckross House Ltd. Open all the year, except Mondays.*

It would be difficult to conceive a more ideal setting for a garden, in the Killarney National Park on the shore of Lough Leane, ringed by mountains and in places fringed with dense woodland to the water's edge.

The garden of this beautiful place is a kind of tamed extension of the scenery itself, smooth lawns taking the place of rough meadows, carefully selected trees underplanted with rhododendrons, azaleas and other exotic shrubs replacing

The woodland garden, Muckross House

the native forest and the natural outcrops of rock groomed and planted to make the perfect rock garden. The style is that of the woodland glade with trees planted in groups and as isolated specimens, big coppices of hardy hybrid rhododendrons, a hillside covered in *Rhododendron ponticum* for background and a well planted water garden to cement still further this firm union with the landscape. There are some very good embothriums and well grown specimens of *Nothofagus cunninghamii,* also big trees of *Abies nordmanniana, Pinus muricata, P. radiata, Sciadopitys verticillata, Sequoiadendron giganteum* and *Tsuga heterophylla.* An unusual feature is a close clipped hedge of *Pernettya mucronata.*

See also illustration on page 47.

MUNCASTER CASTLE, *Ravenglass, Cumbria. On A595, 1 mile east of Ravenglass. Peak season May–June. Privately owned. Open occasionally, usually on Sundays.*

The grass walk above the Ghyll, Muncaster Castle

Today this garden is chiefly famous for its great collection of rhododendrons and azaleas made during the last hundred years in a site of great natural beauty. But man had also added to the quality of the site before rhododendron planting began. The castle is a romantic building made of red sandstone, parts of it as early as the thirteenth century. It is placed on top of a hill facing up Eskdale, with distant views of the highest Cumbrian mountains. To one side is a narrow but deep valley, the Ghyll, and beyond this, around the bluff of the facing hill, there is a very long level grass walk with a well-trimmed hedge on its outer edge. It is an extraordinarily formal feature to be found in such a wild spot, and since it was made about 1780 with the obvious purpose of exploiting the view, it may be compared with similar terraces at Duncombe Park, Rievaulx and Polesden Lacey.

Much of the rhododendron and azalea planting is in the Ghyll and other ornamental trees and shrubs have also

185

been planted here, including purple-leaved maples, so that the display of colour in May and June can be fantastic. Still more rhododendrons, including the best species and pedigree hybrids, are in the surrounding woods and in clearings made through them. There is also a more formal garden beside the castle, though even here beds once used for flowers in season are now permanently planted with shrubs, including evergreen azaleas, and herbaceous perennials.

Eucryphia cordifolia thrives at Muncaster and there is a notably fine specimen of *Nothofagus procera*.

NEWBY HALL, *Skelton, North Yorkshire. Entrance on A1 at Boroughbridge. Peak season summer. Privately owned. Open spring to autumn, very frequently.*

Newby Hall is an old house with a new garden, though they fit so well together that it would not be obvious to the visitor who knew nothing of their history. The original house was built in the late seventeenth century, but was altered in the mid-eighteenth century by Robert Adam. Early prints show a very formal garden, a series of symmetrical terraces and parterres, but little of this remains today except in the immediate vicinity of the house. The rest has been almost completely redesigned since 1923 by Major Edward Compton, though his mother had started to replant eight years earlier.

The River Ure bounds the garden to the south and Major Compton laid out enormous twin borders separated by a wider grass path to continue the central axis of the south terrace almost to the river's edge. On each side of this

Sylvia's Garden, Newby Hall

central walk he placed small gardens or enclosures or made special features. Sylvia's Garden is completely self-contained, a sunken rectangle with formal beds and flagged paths, but informally planted with small perennials and shrubs. The rose species garden is also sunken and rectangular, but its shape is partly concealed by the luxuriance of its planting, not only with rose species but also with shrub and old-fashioned varieties, philadelphus, kolkwitzia and other shrubs, the whole enclosed by a purple beech hedge. Then there is a little autumn garden, an orchard garden, two quite separate rock gardens, a water garden and a wild garden with many species of rhododendron.

Through it all, binding the whole together, are trees and shrubs, many of them grown to considerable size though few are really old. Visitors who think of Yorkshire as a cold place will be surprised to find *Eucalyptus gunnii* growing out of doors. A specially hardy form known as montana has been selected. There are also eucryphias, embothriums and *Koelreuteria paniculata*, as well as more obvious things for a twentieth century Yorkshire garden such as *Acer griseum*, many magnolias, cherries and a good collection of malus and sorbus species and varieties.

As labour has become more difficult to find, the herbaceous borders have somewhat changed their character and are now mixed borders with shrubs and roses as well as herbaceous plants. But the great central vista to the river, or back to the house, still remains one of the most impressive of its kind.

NEWSTEAD ABBEY, *Ravenshead, Nottinghamshire. On A60, 9 miles north of Nottingham. No peak season. Nottingham Corporation. Open all the year.*

Lord Byron lived at Newstead Abbey, but it had belonged to the Byrons long before that, and before they came there in 1540 it had already been an abbey for centuries. A mediaeval fish pond is still to be seen and there is also a large green parterre with a raised walk against its outer wall and a sunken rectangular

The landscape lake at Newstead Abbey

pool as its central attraction. All these must be very old, but garden making has been an almost continuous process at Newstead Abbey and it contains characteristic elements from all the centuries; a landscape garden and lake, many fine specimen trees, shrubs in plenty including rhododendrons, a Japanese garden, and a rose garden. Now it is a public park and still more additions are being made to suit its new purpose, but the old still remains and is full of interest.

NUNEHAM COURTENAY ARBORETUM, *Nuneham Courtenay, Oxfordshire. In Nuneham Courtenay on A423, 2½ miles south of Cowley. No peak season. University of Oxford. Open on weekdays from April to October.*

This fifty-acre arboretum is now run as an extension of the Oxford Botanic Garden, but began in the 1830s as a pinetum attached to the landscape garden at Nuneham. William Sawrey Gilpin laid out the original eight acres and his serpentine ride still gives access to it, creating convenient bays for planting and greatly increasing the apparent extent of this portion. There are many old trees including araucarias, cedars, sequoias, sequoiadendrons and Douglas firs, and also a great deal of new planting to bring the collection right up to date. There are also underplantings of rhododendrons, camellias, heathers and other shrubs.

NYMANS, *Handcross, West Sussex. At Handcross on B2114, off A23, 2 miles south of its junction with M23. Peak season April to August. National Trust. Open frequently from spring to autumn.*

In this lovely garden many of the elements that have been most characteristic of garden making are brought together. It is a collector's garden, yet it is also a designed garden. It is divided into a number of separate sections, as so many twentieth century gardens are, but the sections at Nymans are mostly too large and insufficiently enclosed to have the character of outdoor rooms. One gets the impression that this method of gardening has been adopted because it permitted the maximum variety of treatments and maybe because it enabled numerous members of the same family to express their own particular ideas.

Plants are used sensitively at Nymans to create pictures and establish moods, but there is not quite the degree of care over every detail that characterizes more self-consciously 'designed' gardens, such as Sissinghurst Castle or Hidcote. Part of the charm of Nymans is its occasional air of casualness, of things having been done just because it gave pleasure to someone to do them and not as part of a master plan.

Ludwig Messel began to plant the garden in 1885 and was succeeded by his son, Lt. Col. L. C. R. Messel. Even today, though Nymans belongs to the National Trust, the Earl and Countess of Rosse, the latter a grand-daughter of Ludwig Messel, continue to manage the garden. As a consequence it has lost none of its intimate, special, family quality.

The range of plants is very great and there are so many rhododendrons that they long since overflowed into a woodland garden on the other side of the road. There are many magnolias, including Leonard Messel, a particularly

good pink flowered form of the hybrid *Magnolia loebneri* (*kobus* × *stellata*) which originated at Nymans.

There is also a good camellia collection, and in this will be found another Leonard Messel, this one a hybrid between *Camellia reticulata* and *C. williamsii* Mary Christian made at Nymans.

There is a big heather garden, part of it cut through by deep, narrow paths like those in a maze, part of it more open with a lawn bounded by a raised walk and pergola on one side and shrub borders on another. Here will be found what must be one of the largest bushes in Britain of *Pieris forrestii* Wakehurst variety.

Yet another Nymans speciality are eucryphias, and in addition to species there are tall columns of *Euchryphia nymansensis*, the special Nymans hybrid between *E. cordifolia* and *E. glutinosa*, which has become one of the most popular kinds.

The big herbaceous borders were designed with the help of William Robinson and so much nonsense is talked about his supposed dislike of all formality that it is interesting to note the elaborately trimmed topiary specimens which punctuate them.

Fuchsias, hydrangeas and old-fashioned roses will be found in plenty and in spring there are meadows filled

Camellias around the dove cote at Nymans

with daffodils. The pinetum beyond the largest of these has strange as well as beautiful specimens including the gaunt weeping form of wellingtonia. Among the oldest trees, all planted in 1898, are *Abies grandis*, *Cupressus macrocarpa*, *Picea omorika*, *P. orientalis* and *Sequoia sempervirens*. There are good specimens of *Abies bracteata* and *Cupressus sempervirens*, and a small but old tree of the rare Chinese swamp cypress, *Glyptostrobus lineatus*. Specially interesting broad-leaved trees include *Gymnocladus dioica*, *Kalopanax pictus*, *Magnolia macrophylla*, *M. sargentiana*, *M. veitchii*, *M. watsonii*, *Nothofagus fusca*, *N. solandri cliffortioides* and *Oxydendrum arboreum*.

This only scratches the surface of the things to be found in this remarkable garden. It is hard to believe that so much could be contained within thirty acres.

See Colour Plate 21 opposite page 163.

THE OWL HOUSE, *Lamberhurst, Kent. On by-road off A21 on north side of Lamberhurst. Peak season May to July. Privately owned. Open frequently all the year.*

A relatively new garden made in meadow and woodland around two old cottages and a converted oast house. Close to these buildings the style is in the familiar English cottage tradition, with flower borders, rose-covered pergolas and clipped box hedges, but elsewhere the planting is much more original with a great many roses, old and new, grown as bushes or trained on

tripods in a meadow. Roses continue deep into the woodland where they are associated with rhododendrons, azaleas and many other flowering shrubs. Though the planting is informal there are numerous architectural features and ornaments to remind visitors that this is man's creation not nature's (*see* overleaf). There are also several small ponds all well incorporated in the overall plan.

Walk to the temple, the Owl House

OXFORD BOTANIC GARDEN, *Oxford. In Oxford, in High Street beside the River Cherwell. No peak season. University of Oxford. Open all the year.*

This is the oldest botanic garden in Britain and one of the smallest, but it is completely charming and fulfils very efficiently both its original purpose of providing a wide range of living botanical material and its more recent role as a delightful garden for public enjoyment. The botanical specimens are still grown in the traditional rectangular beds set out in straight rows separated by grass or gravel paths. In a separate section beyond a high wall there is a lavishly planted water garden, a fine herbaceous border, a well stocked rock garden and plenty of good trees and shrubs, including large specimens of *Fraxinus pennsylvanica, Ginkgo biloba, Koelreuteria*

paniculata, Morus alba and *Salix matsudana tortuosa*. Outside the botanic garden facing the High Street is a formal rose garden designed after the last war as a memorial by Sylvia Crowe.

190

The herbaceous border, Oxford Botanic Garden

PACKWOOD HOUSE, *Packwood, Warwickshire. Off A34, 2 miles east of Hockley Heath. No peak season. National Trust. Frequently open, spring to early autumn.*

Here is the most extraordinary topiary garden in the British Isles, made about 1650 shortly after the execution of Charles I and the establishment of a Commonwealth, and apparently meant to represent the biblical story of the sermon on the mount, though this is denied by some authorities. What is beyond dispute is that at the far end of the garden on a conical mount is a huge cone of yew, ranged at its foot in a straight line are twelve more yews, with many more scattered more or less indiscriminately over the rest of a considerable rectangular enclosure. The mount itself may well have been there

Topiary representing 'the multitude', Packwood House

before John Fetherston planted his yew trees, for the house is Tudor. Perhaps its original intention was as a look-out, a common feature of sixteenth century gardens. In John Fetherston's lifetime the yew trees would only have grown to moderate height and he could have no idea of the overpowering impact of the giant specimens that crowd his garden today.

The topiary garden is the outer of two enclosures, the other, beside the house, being bounded by brick walls with a brick gazebo at each corner. Though these elegant little buildings look alike they were made at different times, the oldest in the north-east corner about 1680, the one in the south-west corner a century later and the other two much more recently. The wall separating the two gardens has niches in which bee skeps once stood.

PENSHURST PLACE, *Penshurst, Kent. In Penshurst on B2176. No peak season. Privately owned. Open frequently from spring to early autumn.*

The garden was made mainly in the mid-nineteenth century in the formal style of the seventeenth century with terraces and *allées* which take in a fish pool. This suits the character of the house, some parts of which are mediaeval with additions up to the seventeenth century. Particularly interesting is the use of solid blocks of box trimmed with almost the precision of slabs of masonry and used to form part of the pattern on the main parterre.

Blocks of trimmed box decorate the parterre at Penshurst Place

PITMEDDEN HOUSE, *Pitmedden, Grampian. On A999, about 11 miles north of its junction with A9. No peak season. National Trust for Scotland. Open all the year.*

Like the delightful garden at Edzell Castle, the Great Garden of Pitmedden represents the taste of the seventeenth century garden makers and exhibits the same delight in patterns made to be looked at from above. As at Edzell this is a rectangular garden and completely enclosed but here by high terraces on three sides and a wall on the fourth with the house at a little distance. It is a much larger garden than Edzell with room for a much more diverse arrangement of 'knots', for that is what these patterns cut in box really are. The garden is overlooked by two elegant gazebos one at each corner of the terraces and is reached from the main terrace by a staircase that divides and rejoins and is placed centrally against the high retaining wall. The garden was originally made about 1675 (that is the date on the lintel of the outer doorway) but in the nineteenth century it was used as a kitchen garden and the parterres

The Great Garden of Pitmedden

disappeared. When the property was handed over to the National Trust for Scotland in 1952 only the masonry remained, some of that in poor repair, and the beds had to be completely redesigned. Since no plans of the originals remained new ones were designed, three based on contemporary plans for the Palace of Holyroodhouse, a fourth an original design for the new garden. All these new plans were made by the same man, employed by the Ministry of Building and Public Works, who designed the new beds for Edzell Castle. A fountain in contemporary style was also made from fragments preserved at Pitmedden plus some of similar date from the Cross Fountain of Linlithgow.

So today the old garden can be seen recreated, if not exactly as it originally was, at least completely in the spirit of the times, except for the gay infilling of flowering annuals which seems to have been regarded as a necessary tourist attraction.

See also illustration on page 5.

POLESDEN LACEY, *Polesden, near Dorking, Surrey. On a by-road 1½ miles south of its junction with A246 in Great Bookham. Peak season May to August. National Trust. Frequently open, from spring to autumn.*

It would be difficult to imagine a more English garden than this, approached by narrow lanes, their hedgerows filled with wild flowers, and planned to take full advantage of the lovely views of the valley in which it is situated and the surrounding woodland and farmland. Richard Brinsley Sheridan lived here from 1796 to 1816 and may well have laid out the long grass terrace along the edge of the valley. Two tall stone pillars mark the entrance, large stone urns and other ornaments with classical inscriptions decorate it and at the far end there is a Doric portico to emphasize the point that this is a sophisticated gallery from which to enjoy a rural scene.

The grass terrace, Polesden Lacey

Shortly after Sheridan's death the old house was pulled down and a new one in neo-Grecian style built in its place. Nothing much more of importance appears to have happened until Mrs Ronald Greville bought Polesden Lacey in 1906 and engaged J. Cheal and Sons to lay out a whole series of gardens, some of them linked enclosures in the style then becoming fashionable, others open and serving as a link between the new development and the old. The enclosures flank a central path and include a rose garden, iris garden, lavender garden and peony borders.

Some are surrounded by brick walls with circular peepholes framing views outside. Nearest the house is Mrs Greville's own burial place, a simple plot of grass backed with yew against which white marble statues are displayed.

Beside the great lawn to the south of the house are many specimen trees, some of which were planted by royal or other distinguished visitors and bearing plaques denoting this. They include large and well shaped blue spruces, Norway maples and copper beeches.

POLLOK HOUSE, *Glasgow, Strathclyde. On A736 in Pollokshaws. No peak season. Glasgow Corporation. Open all the year.*

Two contrasting styles of garden making meet here, a formal arrangement of terraces adorned with handsome stone gazebos around the house, and as a quite separate unit on a ridge of land to one side, a woodland garden with many good trees and shrubs, including a large number of rhododendrons, mainly hardy hybrids. The formal garden may well be the work of William Adam, the eighteenth century architect who designed the house; the woodland garden is twentieth century.

Please check actual dates and times of opening in the various guides and lists given on pages 68–69.

Pollok House gazebo and box-edged beds

Buildings around the 'village green', Portmeirion

PORTMEIRION, *Penrhyndeudraeth, Gwynedd. On by-road off A487, 2 miles south-east of Portmadoc. Private company. Peak season May to August. Open throughout the year.*

This is the ultimate example of the picturesque movement – a whole garden village in an idyllic cove on the northern shore of Traeth Bach, an almost landlocked estuary in north Wales. The story of its creation is as fantastic as the place itself. The architect and author, Clough Williams-Ellis – later knighted for his many services to the country – was looking for a safe anchorage for his yacht. He discovered in this sheltered cove precisely what he required, but he also found a derelict Victorian mansion and a woodland garden stretching around the headland and filled with rhododendrons, azaleas and other shrubs. So he decided to exploit commercially the romantic qualities of the site by creating a fantastic dream village, strongly Italian in spirit, yet drawing on architecture from many centuries and various parts of the world. The tiny village is overtopped by a slender Italian campanile and many of the buildings are plaster faced and painted with Mediterranean style colour washes. But there are also buildings in many other styles, including the original Victorian house converted to a modern hotel beside the little quay.

The whole collection clusters around what must be the most sophisticated village green in the world (*see* page 195) – a tiny formal park with a shapely pool flanked by columns bearing gilded figures of Siamese dancers and overlooked by an elaborate colonnade, a pink washed gothic pavilion and a Jacobean town hall. In spring the whole place seems embowered in rhododendrons, azaleas, embothriums, lilacs and many other shrubs, to be followed in summer by hydrangeas and gay bedding plants. Immediately behind the village there are some fine old specimen rhododendrons retained from previous planting, but regrettably the extensive woodland gardens laid out in the nineteenth century have become very overgrown.

POWERSCOURT, *Enniskerry, Co. Wicklow, Eire. On T43a, just south of Enniskerry. No peak season. Powerscourt Estate. Open daily from Easter to October.*

Here is the most magnificent example of the Victorian rediscovery of the glories of Italian gardening. The site is ideal for the purpose with the land falling quite steeply from the mansion to the south, then levelling out before rising again to the sharp cone of the Sugar Loaf mountain. Even without a garden this would be a memorable landscape. The great formal terraces with their elaborately patterned pavements and balustrades, the huge circular pool and the columns of mighty conifers emerging from broadleaved trees give it a theatrical quality unsurpassed by any garden in the British Isles.

The Japanese garden, Powerscourt

23. Skilful use of plants, Sutton Park (*see* page 220)

24. The rock garden, Threave (*see* page 222)

25. Azalea Valley in Windsor Great Park (*see* page 230)

No doubt most visitors seeing Powerscourt for the first time will imagine it to be the work of some great master of the seventeenth or early eighteenth century. The mansion, now gutted by fire, was in fact built in 1743 and the grotto built of tufa stone below the Triton pool is also eighteenth century. But work on the great formal garden did not start until 1843 and it took thirty-two years to complete. It was, as far as can be gathered, the only important work of its creator, one Daniel Robertson, of whom little seems to be known except that he was a heavy drinker, suffered from gout, and often directed the work from a wheelbarrow.

Powerscourt is famous for its trees, its park and its waterfall as well as for its terrace gardens, but both visitors and writers often overlook the Japanese garden made in a dell beside the grotto already mentioned. It is a charming example of its kin'! with a blue and white pavilion as its centrepiece, several lacquer-red bridges, the usual stone 'mushrooms' and lanterns and good planting with cherries, magnolias, Japanese quince, etc.

There are many fine trees at Powerscourt, some of them planted early and now well over a century old. These include *Abies concolor lowiana*, *A. grandis*, *A. nordmanniana*, *A. spectabilis*, *Chamaecyparis nootkatensis*, *Cupressus macrocarpa*, *C. funebris*, *C. sempervirens*, *Eucalyptus globulus*, *Fitzroya cupressoides* and *Pinus jeffreyi*. A fine avenue of *Araucaria araucana* extends

Spitting men fountain and sundial, Powerscourt

the line of the house terrace towards the west and a specimen of *Abies delavayi faxoniana* is one of the largest of its kind in the British Isles (16·5 metres in 1966). There is also a big specimen of *Picea likiangensis*, which Alan Mitchell describes as 'superb, very blue'. But to see all these the visitor must be prepared to explore the park as well as the garden and it extends for 2 miles to the waterfall, itself 121 metres high and said to be the highest in the British Isles.

POWIS CASTLE, *Welshpool, Powys. Entrance in Welshpool (pedestrians only) and for cars from a by-road off A483, 1 mile south of the town. No peak season. National Trust. Open frequently from May to September.*

Of this garden Christopher Hussey said that it 'reproduces more nearly an Italian baroque terraced garden than any other surviving in England'. The old red sandstone castle is strategically placed on a ridge with extensive views of the hilly Welsh countryside and when, in the 1790s, the Earl of Rochford started to make a garden there the steep slope below the castle had to be terraced in the

Italian manner. Each terrace differs in depth, breadth and treatment, two are ornamented with stone balustrades and these are themselves further decorated with urns and lead figures of shepherds and shepherdesses. The result seen from below is of a pattern, as in all these early gardens, but in this instance a vertical pattern instead of one laid out on the flat. The earl did in fact make a horizontal pattern too, a water garden in the Dutch manner, on the level land 30 metres below the castle, but this has disappeared, its place being taken by a simple lawn, though to one side what was once a kitchen garden has been converted into a series of formal gardens with some old pyramid-trained apple trees retained in one section as an ornamental feature.

As the centuries have passed Powis Castle has also acquired a woodland garden made on the curl of the ridge which partially encloses the place, and this in turn has been underplanted with rhododendrons and other exotic shrubs in the modern manner. The warmth and shelter of the terraces (they face south-east) has also been exploited by twentieth century gardeners for the cultivation of many choice shrubs and herbaceous plants, so that today Powis Castle is interesting to plant lovers as well as to those whose main gardening interests concern history or design.

A feature of the old garden is an orangery actually built into one of the terraces, and on the terrace above there is a brick-faced loggia with seven arches, possibly the place originally used as an aviary, for this is known as the Aviary Terrace.

Also remarkable are the huge yew buttresses to one side of the castle, the great box hedges that line the winding ascent from the old kitchen garden, and the great domes of clipped yew which seem to sprout out of the topmost terrace.

The terraces, Powis Castle

A pinetum started in 1932 already contains outstandingly fine specimens, including *Abies alba* and *A. delavayi georgei*. In the garden itself there is a good *Ginkgo biloba, Pinus ponderosa, Sequoia sempervirens* and *Davidia involucrata*, while in or around Gwen Morgan's wood in the Powis estate (but outside the National Trust garden) are some more remarkable specimens, including another *Pinus ponderosa* and a *Pseudotsuga menziesii* described by Alan Mitchell as respectively 'easily the finest known' and 'tallest tree in Britain'.

Prior Park from the lake spanned by the Palladian bridge

PRIOR PARK, *Bath, Avon. On the eastern outskirts of Bath. No peak season. Privately owned. Open occasionally.*

Here is an eighteenth century landscape chiefly famous now because its main architectural feature is the last to be made of the three covered or Palladian bridges; the other two, in order of construction, being at Wilton House and Stowe. These bridges are not copies one of another, nor were they copied from designs by Andrea Palladio as their name might suggest, but they are similar in appearance and perform a similar function in the landscape composition. From this point of view the one at Prior Park, probably built in 1756, is perhaps the most important since without it there would scarcely be a composition at all. It could not be placed more felicitously. From the great Georgian mansion which overlooks Bath from the south the ground falls very steeply to two lakes separated by a long straight dam. The bridge spans the nearer of this pair and is built to just the right height to conceal the dam from the mansion. The rest of the slope is green meadow in which cows graze, closed in by trees on each side and with Bath spread out over the valley of the River Avon and the sides of Landsdowne to the north. Nothing could be much simpler in design, few landscapes are more impressive in realization. It was made by Ralph Allen who popularized Bath stone and was concerned with the rebuilding of Bath in that material.
See illustration on previous page.

PUSEY HOUSE, *Pusey, near Faringdon, Oxfordshire. On B4508, 1 mile south-west of its junction with A420. Peak season summer. Privately owned. Open about twice weekly from spring to autumn.*

Here is another example of an eighteenth century landscape used for a twentieth century plant garden, but on a relatively modest scale. The house was built in 1748 and the landscape was made at that time, but not by Kent, Brown or any other famous name. Yet all the elements of the style are here, a lake in the middle distance, this one long and narrow like a river, parallel with the south front of the house, and then, beyond, a vista of countryside framed in trees. A white Chinese style bridge crosses the lake to the east, and to the west there is a small classical temple. In this charming setting the present owners have, since 1935, made an entirely new garden with a house terrace designed by Geoffrey Jellicoe and great numbers of shrubs, herbaceous plants, roses and new trees disposed in such a way as to give new life and interest to the garden without destroying its basic form. There are some fine old trees including swamp cypress, plane, cedars, beeches and a black walnut said to be among the largest in Britain. It was over 27 metres high when measured in 1968, and is described in *Trees and Shrubs Hardy in the British Isles* as 'a superb tree'.

Bridge and lake from the house terrace, Pusey House

QUEEN MARY'S GARDEN, *Regent's Park, London. In the Inner Circle, Regent's Park. Peak season June to September. Crown Property. Open all the year.*

Most rose lovers would agree that this is the finest rose garden in the British Isles and one of the best in the world. It was made in 1932 when the lease on the Inner Circle, held by the Royal Botanical Society, expired and the area was redesigned as part of Regent's Park. It was originally a large circle of beds, and this arrangement is still there, but the roses have now spread far beyond it and cover a considerable acreage, along one side of a lake and down an avenue. It is a lovely setting, the beds are of generous size, usually each restricted to one variety planted rather closely and grown superbly well, so that the display at the peak flowering periods is terrific. Great efforts are made to keep the collection up to date and new varieties are often added before they are available for general release.

Queen Mary's Rose Garden, Regent's Park

RIEVAULX TERRACE, *Rievaulx, North Yorkshire. On B1257, 2½ miles north-west of Helmsley. No peak season. National Trust. Open frequently from spring to autumn.*

This terrace is related to the Duncombe terraces described on page 128. The latter, started by Thomas Duncombe in 1713, were completed by his son, another Thomas, about 1730. A grandson, also named Thomas, made the Rievaulx terrace about 1758 and there are some indications that he intended to link it with the Duncombe terraces by means of a viaduct, though there is no

The ruined abbey viewed from the Rievaulx Terrace

proof of this. What is certain is that the Rievaulx terrace was designed to exploit the magnificent view of the ruins of Rievaulx Abbey in the valley below it. The terrace is of grass, curving, like the east terrace of Duncombe Park, to follow the line of the escarpment, and also like that terrace, with a temple at each end. Also as at Duncombe, by the present century trees had grown up so thickly on the slopes as to obscure the views the terrace was created to reveal. Now, since the National Trust purchased this terrace in 1972, great swathes have been cut diagonally through the trees at numerous points so that new vistas of ruins and countryside are revealed to the visitor prepared to walk the half mile from one end to the other. If any doubt remained as to the original intention of the Duncombe terraces this Rievaulx revelation should remove it.

ROCKINGHAM CASTLE, *Rockingham, Northamptonshire. In Rockingham on A6003 from Kettering, 2 miles north of Corby. No peak season. Privately owned. Open about once a week from spring to early autumn.*

The interest here lies mainly in the ancient castle, but the garden with its huge yew hedges and alleys, its rose garden enclosed within a great circle of yew, and the good planting in ruined walls and foundations fits it well and is very romantic. There are also extensive views to east, north and west.

ROUSHAM HOUSE, *Rousham, Oxfordshire. On by-road to Rousham off B4030 at Hayford Bridge. No peak season. Privately owned. Open fairly frequently in summer.*

This garden, which is more fully described on page 14, is the most complete example of the landscape style of William Kent. It is much smaller than Stowe, where Kent also worked, but there many additions were made after his death and even during his lifetime others, including Lord Cobham, were playing some part in what was happening. At Rousham Kent carried out his own ideas and then for two centuries successive generations of the Dormer family, who continued to live there, felt no urge to alter it in any way. Only age and the inevitable growth and decay which it brings have wrought any change in what Kent so ingeniously planned.

The rose garden, Rockingham Castle

The upper cascade, Rousham House

Rowallane – a garden that steps over farm walls

ROWALLANE, *Saintfield, Co. Down, Northern Ireland. 1 mile south of Saintfield. Peak season April to June. National Trust. Open all the year.*

There is no garden quite like Rowallane for no other has simply jumped its original confines and spread across the surrounding fields without making any attempt to remove or conceal their walls. This is an area of poor soil where the rock frequently crops out on the surface, and for centuries farmers have been accustomed to enclose their fields with dry stone walls. At Rowallane the rock gardens were made by the simple process of baring a little more of the already exposed rocks, and as for the walls, they are still there and the visitor must pass through them by gates or climb over them by stiles to get from one plantation to another. So it is neither quite a wild garden nor yet wholly a woodland garden, but a mixture of both these with a peculiarly agricultural overtone all its own. There are more formal elements in the design, particularly in the old walled garden near the house, where the straight paths and rectilinear beds that no doubt were once used for fruit and vegetables remain, though now used exclusively for ornamental plants.

This is in short a collector's garden and one of the finest of its kind. There was not much except some shelter trees when Hugh Armytage Moore began to plant in 1903, but by the time the National Trust took it over in 1955 it

203

had grown to fifty acres filled with a magnificent variety of woody and herbaceous plants.

The most colourful period is in late spring when thousands of rhododendrons and azaleas are at their best, but for the plant lover there is always something of interest at Rowallane, so catholic was the taste of its creator. In early summer there are numerous meconopsis species and varieties. *Olearia macrodonta* has grown to great size and there are also fine specimens of various cornus species, eucryphias, eucalyptus, and nothofagus. In the walled garden is an *Azara microphylla variegata* grown to tree size.

It was Mr Moore's practice to look out for specially good forms of plants and also to make hybrids of his own, and several bear the name of his garden, e.g. *Hypericum* Rowallane, a slightly tender hybrid between *H. hookeranum rogersii* and *H. leschenaultii, Viburnum plicatum* Rowallane which received the Royal Horticultural Society's Award of Garden Merit in 1969, and *Chaenomeles superba* Rowallane with large crimson flowers which received the A.G.M. in 1957.

The largest of the rock outcrops is in one of the more remote parts of the garden, but it is worth seeking out as it contains many good plants including meconopses, lilies, hardy geraniums, lithospermums and celmisias.

ROYAL NATIONAL ROSE SOCIETY'S GARDEN, *Chiswell Green, St Albans, Hertfordshire. In Chiswell Green Lane at Chiswell Green between St Albans and M1 (Exit 6). Peak season June to September. Royal National Rose Society. Open daily from mid-June to late September.*

Part of this garden is laid out to display the ornamental use of roses of all kinds and part is a trial ground in which new varieties of rose are tested and given awards if of sufficient merit. The display section is designed mainly as one large garden with a pavilion, pool, pergolas etc. and is planned to show both the use of roses in formal beds and in more informal plantings, including ground cover, hedges and as shrubs. There are in addition several model plots designed to show various ways of growing roses in small gardens.

This is a beautiful garden as well as a highly instructive one, and its value to garden makers has been enhanced in recent years by the inclusion of many hardy perennials that associate well with roses.

See also Colour Plate 22 opposite page 163.

RUDDING PARK, *Follifoot, North Yorkshire. Just south of A661, 1½ miles east of Harrogate. Peak season May to July. The Mackaness Organization. Open daily from late May to mid-September.*

Humphry Repton prepared plans for the landscape at Rudding Park, though how much of his design was carried out or still remains is not clear. The park certainly has a Reptonian look and the views across the Vale of York are magnificent. But what is of greatest interest to garden lovers today is the new garden made by the late Captain Sir Everard Radcliffe with the assistance of James Russell from 1945 in what was presumably part of Repton's woodland. This is very typical of the modern trend in woodland gardening which succeeds in

The Royal National Rose Society's garden and offices

introducing a considerable degree of formality into what is basically a natural style of planting. Here, as in other woodland gardens, there are large plantations of rhododendrons, drifts of candelabra primulas looking as if they must always have been there, lilies, hydrangeas and many other plants grouped in island beds of irregular shape or simply in groups among the trees. But at the heart of it all is a large marble vase on a pedestal in the middle of a circular clearing from which straight alleys radiate in all directions, linked by cross alleys which are not immediately visible. One of these walks leads through a rose garden to a fine pair of wrought iron gates giving access to the old walled kitchen garden. Here vegetables have given place to wide twin borders separated by a grass path leading to a little brick pavilion built in the style of a seventeenth century orangery. This is a romantic garden portraying a longing to capture the best of the past and link it with the best of the present.

Radiating avenues in the woodland garden, Rudding Park

SALTRAM HOUSE, *Plymouth, Devon. Off A38 between Plymouth and Plympton. No peak season. National Trust. Open very frequently from April to September.*

Saltram House is famous for its Adam interiors and fine collection of paintings. It stands in a pleasant eighteenth century landscape park and there are some fine trees, but its most distinctive garden feature is a very attractive orangery, unusually framed in wood, and built in 1775. Oranges are still grown in it in ornamental tubs which in summer are moved to an outdoor standing ground surrounded by tall eucryphias, hoherias and other exotic trees and shrubs not known when the garden was originally made.

The orangery, Saltram House

SANDRINGHAM, *Dersingham, near Kings Lynn, Norfolk. On B1440, 2 miles north of its junction with A148. Peak season spring and summer. Her Majesty the Queen. Frequently open from spring to early summer, except when the Royal Family is in residence.*

Great changes have been made at Sandringham in recent years to reduce the expense of what was originally a great early twentieth century garden. The house has also been simplified and reduced in size. But there have been additions as well as deletions, including the improvement of the park and woodland with the help of T. H. Findlay who for many years assisted Sir Eric Savill in the development of the Savill Garden and the Valley Gardens in Windsor Great Park. There is also an interesting formal garden, designed by Geoffrey Jellicoe for King George VI. This is long and narrow, enclosed with lines of pleached lime trees and subdivided by clipped box hedges into numerous compartments, individually treated in sharply contrasting ways.

THE SAVILL GARDEN, *Windsor Great Park, Berkshire. Entrance in Wick Lane, Englefield Green, reached from Wick Road off A30, 1 mile south of Egham. No peak season, but flowering trees and shrubs are at their best from April to early June. Crown Property. Open daily from March to October.*

This was the first of the gardens to be made by Sir Eric Savill in Windsor Great Park, to be followed, after the Second World War, by the series of gardens further west and adjoining Virginia Water, collectively known as the Valley Gardens. When work started in 1932 the intention was simply to make a bog and water garden in a rather damp spot adjoining Englefield Green, but one thing led to another and by the time the garden was complete it included most of the features characteristic of any large garden made in the twentieth century and had even acquired a high brick wall to simulate a building where none in fact existed.

The garden is remarkable for its complexity of design, amazingly varied collections of plants and for the skill with which these have been associated. The result is one of the outstanding achievements of twentieth century garden making in Britain.

In one sense the visitor is forced to see this remarkable garden in the wrong sequence since the public entrance is to the original woodland glade in which the ponds and bog garden were made and which is treated in a semi-wild way, though it must be understood that here the term 'wild' is used to describe a style and not a lapse in care, since the cultivation throughout is of the highest order.

Yet logically a garden such as this would be seen from the house outwards, that is to say the more formal features would come first and the progression would then be towards a 'natural' style.

In the Savill Garden the formal features are a terrace with a series of raised rectangular rock beds for alpines, then a rose garden leading to long double herbaceous borders, then another garden in which roses play a major part, but this time mostly shrub and informal roses associated with other plants.

So the transition is made step by step to miscellaneous shrubs, a woodland garden, peat beds and an alpine meadow.

In early spring the place is full of daffodils and crocuses naturalized in the

Rhododendron Polar Bear flowering in early August, Savill Garden

grass; soon it is ablaze with rhododendrons and azaleas, to be followed swiftly by primulas, meconopses, roses and all the summer flowers. In autumn there are berries and other ornamental fruits and the rich colours of autumn foliage and even in winter various willows and dogwoods, kept pollarded for the purpose, contribute their own distinctive bark colours. As a result this is a garden that is full of beauty and interest throughout the year. There is also a large temperate greenhouse used chiefly for those rhododendron species and other shrubs too tender to be safe outdoors in this rather cold part of Britain.

Notable trees include a very beautiful specimen of *Picea omorika pendula* and some big *Metasequoia glyptostroboides*, grown from the original importation of seed.

See also illustration on page 38.

SCONE PALACE PINETUM, *Scone, Tayside. On A93, 2 miles north of Perth. No peak season. Privately owned. Open frequently from spring to autumn.*

The name of David Douglas, the explorer who did so much to introduce north-western conifers to Britain, is closely connected with Scone. He was

The pinetum, Scone Palace

born there and as a lad worked in the garden of Scone Palace. Some of his earliest seed was sent here and there are Douglas firs in the palace garden which were planted in 1834, the year Douglas died, from seed sent home in 1827. These are not actually in the pinetum but near to it. The pinetum was started in 1848 and has been well maintained ever since. There is no attempt at landscaping and the spacing of the trees is fairly even, though there are several wide walks through it, one lined with immense western hemlocks (*Tsuga heterophylla*), another with noble firs (*Abies procera*). A tree of *Pinus jeffreyi* is described by Alan Mitchell as the largest he has seen. There are very big specimens of *Abies concolor lowiana*, *A. grandis*, *A. nordmanniana*, *Libocedrus decurrens*, *Cedrus atlantica glauca*, *Chamaecyparis nootkatensis*, *Picea orientalis*, *P. sitchensis* (one 44·5 metres in 1970), *Pinus monticola* and *Sequioadendron giganteum* and also smaller but interesting trees of *Picea brewerana*, *Abies delavayi* and *Torreya californica*.

SCOTNEY CASTLE, *Lamberhurst, Kent. On A21, ½ mile south of Lamberhurst. No peak season, but this garden is most colourful in May and early June and again in October. National Trust. Open frequently from April to October.*

This is probably the most beautiful and best preserved of all the early nineteenth century picturesque landscapes. Garden making began at Scotney Castle in 1836 when the owner, Edward Hussey, decided to build himself a new house on the summit of the ridge overlooking the valley of the little River Bewl in which his existing residence was situated. This was a beautiful seventeenth century villa standing beside the round tower of a fourteenth century castle and its sixteenth century wing, the whole group of buildings surrounded by a moat which on the south-west side attained the proportions of a lake. It was an exceedingly romantic spot surrounded by woods and meadows, but damp, old and inconvenient. So Mr Hussey engaged the architect, Anthony Salvin, an exponent of the neo-Tudor style, to build him a new house, for which purpose a stone quarry was opened just below the chosen site, and consulted William Sawrey Gilpin, a leading advocate for the picturesque landscape, to advise on the new garden.

Everything was propitious. The group of old buildings, the seventeenth century villa partially demolished to

The new house from the ruins, Scotney Castle

make it a romantic ruin, provided exactly the right focal point for a living picture to be viewed most effectively from the new mansion and a balustraded belvedere constructed above the quarry. This itself became a rock garden, groups of trees and shrubs were carefully placed on the slopes to create vistas and an interesting foreground and a cedar of Lebanon was as meticulously sited in a meadow on the far slope to embellish the already lovely backdrop. Even the American conifers, so often criticized as alien to the English landscape, look right at Scotney Castle, the tall columns of incense cedar and selected forms of Lawson cypress making strikingly dramatic accents among the soft and rounded outlines of native oak and beech. Notable trees include *Sequoia sempervirens*, a fine *Sequoiadendron giganteum*, *Thuja plicata*, *Pinus ponderosa*, *Picea orientalis*, and *Chamaecyparis lawsoniana erecta*. There are also large trees of *Cedrus deodara*, *Picea sitchensis*, *Pinus nigra maritima* and *Pseudotsuga menziesii* and an immense bush of *Kalmia latifolia*.

Edward Hussey's creation has been lovingly maintained by successive generations and has finally been entrusted to the National Trust.

See illustration on page 21 and Colour Plate 2 opposite page 16.

SEZINCOTE, *Moreton-in-Marsh, Gloucestershire. On A44, 1 mile west of Moreton-in-Marsh. Peak season summer. Privately owned. Open very occasionally.*

Sezincote is a Georgian country mansion with Indian decorations, including a great onion-shaped dome. It was built about 1805 by Sir Charles Cockerill to the design of Thomas Daniell, who had written a book on Indian architecture. Humphry Repton was also involved, apparently in the house as well as in the garden, and John Nash appears to have visited the place and given some advice. This was before his own Indian design for the Prince Regent's Pavilion at Brighton.

The result is completely unique since the garden also contains Indian features to match the house. It is not in any way modelled on actual Indian gardens, but merely decorated with Indian ornaments and architecture. This is mainly in a little glen between the house and the road, some distance away. The long entrance drive crosses this ravine on a substantial stone bridge based on an Indian design and ornamented with crouching bulls executed in Coade stone. A stream tumbles rapidly down the quite steep glen, splashing over rocky cascades on the way and seemingly having its source in a circular pool higher up the valley. This has a curious fountain as its centrepiece, spouting an umbrella-shaped

The canal pool, Sezincote

spray of water. It is backed by a little Indian temple containing a Coade stone figure of the goddess Souriya, and behind this again, tucked into the hillside, is a grotto or cave. Below the bridge a bronze serpent ascends a bronze pole in the centre of another pool. Everywhere there is lush planting, bamboos, hardy palms, aruncus, gunnera, irises, *Campanula lactiflora*, primulas, lilies and much else, some of it possibly old, but most of it fairly recent and designed by Graham Thomas. Mr Thomas also designed the narrow canal pool flanked by pencil-slim cypresses which cuts across a terrace enclosed by the mansion itself and a curving conservatory which extends like a wing from it. Overlooking this is an elegant little pavilion in Indian style designed by the present owner, Cyril Kleinwort.

SHAKESPEARE GARDENS, *Stratford-upon-Avon, Warwickshire. Peak season May to August. Shakespeare Birthplace Trust. Open daily from spring to autumn.*

Several gardens in and around Stratford-upon-Avon have been re-made and are maintained because of their connection with Shakespeare. No attempt has been made to replace what was originally there, since no records exist to

The Knot Garden, Stratford-upon-Avon

indicate what that was. Instead gardens have been made which suit the sites, set off the buildings, if any, and contain many plants mentioned by Shakespeare and other writers of the period. The one that comes nearest to a genuine sixteenth century garden is the little Knot Garden in Chapel Street. This occupies a rectangular enclosure between a garden made in the ruined foundations of New Place, Shakespeare's last home, and a much larger enclosure, the Great Garden, where Shakespeare probably grew fruit and vegetables. A few streets away, in Old Town, is a garden behind Hall's Croft, where Shakespeare's daughter lived. Anne Hathaway's cottage at Shottery, about a mile away, has a charming cottage garden more nineteenth century than sixteenth century in the profusion of its overflowing flower beds. Other gardens are at Shakespeare's Birthplace, which was restored in 1847 and at Mary Arden's house a few miles away at Wilmcote.

SHARPITOR, *Salcombe, Devon. On a lane 1½ miles south-west of Salcombe. Peak season spring and early summer. National Trust. Open all the year.*

This is quite a difficult place to find and a long way from main roads, but it is worth while making the journey if only to enjoy the superb views down on the Salcombe estuary and along the steep south Devon coast. In fact there is a lot

Sharpitor – view of the Salcombe estuary

more than views to attract plant-loving visitors to Sharpitor, for the six acre garden is full of good plants. There are many well grown rhododendrons, azaleas, magnolias, tricuspidarias and acacias, as well as crinums, agapanthus, calceolarias, cupheas, fuchsias and many more plants that thrive in this mild maritime climate. The collection, for such it is despite quite a pleasing design, was made by a wealthy business man, Otto Overbeck, between 1912 and 1937 and has been well maintained by the National Trust.

SHEFFIELD PARK, *Near Uckfield, East Sussex. On A275, 5 miles south of junction with A22. Peak seasons May – June and October – November. National Trust. Open frequently from spring to autumn.*

The garden at Sheffield Park began in the eighteenth century as a 'Capability' Brown landscape, developed a hundred years later into a picturesque landscape with two more lakes linked by a rock garden and cascade, and finally in the present century acquired a collection of trees and shrubs to bear comparison with any in the country. It thus portrays the changing tastes of three centuries and perhaps better than any other garden shows how these can combine to produce a superb result.

The house was built for the 1st Lord Sheffield by James Wyatt and is castellated in the Gothic style. From the house the land slopes to the south-east to a wide, shallow valley. It was in this valley, at some distance from the house, that 'Capability' Brown placed the first two lakes, set across the view, with grass sweeping up to the house, and with tree belts and clumps to frame the whole vista. More than a century later the 3rd Earl, with the aid of James Pulham, made two further lakes by enlarging

three little pools already there, this time following the line of the subsiduary valley towards the house and so, with the first two, making a kind of gigantic letter T with its head in the main valley, where a tributary of the River Ouse had been dammed. There was no water in the subsiduary valley to the house and a large reservoir was constructed, into which water was pumped from lower down, to supply these new lakes. There is a considerable drop from the top to the second lake and this was filled with a

Gunnera manicata **beside one of Capability Brown's lakes at Sheffield Park**

large rock bank and a stream and cascade made to connect the two lakes.

Finally came the planting of A. G. Soames, who purchased the property in 1909 and continued to live there until his death in 1948. An enthusiastic plant lover, he stocked the woodlands and the water sides with choice trees and shrubs and raised many rhododendrons himself, including hybrids between *Rhododendron discolor* and *R. griffithianum* which bear the group name Angelo and add greatly to the beauty of Sheffield Park in early June. There are also, in May and June, thousands of other rhododendrons including the hardy hybrids, together with azaleas, cornus species, kalmias and many other flowering shrubs. In autumn the place is ablaze with foliage colour provided by taxodiums at the water's edge (both *Taxodium distichum* and *T. ascendens* are planted), maples of many kinds, amelanchiers, *Nyssa sylvatica*, beeches, aza-

Exotic trees and shrubs at Sheffield Park

leas, parrotias, cornus species, *Betula pendula dalecarlica* and many other trees and shrubs.

The conifer collection is particularly fine with many of the coloured forms of

The Chinese pavilion, Shugborough

Lawson cypress adding to the richness of the scene at all times of the year and specially notable specimens of *Cunninghamia konishii, Picea brewerana, P. omorika* and *Libocedrus decurrens*. Other interesting trees are an umbrella pine (*Sciadopitys verticillata*), near the second lake from the house and a very tall *Sequoiadendron giganteum* in this same area. There are numerous fine specimens of *Abies procera*, all over 30 metres high, and also a very big *A. grandis*. But there are some much older trees than these, notably a *Pinus montezumae* and two *Pinus pinaster*, believed to have been planted about 1800 and really part of the original green landscape.

SHUGBOROUGH, *Great Haywood, Staffordshire. At Milford on A513, 5½ miles southeast of Stafford. No peak season. National Trust and Staffordshire County Council. Open all the year.*

Shugborough is of special interest to garden historians because it contains so many buildings and monuments in the neo-Grecian style, some, including the Temple of the Winds, designed by James Stuart, often nicknamed 'Athenian' Stuart because of the leading role he played in this particular fashion. In the park at Shugborough, created from about 1740 onwards, these buildings appear all over the place, not always with any clear purpose in design but fascinating in their own right. More obviously contributing to the landscape is a Chinese pavilion, designed by Sir Peircy Brett, which stands on a little knoll beside the River Sow which winds through the park. A more formal garden with terraces, topiary and rose beds was made between mansion and river in the nineteenth century.

SISSINGHURST **C**ASTLE, *Sissinghurst, Kent. Approached by a lane on the north side of A262, ½ mile east of Sissinghurst. No peak season. National Trust. Open daily from April to mid-September.*

This garden, made by the late Vita Sackville West and her husband, Sir Harold Nicholson, from 1930 onwards, shares with Hidcote the distinction of having almost certainly exercised the greatest influence on subsequent garden design in Britain. These two gardens have much in common. Both are divided into numerous compartments in the sixteenth and seventeenth century manner. Unlike these early gardens both make great use of plants of many kinds and obtained from many countries so that the profusion of planting often tends to mask the essential regularity and firmness of the underlying design. And in both colour is used thoughtfully and well, though with perhaps an even greater fastidiousness over detail at Sissinghurst than at Hidcote.

The rose garden, Sissinghurst Castle

The 'castle' is a fragment of an Elizabethan house, never intended for defence and entirely devoid of fortification, though it has a slender twin turretted tower from which wonderful panoramic views of the garden and the surrounding countryside can be obtained. Indeed this is the best vantage point from which to appreciate the rather complex design of the garden and the clever way in which Sir Harold Nicolson, who was mainly responsible for the plan, succeeded in producing an apparent degree of symmetry out of a very irregular plot, rendered yet more difficult by the presence of several scattered buildings. Despite these obstacles he contrived to make long vistas and alleys linking the smaller and more intimate gardens which include a white garden, a yellow and orange garden, a garden of old roses, a rondel of clipped yew, a lime walk, a herb garden and an orchard filled with daffodils in spring and dripping with roses in summer, since the old apple trees have been preserved mainly as natural supports for climbers. It is an enchanting place at all times of the year since it has been planted for all seasons and as a place to be lived in at all times.

See page 54 and Colour Plate 9.

SIZERGH CASTLE, *Kendal, Cumbria. On A6, 3½ miles south of Kendal. No peak season. National Trust. Fairly frequent opening from spring to early autumn.*

For the garden lover there are many good things at Sizergh Castle; island beds well stocked with shrubs and old roses; some good perennials including large drifts of hostas; a lake several hundred years old, now flanked with more shrubs, and a recently planted avenue of the hybrid lime, *Tilia euchlora*, which because of its relatively small size is particularly suitable for garden planting.

But what really draws the knowledgeable gardener to this ancient castle (the pele tower was built in the fourteenth century) is the large rock garden built in 1926 by T. R. Hayes and Son.

During the first quarter of this century the fashion for 'natural' rock gardens was at its height and Hayes were acknowledged masters of the art. They used the best Westmorland limestone taken from the surface with all its natural weather and water markings, and they re-set it so cunningly that it appears to be an outcrop native to the site. Unfortunately rock gardens of this kind, though beautiful in themselves, were not really very satisfactory places

The rock garden, Sizergh Castle

in which to grow alpine plants, and they were also extremely costly to make and maintain.

The Sizergh Castle rock garden is large (about ¼ acre) and a first class example of its kind. Though little attempt is now made to use it for its original purpose it is most effectively planted with hardy herbaceous plants, including the willow gentian (*Gentiana asclepiadea*), small shrubs including dwarf conifers and Japanese maples, as well as a really notable collection of hardy ferns. There is a good deal of water in the rock garden, really a series of small pools arranged roughly in an oval and linked by an artificial stream, and this has given scope for the cultivation of many moisture-loving plants, such as astilbes and Asiatic primulas. Outside this main area, which fills a little dell, there is a dwarf conifer collection containing over sixty species and varieties.

SPETCHLEY PARK, *Spetchley, Hereford and Worcester. On A422, 3 miles east of Worcester. Peak season May to August. Privately owned. Open about once weekly from April to September.*

Here the visitor can see many of the aspects of British garden making in the past two centuries. There is a fine landscape park and lake, a big walled garden, lawns, flower beds and a good collection of trees and shrubs. There is also a fascinating series of enclosures made with box and permanently planted with trees and shrubs – the kind of formal design coupled with informal planting that Miss Jekyll often adopted, though there is no evidence that she actually worked here. There is a particularly good specimen of the dawn redwood, *Metasequoia glyptostroboides.*

STOURHEAD, *Stourton, Wiltshire. On B3092, 1½ miles north of junction with A303 near Mere. No peak season. National Trust. Open all the year.*

Many would agree that this is the most beautiful of all eighteenth century classical landscape gardens. It was made by the owner, Henry Hoare, from about 1744, with the assistance of Henry Flitcroft, a civil servant in the Office of Works, who designed the various buildings used to decorate the landscape. The site was a bare valley in which the River Stour rises. By damming this little stream at several points Hoare created a series of lakes, and made the largest of these the centrepiece of his landscape. He planted trees on the valley sides, principally beech and spruce, taking great care, in his own words, to arrange them 'in large masses as the shades are in painting, to contrast the dark masses with the light ones, and to relieve each dark mass itself with sprinklings of lighter green here and there'.

Fountain among the box-edged enclosures, Spetchley Park

View to the Pantheon, Stourhead

The early Georgian mansion, built by his father on level ground above the valley, was out of sight of the new landscape, but it was Henry Hoare's idea that the visitor should start from this point and proceed by a definite route. First as he came over the lip of the valley the Temple of Apollo would appear apparently floating in the trees above the water; then descending by a winding path the Pantheon and Gothic Cottage would be seen briefly. The journey would continue across the northern neck of the lake, through a grotto (its fountain fed by the source of the River Stour) which frames the view of the Temple of Flora on the opposite side of the lake, then past the Gothic Cottage and Pantheon with views of the Stone Bridge and the Bristol Cross, across the largest dam, up the hill to the temple of

Apollo from which there are some of the most extensive views of the whole landscape, and finally down to the Stone Bridge and the tiny village of Stourton. This is still the most dramatic way to see Stourhead, though most visitors now enter from the village and see it first from a low and not a high vantage spot.

Many changes have taken place since Henry Hoare's time, some of them made by his grandson, Sir Richard Colt Hoare, who succeeded him in 1785. The main effect of these has been to increase greatly the diversity of the planting, so that today Stourhead may be regarded almost as an arboretum as well as a landscape. Inevitably this has altered the simplicity of the original design, but Stourhead remains a ravishingly beautiful place and those who find the colour of rhododendrons offensive can avoid visiting it in May and June when they are in bloom. In Henry Hoare's planting there were geans and lilacs.

Trees of particular note are *Abies procera* and its variety glauca (one tree planted in 1841 was 43 metres high in 1970), *Cedrus atlantica glauca, C. libani* and *C. deodara, Chamaecyparis nootkatensis, Cunninghamia lanceolata, Liriodendron tuli-pifera* and its variegated variety, *Picea brachytyla, P. polita, Pinus peuce,* (28·5 metres in 1970 and one of the tallest in the country), *Sequoia sempervirens, Sequoiadendron giganteum* (the tallest being 40 metres in 1970), *Torreya californica* and *Tsuga heterophylla* planted in 1871 and very large.

See also illustration on page 17.

STOWE, *Buckingham, Buckinghamshire. On the road from Buckingham to Silverstone, 3 miles north-west of Buckingham. No peak season. Stowe School and National Trust. Open occasionally during school vacations.*

Though Stowe lacks the compactness of Rousham, the pictorial perfection of Stourhead, the grandeur and breadth of Blenheim Palace, or the repose of Bowood, yet it remains one of the greatest landscape achievements of the eighteenth century and illustrates better than any of those just named the progression of ideas which marked that revolution in English garden making. For at Stowe Bridgeman was followed by Kent, who later had the assistance of Brown, with Lord Cobham himself actively engaged in all that went on up to the time of his death in 1749. After that Cobham's nephew, Earl Temple, continued to develop the landscape and improve the mansion with the aid of Robert Adam and others. The landscape, commenced about 1710, was not completed until about 1780. Few gardens have enjoyed such an extended, continuous and intensive development. Nor is any other garden of this period and style quite so complex as Stowe, which is not so much a single landscape as a series of interlocking landscapes around the great central view from the mansion, down to the upper lake framed by trees and a pair of classical pavilions to the great Corinthian arch surmounting the opposite hillside ¾ mile away. Very approximately this is a north to south prospect. To the east of it are the Elysian Fields in a small cross valley at right angles to the main valley and embedded in trees. An artificial river flows through it, a Shell Bridge spans it and various temples, columns and monuments decorate it. Continuing northwards the visitor enters the much more open, waterless Grecian Valley, overlooked by the Temple of Concord and Victory.

The upper lake, still known as the Octagon Lake from the shape Bridgeman gave it, though it is now completely informal, not only receives the water from the Elysian Fields, but itself narrows to river-like proportions to the east, where it is crossed by the Palladian Bridge. Above this, on the hillside, surrounded by just a few rather gaunt trees,

The Pebble alcove at Stowe designed by William Kent

The Elysian Fields and Temple of British Worthies, Stowe

is the extraordinary Gothic Temple with the Cobham Monument rising above the woodland to the north.

Turning westward the visitor will find a second lake fed by a cascade from the Octagon Lake and overlooked by a Rotunda perched on a rounded knoll and also by the Temple of Venus at its lower (western) end.

Stowe is approached from the road across the elegant Oxford Bridge, between the twin Boycott Pavilions and through a long avenue of limes fairly recently replanted, but all this, though fine in itself, is outside the main landscape.

See also page 15.

STUDLEY ROYAL AND FOUNTAINS ABBEY, *Studley Roger, North Yorkshire. Off B6265 either at Studley Roger or on by-road to Fountains Abbey, 3 miles west of Ripon. No peak season. Department of the Environment. Open all the year.*

Studley Royal and Fountains Abbey must be considered together since they are linked by one of the most original gardens in Britain. Here, as at Castle Howard, the history can be studied of the first half century of landscape

gardening in Britain, though the effects in the two places are very different.

The garden of Studley Royal, or more accurately the garden in the valley about a quarter of a mile to the south of the house, was made by John Aislabie

218

Moon Ponds and Temple of Piety, Studley Royal

between about 1720 and his death in 1742. The later development which links this garden with Fountains Abbey still further up the valley was made by his son William from 1768, when he was able to purchase the ruined abbey, but the conception of a continuous planned elysium right to the abbey was probably in John Aislabie's mind from the outset.

The sides of the valley are steep and craggy, especially on the eastern side. The little River Skell flows through it and John Aislabie used the waters of this to create a series of canals and pools, filling the whole northern half of the valley. All are geometric in shape, but the setting is completely natural, the valley sides densely covered with trees. Colin Campbell, one of the greatest exponents of the Palladian style, was Aislabie's architect and the white Doric temple which stands silhouetted against the trees on the east side looking across the valley, is probably his design. In front

Fountains Abbey and widened River Skell

are three ponds, one circular and two crescent shaped, known as the Moon Ponds, and in front of them is a long canal pool. This takes the main flow of the river and further on discharges over a formal cascade into a large semi-circular pool where the valley suddenly widens out. There are other pools and buildings as well as statues, the whole creating what is almost certainly the finest formal waterscape in the British Isles. It is a scene of extraordinary peacefulness, out of sight of any habitation, a place to be visited, enjoyed and then left to its own almost magical life.

By the time William Aislabie was able to purchase Fountains Abbey and the adjacent Fountains Hall the landscape movement was in full swing and it would have been ridiculously old-fashioned to contain water within formal shapes. So the rest of the stream was simply widened to make it a fitting setting for the tall vertical lines of the splendid ruin which was to be the climax of this progression from the classic to the gothic. Low weirs were built across the widened stream, both to retain an adequate volume of water and to create a series of small cascades. On the hill top to the east there is a viewpoint from which one can look down on the abbey and the approach to it. It is a memorable scene.

Studley Royal itself was destroyed by fire in 1946, but it never played any part in the Aislabie landscape schemes which were out of sight of it. A handsome stable block, designed by Colin Campbell and Roger Morris, remains and has been converted into a house.

SUNTRAP, *Gogarburn, near Edinburgh, Lothian. On by-road to East Hermiston off A8 at Gogar. No peak season. National Trust for Scotland. Open all the year.*

This little garden has been laid out in demonstration areas by the National Trust for Scotland to show members what can be done in quite small plots. There are plenty of good shrubs and herbaceous perennials, an attractive, well planted rock garden, island beds, a mini-pinetum, a model vegetable garden and several small greenhouses variously equipped and stocked. Courses are held and demonstrations given from time to time.

SUTTON PARK, *Sutton on the Forest, North Yorkshire. In Sutton on the Forest on B1363, 8 miles north of York. Peak season April to August. Privately owned. Open fairly frequently from spring to autumn.*

Sutton Park is a lovely medium size Georgian house overlooking an extensive eighteenth century park. Since 1962 it has been given two entirely new gardens of its own, one a series of terraces flanked by lawns and island beds, designed by Percy Cane, the other a woodland walk leading to a temple, made by the present owners, Major and Mrs Reginald Sheffield, who have also arranged all the planting. The result is a fine example of the twentieth century synthesis between formality and informality; firm design overlaid with a rich covering of plants carefully chosen for controlled colour effects. This is a garden in which flowers are used as an artist would use paints and the whole makes a fine setting both for the house and for the landscape.

See also Colour Plate 23 opposite page 196.

SYON HOUSE, *Brentford, Greater London. Off Twickenham Road, 2 miles west of junction with M4 at Gunnersbury. Peak season May to September. Privately owned. Open frequently from spring to autumn.*

The garden of Syon House as it is known today effectively began about 1770 when the Duke of Northumberland asked his friend and neighbour 'Capability' Brown to design a landscape for him. Brown's long, river-like lake on the north remains much as he made it, and there are still some tree clumps which may have been his planting, but everything else has changed. Succeeding Dukes of Northumberland nearly all seem to have been tree lovers so that gradually the park around the lake acquired more the appearance of an arboretum than of a landscape. Many fine specimens still remain, including numerous exotic oaks, maples, a good zelkova, and beside the lake some tall taxodiums with very pronounced 'knees' (the curious breathing roots which the swamp cypress produces when growing in water), and a fine *Pterocarya fraxinifolia*.

In the 1820s Syon acquired a beautiful conservatory designed by Charles Fowler, a very advanced piece of horticultural architecture for its date. It has a large central glazed dome flanked by curving wings and it was originally heated by air ducts beneath the floor.

The final metamorphosis began in the 1960s when part of Syon Park was adapted for use as a permanent exhibition of gardening. For this purpose a six acre rose garden was made on the south side and planted with many new varieties. To the north, beside the lake in an area known as Flora's lawn, because it is overlooked by a statue of the Goddess Flora on a high column, island beds were made for herbaceous perennials. Various prominent landscape architects, including Russell Page and John Brookes, gave advice or designed special features; new buildings were created to house exhibits of machines and garden equipment and the old riding school was turned into a garden centre.

Inevitably this has changed the character of Syon House, though the old features are still there and the conservatory has been splendidly restored.

See also illustration on page 44.

The conservatory, Syon Park

TATTON PARK, *Knutsford, Cheshire. Entrance in Ashley Road on the northern outskirts of Knutsford, reached from A50 via A5034. No peak season. National Trust and Cheshire County Council. Open very frequently from spring to autumn.*

This garden has the distinction of attracting more visitors than any other belonging to the National Trust. This must not be taken solely as a criterion of its excellence, since it must in part be due to its situation on the south-western fringe of the great industrial complex which extends from Leeds to Liverpool. Yet this is a fine garden standing in an even finer park, very old and very large and some of its features remodelled by Humphry Repton in the early nineteenth century. The garden itself is an eighteenth century landscape which probably originally blended almost imperceptibly into the park, but has since acquired so many additions of its own that it has become a completely separate entity. These include exotic trees and shrubs, groves of rhododendrons, many of them around the lake, and a large Japanese garden said to have been made early in the present century by Japanese workmen who also brought with them the elegant little Shinto temple which forms its centrepiece. An orangery was built soon after the mansion was completed about 1811, and nearby is a well stocked fern house, a most attractive

The Japanese garden, Tatton Park

legacy from Victorian times. In front of the mansion there is an elaborate sunken terrace garden with stone balustrades, said to have been designed by Sir Joseph Paxton and certainly also a Victorian addition. (*See also* page 27.)

THORNBURY CASTLE, *Thornbury, Avon. In Thornbury on B4061, 1 mile north of junction with A38 at Alverton. No peak season. Restaurant.*

Here are the remnants of an early Tudor garden, chiefly of interest to students of garden history and particularly to those

with sufficient knowledge to recreate in imagination what must have been there. It is more fully described on page 2.

THREAVE SCHOOL OF PRACTICAL GARDENING, *Castle Douglas, Dumfries and Galloway. Garden entrance on old military road off south side of A75, 1 mile west of Castle Douglas. No peak season. National Trust for Scotland. Open all the year.*

The mansion house and estate of Threave were presented to the National

Trust for Scotland in 1948 by the owner, Major Alan Gordon, but it was not until

26. Part of the flowery streamside at Wallington (*see* page 232)

27. Japanese maples at Winkworth Arboretum (*see* page 240)

28. Wisley – the lake in autumn (*see* page 240)

Rock beds and daffodils, Threave School of Practical Gardening

after his death in 1957 that the Trust was able to proceed with its plan to establish a school of gardening there with all the necessary adjuncts to permit a comprehensive course in the principles and practice of horticulture. For this purpose an entirely new garden was laid out around the mansion and this has developed so well that already it is a major attraction to garden-loving visitors to Scotland.

To an almost unprecedented extent design is based on the island bed principle which at Threave is used for roses, heathers, shrubs and herbaceous plants. Even the rock garden and scree conform to this same general pattern of irregular areas of cultivated ground within an all-embracing groundwork of mown turf.

Only the old walled garden, the nursery and vegetable gardens and some areas of woodland stand outside this plan.

Peat and rock gardens are linked together in one unit and are exceptionally well designed and planted. One woodland area has been underplanted with rhododendrons, lilies and a considerable variety of ground covering plants arranged in bold drifts of a kind and producing some very agreeable foliage and floral effects. The rose garden is large and contains both bedding and shrub varieties.

In the walled garden there are annuals, herbaceous perennials, bulbs, shrubs and climbers and also a range of greenhouses linked by a glazed corridor in which some specially interesting plants are permanently planted in beds. A pool for moisture-loving plants and aquatics has been added near the rock garden and there is another bog garden near the entrance. In the nursery garden various propagation techniques are used and plants are reared to planting-out size. There is a well stocked vegetable garden and on the hill behind the house a small orchard.

In spring daffodils naturalized in the grass bloom in their thousands and this is also a good time to see the rock garden, but really this is such a well stocked place that it has something to show throughout the year.

See Colour Plate 24 opposite page 197.

TINTINHULL HOUSE, *Tintinhull, Somerset. In Tintinhull, off A303, 2 miles south-west of Ilchester. No peak season. National Trust. Open frequently from spring to early autumn.*

This is an early seventeenth century house to which a beautiful Queen Anne facade has been added. It is quite small and so is its garden, but both are exquisite. The garden, made since 1933 by Captain and Mrs F. E. Reiss, is formal in design but informal in planting. It is divided into three roughly rectangular

sections each of which has received quite different treatment. The largest, virtually square, is an expanse of lawn dominated by a big cedar of Lebanon and several old yews. Next to it is a garden full of flowers, but in very carefully chosen colours. This section has a canal pool as its central feature, with

The main path, Tintinhull House

strip centred on the house and partially divided into three nearly equal parts by wing walls and hedges. A path goes straight down the centre to a little circular lily pool in a tiny parterre at the end. The wall piers are topped by eagles, and trim cones of box line the path, emphasizing its length and its straightness. The middle section is largely in shade because of a very large holm oak in one corner, but from this point one can look across into the cheerful, flowery pool garden.

All the best elements of what may be termed Jekyllian garden making are here compressed into a small space and used as a setting for an exceptionally attractive building. It is a garden full of design and planting lessons for other would-be garden makers.

flanking borders and several well filled plant containers.

The third section is the most fascinating of all, a long, almost corridor-like

TRELISSICK, *King Harry Ferry, Cornwall. On B3289, 1½ miles from its junction with A39. Peak season April to August. National Trust. Open very frequently from spring to autumn.*

This is another of the Cornish woodland gardens and an exceptionally beautiful one, partly because of its fine trees – including some immense cryptomerias – and varied underplanting of camellias,

rhododendrons, azaleas, etc., and also because of its position well above the estuary of the River Fal with fine views both of it and southwards down Carrick Roads to Falmouth. The garden is on

In the woodland, Trelissick

Rhododendrons at Trengwainton

both sides of the road and in the far section there is a very large collection of hydrangeas which should not be missed in late summer.

TRENGWAINTON, *Heamoor, near Penzance, Cornwall. On B3312, ½ mile from junction with A3071. Peak season April to June. National Trust. Open frequently from March to September.*

No mainland Cornish garden has a more comprehensive collection of exotic plants than this. There are rhododendrons in hundreds, including exceptionally large bushes of *Rhododendron falconeri, R. lindleyi, R. taggianum* and other species, many grown from Kingdon Ward's seed. *Michelia doltsopa* flowers freely here and so does *Prostanthera rotundifolia.* There are many good acacias, azaras, heathers (including *Erica canaliculata*), eucryphias, myrtles, hydrangeas, primulas, nerines etc. The arrangement is unusual, partly in a series of walled gardens near the entrance where some of the more tender species are grown, partly in woodland and beside a stream at the edge of a very long drive to the house. Here there is a more conventional garden with lawns and glades and, almost hidden away, yet another enclosure with some of the choicest rhododendrons.

See also illustration on page 37.

TRENTHAM GARDENS, *Trentham, Staffordshire. On A34, 3½ miles south of Stoke on Trent. Peak season April to August. Trentham Gardens Ltd. Open all the year.*

'Capability' Brown not only planned the landscape at Trentham but also had a hand in reshaping the mansion. Unhappily the latter has now been almost completely razed to the ground, but Brown's mile long lake can still be admired. It was made by enlarging an existing formal pool which had itself been made half a century earlier by diverting water from the adjacent River Trent, so providing some control over its flow and the frequent flooding which it caused.

Still more changes were to come. In 1834 the 2nd Duke of Sutherland engaged Charles Barry (later to design the Houses of Parliament and be knighted) to restyle the house and gardens. With the assistance of W. A. Nesfield, Barry laid out very large and elaborate terraces in the Italian style between the house and Brown's lake, and these, now gaily adorned with bedding plants in season, are a principal attraction at Trentham. A model train chuffs around Nesfield's elaborate parterres, pleasure boats sail on the lake and many other gay things happen in these once highly dignified surroundings since Trentham Gardens are preserved as an amusement park.

There are some first rate trees including large specimens of cedar of Lebanon, *Abies concolor lowiana, A. procera, Pinus jeffreyi, P. parviflora, P. ponderosa, P. strobus, P. wallichiana, Sciadopitys verticillata, Sequoia sempervirens, Sequoiadendron giganteum* and *Taxodium distichum.*

Brown's landscape from Barry's terraces at Trentham Gardens

Agave and aeoniums, Tresco Abbey

TRESCO ABBEY, *Tresco, Isles of Scilly. Access by ferry boat from Hugh Town, St. Mary's, Isles of Scilly. No peak season. Privately owned. Open all the year, except Sundays.*

The Isles of Scilly enjoy the mildest climate of any part of the British Isles, thanks to their situation in the Atlantic Ocean off the extreme south-western tip of Cornwall and in the full flow of the warm Gulf Stream. Augustus Smith acquired a lease on the islands in 1834 and soon after built himself a house of local granite on a little hill in the middle of Tresco, an island of only 750 acres. Then it was windswept and barren, but Augustus Smith determined to make a garden and for this purpose cut terraces beside and below his house. He also realized the necessity for a shelter belt of evergreen trees, especially to the west and north, and among those he chose for

the purpose were the Monterey cypress (*Cupressus macrocarpa*) and the Monterey pine (*Pinus radiata*), both recently introduced from California. It was a fortunate choice for these two species were to prove the toughest in surviving the fierce Atlantic gales. Some are now 30 metres high and within their shelter and that provided by the terrace walls Tresco has developed into a sub-tropical garden with plants thriving that are not to be found outdoors in any other British garden. Some exotic plants have leapt the garden walls and established themselves outside, so that clumps of African lilies (agapanthus) greet the visitor who approaches from the south across sand dunes, while *Sparmannia africana* and *Curtonus paniculata* lie in wait beside the road to Tresco Abbey from the tiny harbour of Old Grimsby.

In a garden of such immense horticultural richness it is difficult to single out any individual plants or families for special mention. Yet it is fair to say that it is in the number, variety and fine condition of plants from the Canary Islands and the Southern Hemisphere that Tresco Abbey most obviously surpasses other British gardens. Aeoniums grow everywhere and so do the brilliantly flowered succulents that gardeners still conveniently lump together as 'mesembryanthemums', though botanists have long since distributed them among numerous other genera. Then there are the giant echiums, aloes and agaves in numerous species, pelargoniums, proteas, leucodendrons, *Greyia sutherlandii*, acacias, eucalyptus, hakeas, banksia, euryops, metrosideros, bomareas, leptospermums and many more too numerous to catalogue.

In the lower garden, not far from an extraordinary collection of old ships' figureheads known as Valhalla, is a perfect specimen of *Araucaria heterophylla* which was 30·5 metres high in 1970. In most parts of Britain it is grown as a small pot plant in greenhouses or rooms. In the same year *Pinus canariensis* was 26

The view from Tresco to St. Mary's

metres high and there was one specimen of the very rare Kauri pine, *Agathis australis*, 20 metres high. In *Trees and Shrubs Hardy in the British Isles* one Tresco specimen of the New Zealand evergreen, *Griselinia littoralis variegata*, is described as 'perhaps the oldest and largest plant in the British Isles', and it produces both types of chimera, i.e. with the golden area sometimes around the edge (the more usual form) and sometimes in the centre. The more tender *G. lucida* also grows at Tresco, and there are fine trees of *Myrtus luma*.

TREWITHEN, *Probus, Cornwall. On A390, 2 miles west of Grampound. Peak season April to June. Privately owned. Open occasionally in spring and early summer.*

This is a collector's garden and one which shows well the trend of garden design in Cornwall when the advantages of its mild climate were discovered. The planting is mainly in woodland style around a long tapering lawn which gives an exaggerated perspective from the house. Beyond this there is a ditch and old cockpit which provide damp and sheltered conditions for numerous shrubs and tree ferns. There are many species and hybrid rhododendrons, evergreen azaleas, embothriums, camellias, azaras etc. In a separate walled garden there are even more tender plants, including *Ceanothus arboreus* Trewithen Blue, a particularly fine form of this tree-like species which was selected here.

See illustration overleaf.

TYNINGHAME, *near Dunbar, Lothian. Off A198, 1 mile north of junction with A1. Peak season June–July. Privately owned. Open occasionally in spring and summer.*

This is a large garden with a long history culminating in some radical changes in recent years that have not only made it more manageable but also more beautiful. Tyninghame was purchased by the 1st Earl of Haddington in 1624 and has remained in the possession of the family ever since. A doorway into the great walled kitchen garden at some distance from the house bears the date 1666, but the biggest development seems to have occurred between 1681 and 1735 when the 6th Earl planted many trees, including a triple avenue of beech, extending the best part of a mile to the sea. This still stands and so do some other trees of similar date, but the pattern of straight alleys and rides which he made is now almost completely obliterated. What began as a formal woodland has become a 'natural' one thanks to the introduction of more trees, many of the exotic ones being planted in a random manner. These include a *Pinus leucodermis* which Alan Mitchell lists as one of the three best in the country (another is far to the south, at Killerton), a western hemlock (*Tsuga heterophylla*) that was 30·5 metres high in 1967 and was planted in 1871 and a tall *Abies procera* planted in 1884.

Tree fern and rhododendrons in the cockpit, Trewithen

However though the trees at Tyninghame are fine and much interesting new planting is being undertaken, including the establishment of a representative collection of eucalyptus species, it is the changes in the flower garden made by Lady Haddington since 1952 that have really brought visitors flocking to the garden. First the terraces around the house, once laid out as a Victorian parterre with bedding plants in season, have been simplified and transformed by permanent planting of roses, shrubs and herbaceous perennials. As in so many modern gardens plants have been used with great attention to the colour effects they will produce. Perhaps the most delightful of all the new features at Tyninghame which displays this skill in plant association most effectively is an enclosed garden beside the upper (east) terrace in a rectangular area that was once a tennis court. Here, almost completely concealed from view, a flowery paradise has been created which, despite the apparent abandon of the planting, is firmly under control, and if stripped of its plants would be seen to be mainly rectilinear in design. It all centres around an elegant treillage arbour, itself covered in flowers and containing a statue of Flora. Old-fashioned and shrub roses abound, but they are associated with lilies and hardy perennials. The design of this garden is said to have been copied from an old French book, but the planting is entirely original. James Russell designed some of these features.

The old kitchen garden has also been transformed with a central walk of mown grass flanked by high yew hedges which serve as a background for statues. This wide alley leads to a little parterre with four knots cut in box. Vegetables and fruit trees are still grown in parts of

The Statue Walk through the old kitchen garden, Tyninghame

the walled garden, but flower borders mingle with them and one complete section has been developed as a 'wilderness', using this word in the eighteenth century meaning of a place in which trees and other plants are associated in a free style. In modern terminology it might be termed an island bed garden. Island beds are also used in a long strip to the west of the house, known as the Grove, and here there are more good trees and shrubs, a heather garden and a colony of the rare and difficult Chatham Island forget-me-not, *Myosotidium hortensia*.

A recent addition is a laburnum tunnel through the arboretum that separates house from walled garden, and outside the walled garden itself is a much older tunnel or pleached alley formed of apple trees and said to have been planted some time in the second half of the nineteenth century.

UPTON HOUSE, *Edgehill, Warwickshire. On A422, 7 miles north-west of Banbury. Peak season June to September. National Trust. Open about twice weekly from May to September.*

Upton House is chiefly famed for its collection of works of art, but the garden also displays art, making clever use of a natural peculiarity of the site. This is a narrow valley which cuts across the land some distance from the house but so steep are its sides that it is completely hidden until one arrives at its edge. So from immediately outside the house one appears to be looking at a typical English park-style garden laid out on level land with a fine sweep of lawn in the foreground, an avenue of trees in the distance and enclosing belts of trees on each side.

Walking towards the avenue the valley is suddenly revealed as an obstacle and also as the site of a series of further features. First there are several terraces cut in the valley side, each level traversed by a path and filled with flowers. These terraces are linked by stone steps. At the foot of the valley is a long, river-like lake and to one side a large sunken garden, actually the drained site of another lake, planted with flowering trees. Proceeding still further the exploring visitor discovers a second smaller valley turning out of the first, with a previously concealed house at its head and

Old roses frame Flora's arbour at Tyninghame

The bog garden, Upton House

a very natural looking water and bog garden which contains a lot of good plants. It is quite an arduous climb back to the starting point but the journey is well worth making.

THE VALLEY GARDENS, *Windsor Great Park, Berkshire. Access as for Savill Garden. Peak season April to June and October–November. Crown Property. Open all the year.*

When after the Second World War the Savill Garden was nearing completion its creator, Sir Eric Savill, sought further outlet for his passion for landscape development in the series of small valleys on the north side of Virginia Water. Here there is plenty of room for extension and planting has gone on almost continuously ever since. The gardens are continuous and all are 'natural' in design with no effort to introduce architecture or formality in any way. The very first garden is almost a green landscape framing a view of the lake, and with colour provided largely by pedigree hybrid rhododendrons confined mainly to the upper end. But two adjacent areas are much more highly coloured, at any rate in spring. One is an Azalea Valley, filled with deciduous azaleas and other shrubs, the other the Punch Bowl, a natural amphitheatre banked tier upon tier with evergreen azaleas, overplanted with maples and with various coloured conifers below. Another area is devoted largely to flowering cherries planted almost as if in an orchard. Dawn redwoods appear frequently, in one place filling most of a valley side. Then there is an attractive heather garden with numerous exotic birch species for contrast, while yet other areas have a wider range of plant species so that it becomes difficult to categorize them in any precise way.

Throughout these gardens there are fine trees, some like the big redwoods and wellingtonias, planted long ago, others, like the rowans and the southern beeches, brought in specially to furnish the new landscapes. These are very beautiful gardens, probably the finest of their kind made this century, and they are packed with interest for the plant enthusiast.

See Colour Plate 25 opposite page 197.

The aviary, Waddesdon Manor

The first 'valley garden' in Windsor Great Park

WADDESDON MANOR, *Waddesdon, Buckinghamshire. In Waddesdon on A41, 5 miles north-west of Aylesbury. No peak season. National Trust. Open frequently from spring to summer.*

Baron Ferdinand de Rothschild, who created Waddesdon Manor, was a collector of furniture and fine art, particularly of the French eighteenth century. In 1874 he engaged a French architect, Gabriel-Hippolyte Destailleur, to build a fantastically ornate mansion in the French Renaissance style and he employed the French garden designer, Louis Laine, to lay out the park, which he then decorated with elaborate fountains and a great deal of French, Italian and Dutch statuary. The park itself is English in manner with many fine trees including cedars, wellingtonias, beeches and limes. Around the house there are formal terraces, some planned for bedding out, one made to display a huge aviary built in the form of a semi-circle of elegant treillage pavilions. Macaws fly about uncaged outside this aviary and the parterre is decorated with bird and animal sculptures as well as with gaily planted flower beds. There is nothing quite like this aviary in any other British garden except Dropmore, near Cliveden, and this can seldom be seen.

WAKEHURST PLACE, *Ardingly, West Sussex. On B2028, 8 miles south of its junction with A22. Peak seasons April to June and October–November. National Trust and Royal Botanic Gardens, Kew. Open all the year.*

The house, built of local sandstone, is Elizabethan and beautiful, the garden is a plantsman's paradise that also contrives to be highly picturesque. In part this is because Gerald W. E. Loder (later to become Lord Wakehurst), who bought the property in 1903, had an already well formed landscape garden within which to work, but also full credit must be given to him for devising means by which the enormously diverse collection of exotic trees, shrubs and herbaceous plants which he amassed at Wakehurst Place could be fitted into this landscape to its ultimate advantage. Around the house he retained simple rectangular areas of lawn, but these were enclosed by irregular beds (what we have later come to know as island beds) separated by further lawns and grass paths and leading by a natural progression to the even more natural setting of the woodland and the lake half concealed in the valley to the west.

Wakehurst Place stands on a ridge, with a second valley to the east, and it is the excellent air drainage which these two valleys provide that gives the garden its relative immunity to late spring frosts and consequent ability to provide a congenial habitat for many plants usually regarded as tender in south-east England.

A large pool, backed by a rock garden and more trees and shrubs, to the south-west of the house increased the beauty of the setting and provided yet more places in which to grow plants, and further smaller pools and streams were made in the woodland on the way to the big lake.

Pool and rock garden, Wakehurst Place

These are the major design features that make the garden of Wakehurst Place so satisfactory. The plants are as varied as those in many botanic gardens, and Wakehurst Place has now become an annexe to the Royal Botanic Gardens, Kew, providing soil and air far better than those at Kew for the cultivation of difficult plants.

Wakehurst Place is mainly famous for its rhododendrons and azaleas, its magnolias, maples, heathers and pinetum, but there are so many good things here that it is impossible to do more than indicate a few of them. Magnolias include a very large *M. campbellii* and good specimens of *M. dawsoniana*, *M. sprengeri*, *M. veitchii* and *M. wilsonii*. In the West Wood valley above the lake, rhododendrons are grouped in their botanical series. Close to the magnolias there is a big handkerchief tree (*Davidia involucrata*). There are many Australian plants including *Hakea lissosperma*, a member of the protea family, *Olearia lacunosa*, *Phyllocladus alpinus* and *Athrotaxis selaginoides*.

The showy parasitic *Lathrea clandestina* is well established on the roots of trees in an area known as The Slips, and is very attractive in March and April.

Notable conifers, other than athrotaxis already mentioned, include *Abies homolepis tomomi*, *A. nephrolepis*, *A. pinsapo*, *A. sutchuenensis*, *Cephalotaxus harringtonia drupacea*, *Chamaecyparis lawsoniana glauca*, *Cupressus goveniana*, *C. lusitanica*, *Keteleeria fortunei*, *Larix gmelini*, *Libocedrus chilensis*, *Picea brachytyla*, *P. morrisonicola*, *P. spinulosa* and *Tsuga caroliniana*.

Notable broad-leaved trees not already mentioned include *Acer rubrum*, *Aesculus indica*, *Catalpa bignonioides* (a very large specimen), *Clethra delavayi*, *Corylus colurna*, *Eucalyptus gunnii*, *Griselinia littoralis* (although strictly speaking a shrub, it is of tree-like proportions, over 12 metres high), *Kalopanax pictus* and the fastigiate form of *Liriodendron tulipifera*.

WALLINGTON, *Cambo, Northumberland. On B6342, 1 mile north of its junction with A696. Peak season June to August. National Trust. Open daily from April to September, weekends only in October.*

Garden making probably began at Wallington in the early 1730s and there is a plan made at this period for a very elaborate series of gardens of which the broad outlines are geometric but the details include many rather aimlessly winding paths – a rather awkward mixture between the old formal and new pictorial ideas of garden making. It is interesting to recollect that at this very time 'Capability' Brown was growing up at Kirkharle, little more than a mile to the south, walking daily to school at Cambo and then finding employment as a gardener at Kirkharle. He must have been very familiar with what was happening at Wallington and some say that he returned in later life to carry out landscape work there, but there is no firm evidence for this.

How much of the original plan was actually carried out is not known. Certainly there is not much trace of it today

Wallington – the old kitchen garden transformed

except two ponds in the woodland to the east of the approach road and a wall with a handsome portico in classical style which is the elaborate facade for a modest little cottage in which presumably a gardener once lived. But still further to the east, beyond the second pond, the visitor will discover a walled garden, not shown on the original plan. It was made, apparently, in the 1760s when the old kitchen garden was remodelled as part of the ornamental garden and a new kitchen garden was made in this little curling valley at the end of the wood.

It is a charming, secluded spot, completely shut off by a high wall. The north side has been built up as a terrace with an elegant two-storey building in the middle which looks like a pavilion but was probably originally a potting shed and bothy. Greenhouses and a large conservatory stand on this terrace and its boundary wall is ornamented with charming lead figures. For the rest the contours of the little valley are almost unaltered and a stream, the overflow of the ponds, flows through it.

Today this garden is the central attraction for garden minded visitors to Wallington. Around the mansion there are good lawns, flower borders and specimen trees but the design is conventional and the effect pleasing but unremarkable. It is the little valley lost in the woods that has been converted into an enchanting secret garden, largely as a result of the devotion to this spot of Sir George Trevelyan who inherited Wallington in 1879 and for nearly half a century thereafter worked almost daily in this place re-fashioning it according to his desire. After his death Lady Trevelyan, who loved flower arranging and grew flowers for cutting in nursery beds at the bottom of the walled garden, continued to live at Wallington and it was she who made the rustic terrace at the top of the garden which provides such a good viewpoint for the whole place.

Since the National Trust took control in 1966 further alterations have been made and a good deal of additional planting undertaken principally by Graham Thomas, the final result being one of the prettiest gardens in Britain.

The charm lies in the contrast between the trim eighteenth century buildings and terrace wall and the apparent artlessness of the stream which alternately flows, disappears underground and then reappears to continue its course between rocky, flower-covered banks. There are flower borders beneath the high terrace wall and Lady Trevelyan's rustic terrace is bowered in roses. At the foot of the lawn ornamental trees are dotted about rather as trees might be planted in an orchard, but each is surrounded by a circle of cultivated ground filled with a particular kind of flower.

The large conservatory on the terrace contains exceptionally large and old fuchsias, including one Rose of Castille Improved which was planted in 1901 and now has a trunk 68·5 centimetres in circumference near the base. Nearby is a heliotrope planted about 1940 and reaching to the roof.

See Colour Plate 26 opposite page 222.

WATERHOUSE PLANTATIONS, *Bushey Park, Hampton, Greater London. On A308 opposite Hampton Court. Peak season April to June. Department of the Environment. Open all the year.*

When Charles I decided to improve the garden at Hampton Court he required a good head of water to operate fountains. To raise this from the Thames would have been too difficult so instead an artificial river was made from Longford eight miles away to bring water from the Colne to a large reservoir in Bushey Park. A little brick shed still stands beside this reservoir, housing the gear to control the flow of water, and so the reservoir came to be known as the Waterhouse Pond. Probably at this same period two large coppices were planted, one beside the reservoir, the second a little closer to the famous avenue of horse chestnuts which runs through Bushey Park.

That was quite early in the seventeenth century; 300 years later J. W. Fisher, recently appointed superintendent of Hampton Court garden, conceived the idea of using these two little plantations and the abundant supply of water adjacent to them to create two woodland gardens in the modern manner. Work began in 1949, slowly at first, but much faster when Mr Fisher was offered working parties of prisoners from Wormwood Scrubs. Water channels were dug, a large lake with two islands constructed, many new trees were planted with open glades and grass walks. In this delightful setting a considerable collection of exotic shrubs and herbaceous plants was established, planted in bold drifts so that within a few years the whole place had an astonishingly mature look and became one of the outstanding examples of woodland gardening in England. The plentiful water and good cover provided by trees and shrubs also encourage birds to colonize the place so that the Waterhouse Plantations (or the Bushey Park

One of the man-made streams at the Waterhouse Plantation

woodland gardens, as some prefer to call them) have become a bird sanctuary as well as a plant paradise.

Since the emphasis in planting is fairly heavily on rhododendrons, azaleas and camellias, the peak flowering season is from April to June, but the design is so good, the water so well used, the trees and shrubs so diverse and well chosen that this is always a delightful place to visit. There is a particularly fine *Metasequoia glyptostroboides* and also some good young trees of *Pinus montezumae*. Other good specimens include *Parrotiopsis jacquemontiana*, a rare shrub from the Himalayas which colours well in the autumn, *Parrotia persica* and *Rhododendron macabeanum*. *Meconopsis betonicifolia* grows with exceptional vigour and there are large plantings of primulas, rodgersias, hostas, irises and astilbes. These two woodland gardens now extend to nearly 100 acres.

Neptune and the T-shaped canal, Westbury Court

WESTBURY COURT, *Westbury-on-Severn, Gloucestershire. At Westbury-on-Severn on A48. No peak season. National Trust. Open frequently from spring to autumn.*

This is the finest example of the Dutch style canal garden several of which were made in this part of England in the late seventeenth century. Westbury Court was started in 1696 and completed in 1705. By the 1960s the house had been pulled down and the garden was rapidly becoming a ruin, but then the National Trust took it over and made a complete restoration of the garden. It is further described on page 8.

WESTONBIRT ARBORETUM, *Westonbirt, Gloucestershire. On A433, 5 miles north-east of junction with A6. No peak season, but autumn colour is specially good. Forestry Commission. Open all the year.*

This is one of the oldest and almost certainly the finest arboretum in the British Isles. Started by Robert Staynor Holford in 1829 it was steadily enlarged and improved by successive generations of the same family until in 1956 it was taken over by the Forestry Commission. It now covers 100 acres, plus an annexe known as Silk Wood, and the design remains basically simple, with wide grass rides or drives dividing the trees into more or less regular rectangular blocks, though there are some deviations from this, including an area enclosed by a Circular Drive and various open spaces and glades within the main blocks. One of these is used for Japanese maples and is a favourite spot with visitors in autumn because of the brilliant leaf colour. But in the main the

In Acer Glade, Westonbirt Arboretum

most spectacular specimens or groups are beside the rides as, for example, the great group of incense cedars (*Libocedrus decurrens*) in Holford Ride, which is probably Westonbirt's most photographed feature. These were planted in 1910 and in 1969 the tallest measured 24·5 metres, but in the ride called Mitchell there is a single specimen 30 metres high.

Other notable specimens are *Abies borisii-regis* in Loop Walk; *Abies fargesii*, *Chamaecyparis lawsoniana Allumii* and *C.l. Intertexta* and *Picea pungens*, all in Willesley Drive; *Picea brachytyla*, *P. hurstii* and *Pinus holfordiana* in Morley Drive; and *Juniperus excelsa* in Mitchell Drive. There are also some attractive groups of *Picea brewerana*, but these are not yet of great size.

In spring many rhododendrons, azaleas and magnolias, including *M. campbellii*, are in flower, particularly in an area appropriately known as Savill Glade.

Westonbirt Arboretum is famous for its autumn colour. *Cornus alba sibirica*, the best variety for bark colour, is popularly known as the Westonbirt Dogwood, because it is so freely planted here. There are large groups of *Euonymus alatus* and many good specimens of parrotia, stewartia, fothergilla and other fine autumn colouring trees and shrubs. There are also many fine birches, including *Betula albo-sinensis*, *B. jacquemontii* and *B. maximowicziana*, as well as maples grown for bark colour, such as *Acer griseum* and the snake-barks, *A. capillipes*, *A. davidii*, *A. hersii* and *A. pensylvanicum*.

WESTON PARK, *Weston under Lizard, Salop. In Weston under Lizard on A5. No peak season. Privately owned. Open frequently from May to September.*

'Capability' Brown designed this park from 1762 onwards and it is a good example of his work, though at a later date formal terraces and bedding have replaced Brown's smooth grass around the house. There are two lakes, one in the usual key position in the middle distance, the other concealed in a wood and with a little stone temple beside it. On the edge of this wood is a handsome orangery, known as the Temple of Diana because it contains panels depicting Diana hunting. It was designed by James Paine and is a focal point in the landscape composition.

WEST WYCOMBE PARK, *West Wycombe, Buckinghamshire. On A40 on the west edge of West Wycombe. No peak season. National Trust. Open frequently in summer.*

Here is one of the great eighteenth century park landscapes made, like Stowe, over a period of at least fifty years, and like Stowe evolving over that long period from a semi-formal design, which still retained some of the straight *allées* and broad walks characteristic of the seventeenth century style, into the completely flowing composition which is to be seen today. The grand architect of most of this development seems to have been the owner himself, Sir Francis Dashwood. He was created Lord le Despencer in 1762 and was founder of the Society of Dilettanti and also of the notorious Hell Fire Club which held its meetings here. He was assisted by various architects who designed temples and other buildings for the garden and also refashioned the mansion. Also towards the end of his

236

The Music Temple, West Wycombe Park

Landscape park from the terraces, Weston Park

life, he engaged Thomas Cook, a pupil of 'Capability' Brown, to advise and assist him, and probably some of the major changes to a completely pictorial style were due to this collaboration.

The site is naturally beautiful, in a well wooded valley of the Chiltern Hills, with a little stream, the River Wye, flowing through it. This was dammed some time in the 1730s to form a lake with islands and cascades, and from then on

until Lord le Despencer's death in 1781, the work of furnishing the landscape with buildings and framing them in trees proceeded almost continuously. After that few further additions were made. Humphry Repton worked at West Wycombe in 1794–5, but appears only to have made minor alterations. The landscape also escaped Victorian interference, acquired no arboretum, pinetum or other accretion of exotic plants, and so, apart from the natural growth and decay of trees over the centuries, remains much as Sir Francis planned it.

Perhaps the loveliest scene of all is across the lake to the elegant colonnaded Music Temple on the island. It was designed by Nicholas Revett, who did a great deal of work at West Wycombe. Of special interest too is the Temple of the Winds, modelled on a classical Grecian temple and built in 1759. It appears to be earlier than other temples of this name in British gardens, e.g. Shugborough and Mount Stewart, but these were designed by James Stuart whereas that at West Wycombe was presumably to the design of Revett.

WHITE CRAGGS, *Clappersgate, Cumbria. On A593, 1 mile south-west of Ambleside. Peak season May and June. Privately owned. Open all the year.*

No garden in Britain better illustrates what can be achieved by utilizing the natural features of a craggy site. The garden occupies part of a hillside with rock outcrops overlooking Lake Windermere, and by exposing a little more rock where necessary or adding extra blocks a massive rock garden has been made. As with so many gardens of this kind little attempt has been made to grow genuine rock plants, though some more artificially created areas are used for them. But the big rock outcrops are clothed with herbaceous plants and small shrubs and it is when the rhododendrons and evergreen azaleas are in bloom that the garden makes its most brilliant effect.

WILTON HOUSE, *Wilton, Wiltshire. In Wilton on A30. No peak season. Privately owned. Open frequently from spring to autumn.*

Garden making and garden destruction have gone on here for over three centuries, and the work of different designers has become so intermingled that it is difficult to disentangle one from another. It is therefore somewhat remarkable that what emerges today appears to be a completely coherent composition including both classical landscape and formal elements harmoniously blended together.

The most recent addition, the work of David Vicary in 1971, is the first to greet the visitor since it nearly fills the forecourt which was formerly a paved rectangle. Here a completely formal garden has been made, enclosed by pleached limes, filled with beds of simple geometric design planted with lavender in several different shades from pink to purple and backed by taller shrubs framing a really exciting fountain spouting a generous volume of water from two levels. The whole scheme is on a scale and of a character entirely suitable for its site.

The garden itself lies beside the little River Nadder, dammed and widened in the early eighteenth century as part of the conversion of what had previously been a series of formal parterres into a more 'natural' garden in the new landscape manner. Some of the huge cedars of Lebanon that are so dominant a feature of this garden were already there before landscaping began, and are around 27 metres high. It is interesting to note that some other cedars, known to have been planted between 1902 and 1907 are already almost as tall, the biggest over 21 metres, so maybe the dates given for the earlier trees should be treated with caution. A wellingtonia known to have been planted in 1858 had reached 31·5 metres in 1971, and

Formal garden and fountain in the forecourt, Wilton House

Cedars at Wilton House

there are also some very big liriodendrons, limes, planes and oaks, including the golden or Concord oak near the bridge. In fact if there were a criticism of Wilton today it might be that the size and number of the specimen trees in the foreground somewhat obscures the beautiful Palladian bridge designed for the 9th Earl of Pembroke by his architect, Roger Morris, as the principal building in the eighteenth century landscape.

Water meadows fill the middle distance and the landscape is completed by a densely wooded ridge where there is a stone pavilion or casino designed by William Chambers, which makes a satisfactory distant eye-catcher.

Finally, visible across the lawn in front of the house, but not open to the public, there is an Italian-style terrace garden overlooked by a triple-arched loggia. These were added in the 1820s when formality in garden design was again fashionable.

See also illustration on page 16.

Cornus kousa **at Wisley**

WINKWORTH ARBORETUM, *Hascombe, Surrey. On B2130, 3 miles south of its junction with A3100 at Godalming. Peak seasons May and October–November. National Trust. Open all the year.*

The arboretum was made in the present century by Dr Wilfred Fox on a hillside overlooking a lake and with extensive views of Weald and down. It was sixty acres in extent in 1952 when given by Dr Fox to the National Trust, who have maintained it well without making any major alterations, but subsequent purchases and gifts have increased it to ninety-nine acres. It has a particularly good collection of deciduous trees, including many species of maple and sorbus, also rhus, cotinus, fothergillas, liquidambar, parrotias, *Disanthus cercidifolius* and azaleas and other trees and shrubs which give good autumn colour. *Nyssa sylvatica* grows well near the lakeside and there are very large trees of scarlet oak. *Arbutus menziesii*, not often seen in good condition in British gardens, grows, flowers and fruits well at Winkworth. There are also many good birches, including a particularly fine form of *Betula ermanii* with white, pink flushed bark, and *B. nigra*. Also notable are the cut-leaved purple beech (*Fagus sylvatica Rohanii*) and *Oxydendrum arboreum*. In May the woodland is carpeted with bluebells.

See Colour Plate 27 opposite page 222.

WISLEY GARDEN, *Wisley, near Ripley, Surrey. On A3, midway between Cobham and Ripley. No peak season. The Royal Horticultural Society. Open all the year.*

This is the official garden of the Royal Horticultural Society and so it has to provide facilities beyond those required solely for amenity. There must be laboratories for scientific work, considerable areas set aside for the trial of new flowers and vegetables, model gardens (including fruit and vegetable gardens) for the instruction of students and members of the society as well as extensive greenhouses for the cultivation of tender plants.

All these things Wisley provides and succeeds in addition in being an extremely beautiful garden with a magnificent range of ornamental plants. When the R.H.S. acquired the property in 1904 there was already an established garden made by G. F. Wilson, an enthusiastic amateur gardener, but it only covered about six acres and its principal feature was a woodland garden made in the style then becoming fashionable and much extolled by writers such as William Robinson and Gertrude Jekyll.

Today the garden spreads over the full sixty acres of the estate, but Wilson's wild garden remains at the heart of it.

On a steep bank to the south of this, with a northerly aspect, is the rock garden, first built in 1911 by Messrs Pulham and Sons to a design by Edward White. This has been extended and modified since then, but still remains essentially the same and a magnificent example of the 'natural outcrop' method of construction which was just beginning to be universally accepted. Beside it is an alpine meadow full of *Narcissus bulbocodium* in the spring.

On the other side of Wilson's wild garden is a park-like area known as Six Acres, which contains one of the best heather gardens in Britain as well as a large lake with a well planted island in the middle and a great many fine trees and shrubs. Beyond this, in the northern neck of the gardens, is the pinetum containing a very representative collection of conifers, some of considerable size.

240

The new canal pool at Wisley

Proceeding the other way the visitor can admire an exceptionally well stocked alpine house above the rock garden, proceed onwards past model vegetable plots, an area for specimen trees, rose borders, a new rose garden, model small gardens and model fruit gardens to arrive at a fine new range of

The Chinese Dairy, Woburn Abbey

glasshouses, including one specially designed for display in which many of the plants can be established in beds and permitted to grow in a natural manner. This house is divided into warm, intermediate and cool sections to permit cultivation of plants requiring many different conditions.

Beyond the greenhouses are the trial grounds and from these the visitor can cross the foot bridge into Battleston Hill, developed in the main since 1950 as a home for rhododendrons, camellias and other shade-loving plants. Another bridge leads back to rhododendron trial beds, a great collection of evergreen azaleas in island beds and wide borders separated by an even wider grass walk and filled mainly with herbaceous perennials and some shrubs.

For years the greenhouses occupied the whole area immediately in front of the house, which was convenient for use but very unfortunate from the standpoint of garden design. So in 1970 the old greenhouses were swept away, a very large formal canal pool with a multiple jet fountain took their place and the old potting shed was reconstructed to make an open loggia looking out on one side at the pool and house, at the other on two parterres made within the walls of the old frame yard. One of these parterres is used for bedding plants in season, the other is permanently planted with old-fashioned and shrub roses as well as other small shrubs and herbaceous perennials – an intimate garden in the Jekyll manner and one that has proved very popular with visitors.

The effect of these innovations, together with the opening up of new vistas to the rock garden and Battleston Hill, has been to bind the whole design of Wisley Garden together by giving it a new centre on a scale and with an impact suited to its greatly increased size and complexity. They are the work of Geoffrey Jellicoe and Lanning Roper.

See illustration on page 239 and Colour Plate 28 opposite page 223.

WOBURN ABBEY, *Woburn, Bedfordshire. In Woburn on A50, 8½ miles north-west of Dunstable. No peak season. Privately owned. Open all the year.*

The huge 3000 acre park at Woburn was landscaped by Humphry Repton from 1806 onwards, but there had been tree planting there long before that. In an area known as the Evergreens, where there are now some particularly fine specimens, planting was started in 1742. The mansion was remodelled at about the same time as Repton was refashioning the park, and many new features were being added to the 40 acre garden around it. These included a handsome curving greenhouse (now used as a camellia house) designed by Sir Jeffrey Wyatville and an octagonal 'Chinese dairy' overlooking a pool. There was also a circular labyrinth with a little painted Chinese temple in the middle, a rock garden, a classical temple and many specimen trees.

A great deal of this remains, though not all of it where it was originally placed and some of it in need of repair. Woburn is now more famous for its safari park than for its garden, but work is in hand to restore the latter and to add new features to it. Even as it is, it contains much that is of interest to those concerned with the history of gardening in Britain. (*See* illustration on page 241.)

WREST PARK, *Silsoe, Bedfordshire. On A6 between Bedford and Luton. No peak season. National Institute of Agricultural Engineering (Department of the Environment). Open from spring to early autumn, mainly at the weekends.*

Much of the garden here was laid out in the French style early in the eighteenth century before the landscape movement got under way, and though later in the century 'Capability' Brown worked here, for once he did not destroy the existing garden. Later still, in the 1830s, the mansion for which these gardens had been created was demolished and a new one built a little further away from them, so that a new garden had to be made to link the new house with its old setting. By this time the Italian style was back in favour and the formal terraces that were made blended well with the early eighteenth century design which still remains the centrepiece. The main feature of this is a very long canal pool between blocks of woodland, extending the vista to a particularly lovely domed pavilion designed by Thomas Archer. The woodlands are themselves cut through by quite a complex pattern of *allées* with statues, urns and other ornaments at some of their inter-sections. This is, in fact, a typical piece of French boskage and there are not many genuine old examples remaining in Britain.

What Brown did was almost to surround this formal garden with an artificial river which issues from a rustic bath house and then winds about in a seemingly natural manner. Brown made one of the bridges which cross this stream and a second, a hump back bridge in Chinese style, was added in the nineteenth century.

The nineteenth century Italian terraces are laid out as matching parterres, with statuary groups on large plinths, and clipped Portugal laurels lining the central broadwalk which is aligned on the old canal and Archer's pavilion. It all makes an impressive composition.

The canal and Archer's Pavilion, Wrest Park

A landscape for modern architecture, York University

YORK UNIVERSITY, *York, North Yorkshire. At Heslington on the south-eastern out-skirts of York. No peak season. University of York.*

The making of this great landscape, one of the largest and most imaginative attempted in Britain since 1950, has already been described on page 62. It all flows from Heslington Hall, a brick built Elizabethan mansion at the south-eastern end of the campus. This has a topiary garden of yew, planted about 1720, and also a little gazebo probably of the same period. This old garden has been cleverly linked with the new by means of a canal pool (there was actually such a pool 200 years previously, but in a different position) and a Henry

Moore group of figures placed very effectively on the edge of the topiary garden. A small fish pool nearby, part of a modest nineteenth century attempt at landscaping, has also been incorporated in the design, becoming the head water of the river-like lake which flows right through the campus and binds the whole design together.

The original suggestion for a water-scape was made by the late Frank (H. F.) Clark, development was in the hands of a committee and much of the detail, including the planting of many thousands of trees, was entrusted to Robert Matthew, Johnson, Marshall and Partners of Welwyn Garden City, under the special supervision of Maurice Lee.

See also illustrations on pages 2 and 67.

Please check actual dates and times of opening in the various guides and lists given on pages 68–69.

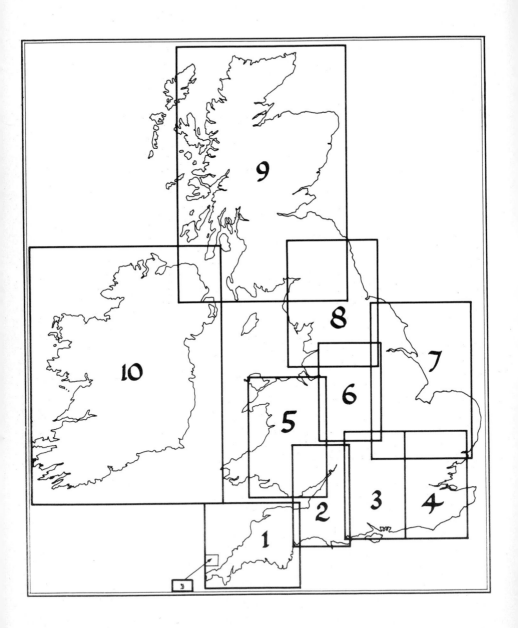

Regional Maps

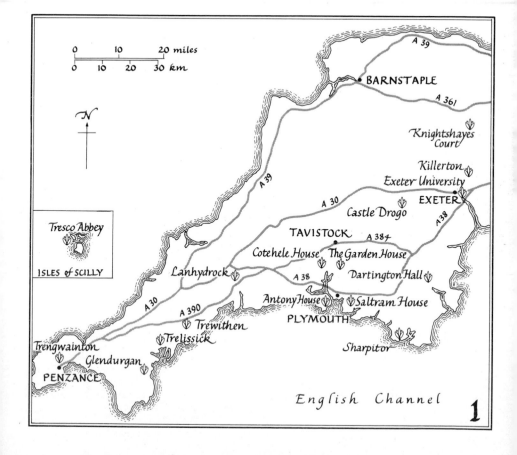

20 miles
30 km

N

BARNSTAPLE

A 39

A 361

Knightshayes Court

Killerton
Exeter University

EXETER

A 38

Castle Drogo

A 39

A 30

TAVISTOCK

A 384

Cotehele House   The Garden House

Tresco Abbey

ISLES of SCILLY

Lanhydrock

A 38

Dartington Hall

Antony House   Saltram House

A 30

A 390

PLYMOUTH

Trewithen

Trelissick

Sharpitor

Trengwainton

Glendurgan

PENZANCE

English Channel

1

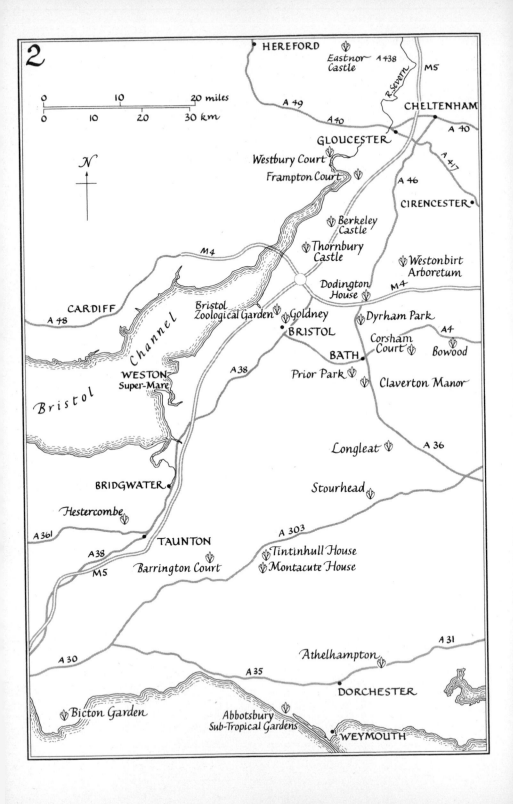

2

HEREFORD

Eastnor A 438
Castle

R. Severn

M5

A 49

A 40

CHELTENHAM

A 40

GLOUCESTER

A 417

Westbury Court

Frampton Court

A 46

CIRENCESTER

N

Berkeley
Castle

Thornbury
Castle

Westonbirt
Arboretum

M4

Dodington
House

M4

CARDIFF

Bristol
Zoological Garden

Goldney

Dyrham Park

A 48

BRISTOL

A4

Corsham
Court

Bowood

BATH

Channel

WESTON-
Super-Mare

A 38

Prior Park

Claverton Manor

Bristol

Longleat

A 36

BRIDGWATER

Stourhead

Hestercombe

A 361

A 303

A 38

TAUNTON

Tintinhull House

M5

Barrington Court

Montacute House

A 31

Athelhampton

A 30

A 35

DORCHESTER

Bicton Garden

Abbotsbury
Sub-Tropical Gardens

WEYMOUTH

0 ———— 10 ———— 20 miles
0 — 10 — 20 — 30 km

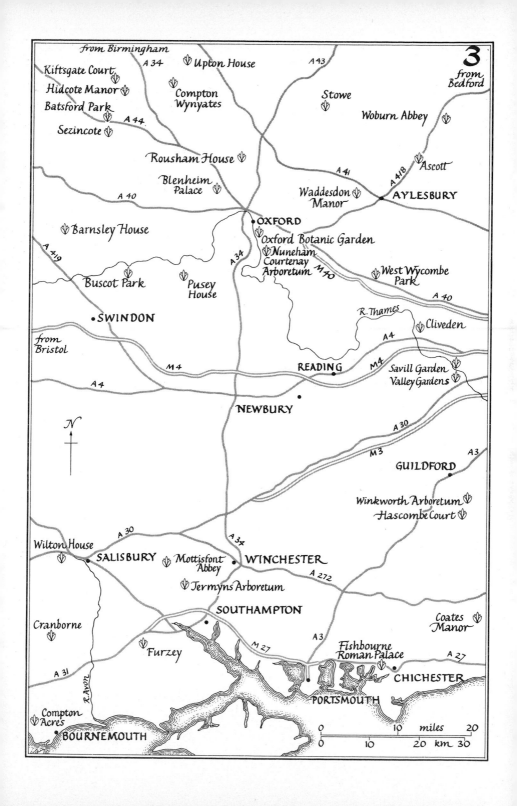

3

from Birmingham

Kiftsgate Court

Hidcote Manor

Batsford Park

A 34

Upton House

A 43

from Bedford

Compton Wynyates

Stowe

Woburn Abbey

A 44

Sezincote

Rousham House

A 41

Ascott

A 418

Blenheim Palace

Waddesdon Manor

AYLESBURY

A 40

Barnsley House

● **OXFORD**

Oxford Botanic Garden

A 419

A 34

Nuneham Courtenay Arboretum

West Wycombe Park

M 40

A 40

Buscot Park

Pusey House

● **SWINDON**

R. Thames

Cliveden

A 4

from Bristol

M 4

READING

M 4

Savill Garden

Valley Gardens

A 4

NEWBURY

A 30

N

M 3

GUILDFORD

A 3

Winkworth Arboretum

Hascombe Court

A 30

A 34

Wilton House

SALISBURY

Mottisfont Abbey

WINCHESTER

A 272

Jermyns Arboretum

Coates Manor

SOUTHAMPTON

Cranborne

A 3

Fishbourne Roman Palace

A 27

A 31

Furzey

M 27

CHICHESTER

R. Avon

PORTSMOUTH

Compton Acres

BOURNEMOUTH

0   10   miles   20

0   10   20   km 30

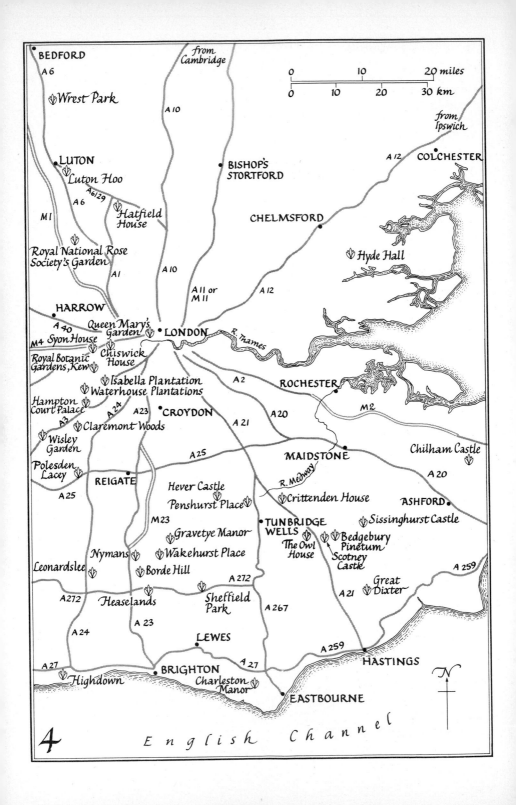

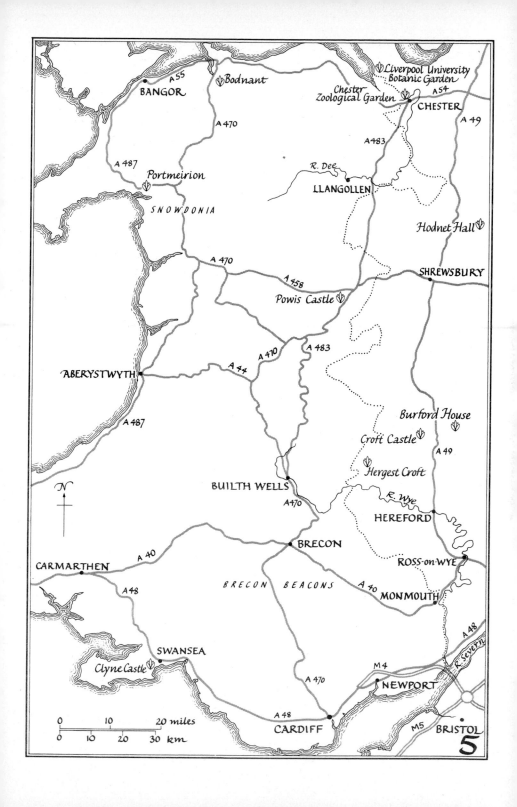

BANGOR · A55 · Bodnant · Liverpool University Botanic Garden · Chester Zoological Garden · CHESTER · A54 · A49 · A470 · A487 · A483 · R. Dee · Portmeirion · SNOWDONIA · LLANGOLLEN · Hodnet Hall · A470 · A458 · Powis Castle · SHREWSBURY · A470 · A483 · A44 · ABERYSTWYTH · A470 · Burford House · Croft Castle · A49 · A487 · Hergest Croft · N · BUILTH WELLS · A470 · R. Wye · HEREFORD · A40 · BRECON · ROSS-on-WYE · CARMARTHEN · A40 · A48 · BRECON BEACONS · A40 · MONMOUTH · A48 · SWANSEA · A470 · M4 · R. Severn · A48 · Clyne Castle · NEWPORT · 0 10 20 miles · 0 10 20 30 km · A48 · CARDIFF · M5 · BRISTOL · 5

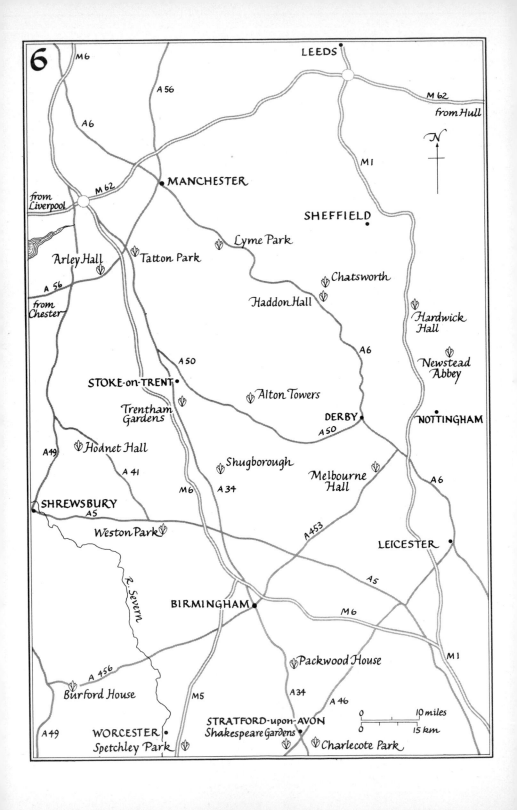

6

LEEDS

M6

A 56

A6

M 62

from Hull

N

M 62

from Liverpool

MANCHESTER

M 1

SHEFFIELD

Lyme Park

Arley Hall

Tatton Park

Chatsworth

A 56

Haddon Hall

Hardwick Hall

from Chester

A6

Newstead Abbey

A 50

STOKE-on-TRENT

Alton Towers

DERBY

NOTTINGHAM

Trentham Gardens

A 50

A49

Hodnet Hall

Shugborough

Melbourne Hall

A 6

A 41

A 34

M6

SHREWSBURY

A5

Weston Park

A 453

LEICESTER

R. Severn

A5

BIRMINGHAM

M6

M 1

Packwood House

A 456

M5

A 34

A 46

10 miles

Burford House

15 km

A49

WORCESTER

STRATFORD-upon-AVON
Shakespeare Gardens

Spetchley Park

Charlecote Park

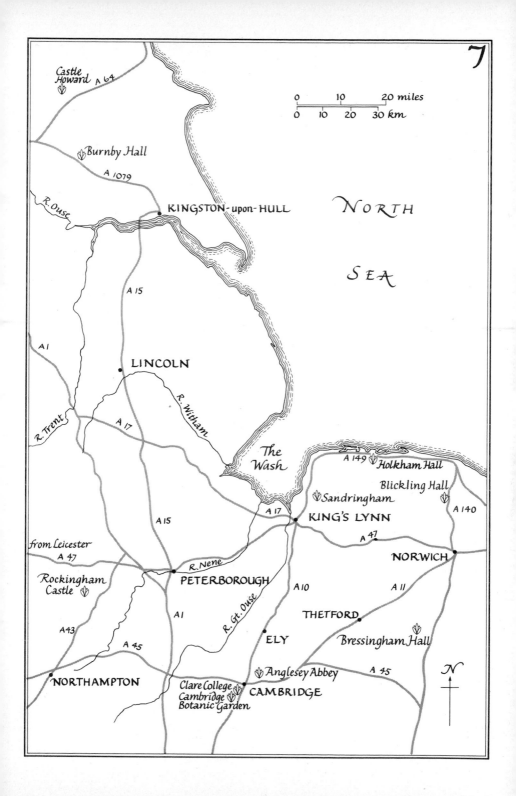

7

Castle Howard A 64

Burnby Hall

A 1079

R. Ouse

KINGSTON-upon-HULL

NORTH

SEA

0   10   20 miles
0 10 20 30 km

A 15

A 1

R. Trent

LINCOLN

R. Witham

A 17

The Wash

A 149 Holkham Hall

Blickling Hall

Sandringham

A 140

A 15

A 17

KING'S LYNN

A 47

NORWICH

from Leicester
A 47

R. Nene

PETERBOROUGH

A 10

A 11

Rockingham Castle

A 1

R. Gt. Ouse

THETFORD

A 43

A 45

ELY

Bressingham Hall

Anglesey Abbey

A 45

NORTHAMPTON

Clare College
Cambridge
Botanic Garden

CAMBRIDGE

N

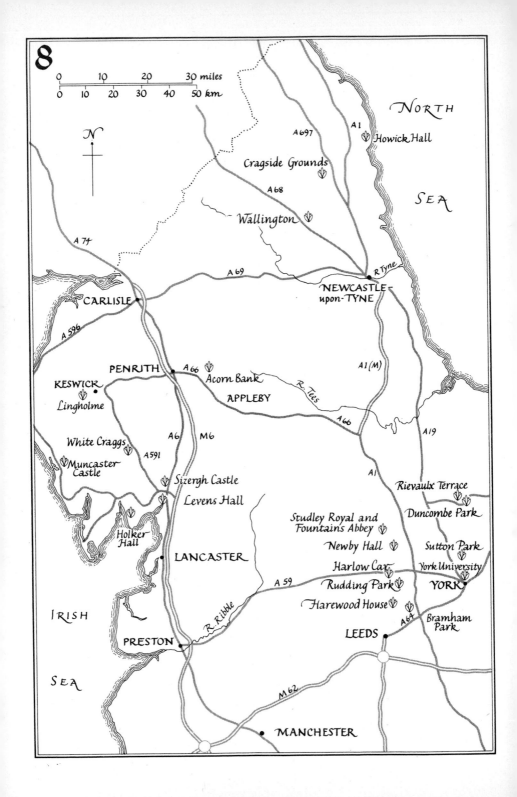

8

0   10   20   30 miles

0 10 20 30 40 50 km

N

NORTH

A1 Howick Hall

A697

Cragside Grounds

SEA

A68

Wallington

A74

A69 R Tyne

NEWCASTLE-
upon-TYNE

CARLISLE

A596

PENRITH   A66   Acorn Bank

KESWICK   APPLEBY   R. Tees   A1(M)

Lingholme

A66   A19

A6   M6

White Craggs

A591

Muncaster
Castle

Sizergh Castle

Levens Hall   A1   Rievaulx Terrace

Studley Royal and
Fountains Abbey   Duncombe Park

Holker
Hall

LANCASTER   Newby Hall   Sutton Park

Harlow Car   York University

A59   Rudding Park   YORK

Harewood House

IRISH   R. Ribble   LEEDS   A64   Bramham
Park

PRESTON

SEA

M62

MANCHESTER

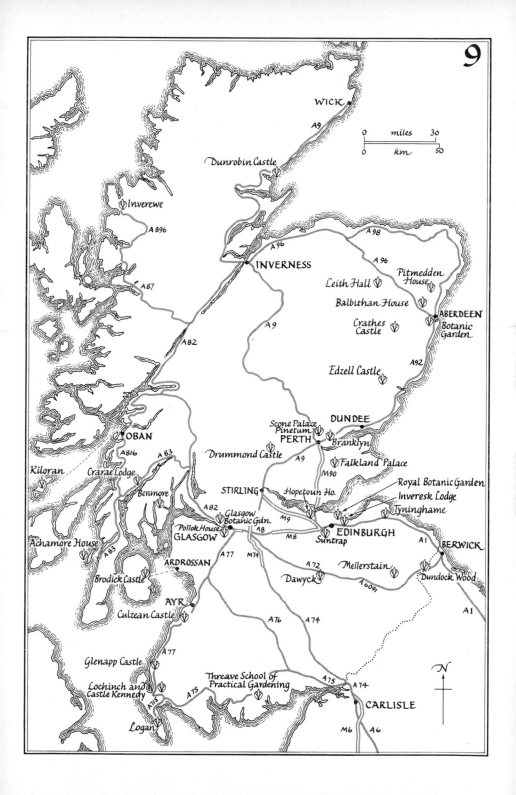

9

WICK

A9

Dunrobin Castle

miles 30
0   km   50

Inverewe

A896

A96   INVERNESS

A98

A96

Pitmedden House

Leith Hall

A87

Balbithan House

ABERDEEN
Botanic Garden

A82

A9

Crathes Castle

Edzell Castle

A92

OBAN

DUNDEE

Scone Palace Pinetum

PERTH

Branklyn

A816   A83

Drummond Castle

A9

Falkland Palace

M90

Kiloran

Crarae Lodge

STIRLING

Hopetoun Ho.

Royal Botanic Garden

Inveresk Lodge

Benmore

A82   Glasgow Botanic Gdn.

M9

Tyninghame

Achamore House

Pollok House

GLASGOW

A8

M8

EDINBURGH

Suntrap

A1

BERWICK

A83

A77   M74

A72

Mellerstain

Dundock Wood

Brodick Castle

ARDROSSAN

A74

Dawyck

A6091

A1

AYR

Culzean Castle

A76   A74

Glenapp Castle   A77

Threave School of Practical Gardening

A75

A74

Lochinch and Castle Kennedy

A75

A75

CARLISLE

Logan

M6   A6

N

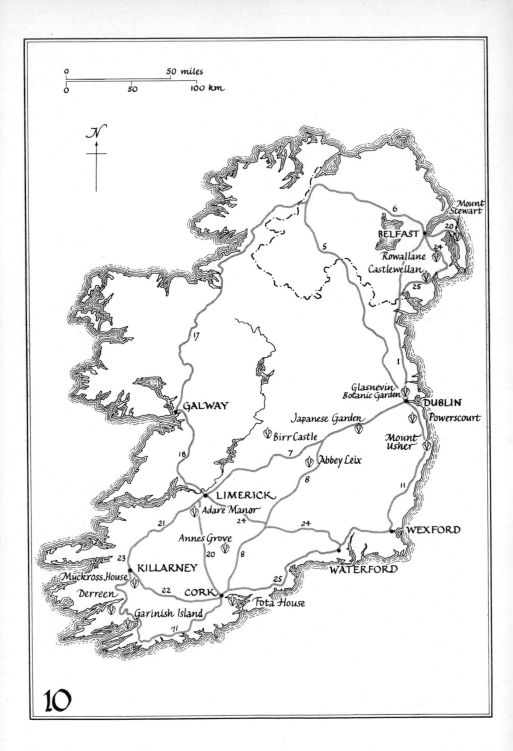

50 miles

50   100 km

N

6

Mount
Stewart

BELFAST

20

5

Rowallane
Castlewellan

24

25

17

1

Glasnevin
Botanic Garden

DUBLIN

GALWAY

Powerscourt

Japanese Garden

Mount
Usher

Birr Castle

18

7

Abbey Leix

8

11

LIMERICK

Adare Manor

WEXFORD

21

24

24

Annes Grove

20

8

23

KILLARNEY

WATERFORD

Muckross House

22

CORK

25

Derreen

Fota House

Garinish Island

71

10

Glossary of Terms

Allée, Alley. The two words may be regarded as virtually synonymous, but the French *allée* is usually cut through woodland, or thickly planted with trees and shrubs between the *allées*, which comes to much the same thing, whereas English alleys are often simply formed with two lines of hedges or trimmed trees, with no infilling beyond.

Belvedere. A structure built expressly as a convenient place from which to admire a view of garden, countryside or both.

Boskage, Bosket. The two words have a similar meaning, being used to describe a dense thicket of trees or shrubs used either for its own sake or as a solid mass to contrast with an open space, or to give greater solidity to *allées* (q.v.)

Eye-catcher. Some object, often a building, but sometimes no more than a facade or a large rock, placed expressly for the purpose of attracting attention from a distance. Eye-catchers are often used in landscapes to call attention to a particularly attractive view or composition.

Gazebo. The word can be used for a variety of very different structures, but in this book I have confined its use to garden pavilions, usually two storeys high. Gazebos of this kind often serve a dual purpose, one as a beautiful object and focal point in the garden, the other as a convenient covered and raised place from which to view it.

Knot. A pattern made with plants, usually small shrubs, such as box, lavender or thyme, kept closely trimmed. The patterns are often elaborate and may simulate the 'over and under' effect of embroidery by using plants of two or more colours. Knot gardens may consist of one or more such patterns, but, though the arrangement of the knots may be regular, the patterns are not, as a rule, arranged in a matching sequence, a feature in which knot gardens differ from those parterres which make use of clipped patterns.

Parterre. A level and regularly shaped area of ground, usually subdivided in a symmetrical way. Often the divisions, which themselves form a pattern, will also carry patterns or designs of their own, and these will always be arranged in a regular, matching way – an important difference between a parterre and a knot garden. A 'green parterre' will have only grass and possibly paving to form the pattern. In more elaborate parterres the patterns may be made with clipped plants (as in knots) with coloured earth, gravel, coal dust and other materials,

257

with a combination of both plants and minerals, or with masonry and water. A *parterre de broderie* is one with a very elaborate pattern, usually in clipped box.

Patte d'Oie. Literally a goose's foot, a term used for a series of *allées* or paths radiating from a central point. It was a favourite device with seventeenth century garden makers.

Vista. A view enclosed on each side, though usually open at the far end. If it is not, it is known as a 'closed vista'.

The parterre at Edzell Castle

Biographical Notes

Robert Abraham (1773–1850). Architect and surveyor who did a good deal of work for the wealthy Catholic landowners, including the Earl of Shrewsbury at Alton Towers, for whom he designed the conservatory and other garden buildings.

Robert Adam (1728–1792). The most celebrated of four architect brothers, the others being John, James and William. Their father, William, was also an architect who redesigned the building and garden of Hopetoun House, near Edinburgh. Robert Adam was even more famous for his interior decorations than for his building, which has sometimes been criticized as inferior in quality.

Thomas Archer (1668–1743). Architect in the baroque style, who is said to have borrowed some of his ideas from the Italian masters Bernini and Borromini. He designed the lovely pavilion at the end of the Wrest Park canal and also redesigned the west front of Chatsworth.

Robert Bakewell. One of the most famous English blacksmiths in the eighteenth century. The Iron Arbour at Melbourne Hall is his work.

Sir Charles Barry (1795–1860). Architect of the Houses of Parliament and many country houses. He also frequently designed terraces in the Italian style for the gardens of houses he was building or altering. His work can be seen at Dunrobin Castle, Harewood House and Trentham.

Guillaume Beaumont. French gardener, said to have been trained by Le Nôtre, who settled in England and became gardener to Col. James Graeme (or Graham) and helped him to make the garden and park at Levens Hall. He died at Levens in 1727 but the date of his birth is uncertain.

Sir Reginald Blomfield (1856–1942). Architect and garden designer. He favoured a formal style in the garden, with architecture dominant, and plants subservient to it. In 1892 he published a book, *The Formal Garden in England*. He wrote frequent articles on the subject, many of which were answered by William Robinson, the great advocate at that period of natural styles in garden making and the supremacy of plants.

Sir Peircy Brett (1709–1781). Naval officer under Lord Anson, probably captain of the Centurion, who led an attack under Anson on Paita, a Spanish settlement on the west coast of South America. He apparently acquired a familiarity with oriental architecture during his voyages. Lord Anson was brother to Thomas Anson who transformed the house and garden at Shug-

259

Robert Bakewell's Iron Arbour at Melbourne Hall

borough, and Sir Peircy designed a Chinese pavilion for the garden.

Charles Bridgeman. Early eighteenth century garden designer (he died in 1738, but the date of his birth is uncertain), who worked at Stowe, Rousham and other gardens before William Kent, and later seems sometimes to have worked with Kent. His own style, though formal to modern eyes, does

Sir Reginald Blomfield's reconstruction of Trinity Manor, Jersey

show the beginnings of a more natural approach.

John Brookes (1933–   ). Contemporary garden designer who has worked on many projects, including the conversion of part of the garden at Syon Park for use as a permanent gardening exhibition. He also writes and lectures on garden design.

Lancelot Brown (1716–1783). Brown was born at Kirkharle in Northumberland, educated in the village school there and at nearby Cambo, and became a gardener in Kirkharle. Later he went to Stowe, at first to the kitchen garden, but later to work on the landscape there under Kent. In 1751 he set up on his own as a garden designer and architect and in the next 32 years did more than anyone else to convert English gardens to the new landscape style. He acquired the nickname 'Capability' because of his habit of assuring potential clients that their estates had great capability for improvement. Examples of his work can be seen at Blenheim Palace, Bowood, Charlecote Park, Chatsworth, Chilham Castle, Claremont Woods, Corsham Court, Dodington House, Harewood House, Kew, Longleat, Luton Hoo, Sheffield Park, Syon Park, Trentham, Weston Park, and Wrest Park. *See also* page 18 *et seq*.

Decimus Burton (1800–1881). Architect who favoured the Grecian style. He designed numerous country houses and also the triumphal arch at Hyde Park Corner, but his garden fame rests mainly on his contribution to the great Palm House at Kew. In fact Burton's part in this is controversial. He certainly appears to have made the first designs to the ideas of Sir William (at that time plain William Jackson) Hooker, but the work was carried out by an Irish constructional engineer, William Turner, who altered Burton's plan so much that some regard the credit as his.

Percy S. Cane (1882–1976). Garden designer and writer. Among the many gardens he has made or added to during his long career are Falkland Palace, Dartington Hall, Hascombe Court, Monteviot and Sutton Park. *See also* page 63.

Sir William Chambers (1723–1796). Architect and writer who was active in introducing oriental buildings and ideas into British gardens. The pagoda at Kew is his. He also designed buildings in classical and romantic styles at Kew and elsewhere, including the little temple or casino at Wilton House.

J. Cheal and Sons. Nurserymen of Crawley, Sussex, who laid out many gardens in the late nineteenth and early twentieth century. The firm was founded in 1871 by two brothers, Joseph and Alexander Cheal, who were later joined by Joseph's son, Ernest, and still later by his son, Wilfred. Joseph Cheal was the one principally concerned with design in the early years, and it was he who directed work at Hever Castle.

H. F. Clarke (1902–1971). Forbes Professor of Architecture at Edinburgh University. Earlier he had worked with Percy Cane and Professor Christopher Tunnard, and had been a lecturer at the Staff College of the Institute of Park and Recreation Administration in Reading. He was a member of the committee advising on the York University campus, and the waterscape there is based on his suggestions.

Dame Sylvia Crowe (1901–   ). Garden architect who has been concerned primarily with large scale landscaping for new towns, including Harlow and Basildon, industrial developments etc., but has also found time to design some relatively small gardens. An example of this side of her work is the memorial garden outside the Oxford Botanic Garden.

Samuel Curtis (1779–1860). First cousin of William Curtis (1746–1799) founder of the *Botanical Magazine* (later known as *Curtis' Botanical Magazine*) in 1787. Samuel became proprietor of the magazine in 1826 and had W. J. Hooker as editor. He was agent at Clumber, Nottinghamshire, from 1816 onwards and was engaged on the laying out of Victoria Park, East London from 1842. About this time he purchased La Chaire in Jersey and began to make terraces and plant many rather tender plants in this sheltered valley leading to Rozel Bay. He lived at La Chaire from 1852 and died there. *See also* pages 30, 34.

William Dallimore (1871–1959). Trained at the Royal Botanic Gardens, Kew, and from 1925–1936 was keeper of the Kew Museum. He also formed the British Forestry Museum. With A. Bruce Jackson he wrote in 1923 the *Handbook of Coniferae*. He was responsible for much of the early design of the National Pinetum, Bedgebury.

Thomas Daniell (1749–1840). An artist who, in 1784, went to India with his nephew, William Daniell, and spent some years there painting. On their return the two Daniells prepared a book, *Oriental Scenery*, which was published in 1808 and had a considerable influence on the decorative styles of the period. Thomas prepared drawings for Sir Charles Cockerill's alterations to Sezincote in the Indian style, and this, in turn, influenced Nash's design for the Brighton Pavilion.

Col. Vernon Daniell. Twentieth century garden designer with a highly individual artistic skill in the association of plants, particularly herbaceous perennials. A fine example of his work is the herbaceous garden at Anglesey Abbey.

A. G. W. Destailleur (1822–1893). French architect who specialized in elaborate buildings in the Second Empire mode. His work at Waddesdon Manor is an almost unique example of his style in Britain.

George Dilliston (1877–1957). Nurseryman, garden designer and author. For many years was landscape manager and later director of the Tunbridge Wells nursery firm, R. Wallace and Co. Published *The Planning and Planting of Little Gardens* in 1914. Was responsible for planting the Lutyens designed garden at Castle Drogo.

David Douglas (1798–1834). Plant hunter who made several explorations of western North America from 1823 until 1833 and was responsible for sending home seed of a great many previously unknown trees, shrubs and herbaceous plants. He introduced the mighty Douglas fir and also the tiny herbaceous genus douglasia.

Achille Duchêne. French garden designer of the late nineteenth and early twentieth centuries, who specialized in making formal parterres in the elaborate seventeenth century manner. Fine examples of his work can be seen at Blenheim Palace.

Henry Flitcroft (1697–1769). The son of John Flitcroft who was head gardener at Hampton Court in the reign of William and Mary. He trained as a draughtsman and architect and became a protégé of Lord Burlington, which ensured his success and earned him the nickname 'Burlington Harry'. He was employed in the office of the Board of Works and designed garden buildings for Stourhead and Woburn Abbey.

George Forrest (1873–1932). Plant hunter who made numerous journeys to the Chinese province of Yunnan over a period of 28 years, and collected a great number of plants and seeds, many of them species not previously known.

Charles Fowler (1781–1867). Architect who made use of the Italian style for utilitarian purposes, as in the floral arcade at Covent Garden and the Old Harringay Market. A splendid example of his work is the great conservatory at Syon House.

William Sawrey Gilpin (1762–1845). Water colour painter and landscape architect who promoted the picturesque style of landscape. In 1832 he published his book, *Practical Hints for Landscape Gardening with remarks on Domestic Architecture as connected with Scenery.* He advised on the landscaping of Scotney Castle and Nuneham Courtenay Arboretum.

T. R. Hayes and Sons. Nurserymen of Ambleside, Cumbria, who for a great many years have specialized in the construction of rock and water gardens on natural lines, using for the most part weather- and water-worn 'Westmorland' stone. Worked at Sizergh Castle.

Nicholas Hawksmoor (1661–1736). Architect who worked with Sir Christopher Wren and Sir John Vanbrugh and, during their lifetimes, tended to be overshadowed by them, though he had a strong and highly individual talent of his own and designed numerous fine buildings. His work can be seen at Castle Howard.

Christopher Hussey (1899–1970). Author of several books and innumerable articles on the great houses and gardens of Britain. Most of his articles appeared in the weekly magazine, *Country Life.* His books include *The Picturesque,* and *English Gardens and Landscapes 1700–1750.* He lived at Scotney Castle and was a grandson of Edward

Hussey who created that supremely picturesque landscape.

W. E. Th. Ingwersen and Son. Nurserymen near East Grinstead on the estate which was owned by William Robinson. They are specialists in alpine plants and rock garden construction, and Will Ingwersen is currently working on a vast rock garden near Teheran for the new Iranian Botanic garden. An example of the firm's work on a much smaller scale can be seen at Bicton.

Gertrude Jekyll (1843–1932). Garden designer and writer who exercised a great deal of influence on British ideas of garden planting from 1891 onwards. In earlier years painting had been one of her principal interests, but she was unable to continue with this because of failing eyesight. She met the young Edwin Lutyens and until the time of her death collaborated with him and other architects in the making of gardens. Her work, or what remains of it, since she was chiefly concerned with herbaceous plants, which can be ephemeral, can be seen at Barrington Court, Folly Farm (Sulhamstead, Berkshire), Glenapp Castle and Hestercombe. *See also* page 49 *et seq.*

Geoffrey Alan Jellicoe (1900–   ). Contemporary garden architect and senior partner in Jellicoe and Coleridge. He has been chiefly engaged in large scale work for public authorities, industrial developments etc., but has also designed many smaller gardens or garden features. Examples of his garden work are to be seen at Pusey, Hever Castle and Wisley, and of large scale work in Hemel Hempstead new town, in the Cheltenham Sports Centre and Plymouth Civic Centre.

William Kent (1685–1748). Painter, architect and garden designer. He became a protégé of Lord Burlington, re-designed the garden of Chiswick House for him and went on to design other gardens in the new landscape style, which he did a great deal to shape and advance. Many of the temples and other classical buildings in these gardens were made to his plans. Examples of his work can be seen at Chiswick House, Claremont, Rousham and Stowe. *See also* page 12 *et seq.*

London and Wise. George London, who died in 1714 (the date of his birth is uncertain), was a gardener who had worked for Charles II and Henry Compton, Bishop of London, before joining Henry Wise (1653–1738) to found the Brompton Park nursery in Kensington. It eventually covered 100 acres and had the best stock of trees and shrubs in the country. The firm not only supplied the plants for a great many of the fine gardens of the period, but also planned some of them. They worked in the grand French manner, laying out symmetrical gardens with parterres, *allées*, formal pools and fountains. Examples of their work are to be seen at Chatsworth, Hampton Court and Melbourne Hall. Many other gardens which they made were swept away during the landscape revolution.

Claude Lorrain (1600–1682). French painter residing for much of his life in Rome. His true name was Claude Gelée and he was born in Lorraine, whence he derived the sobriquet by which he is known. He painted mythical scenes, but set them in splendid landscapes representing his idealized vision of the Roman Campagna. Half a century later these paintings and also those of other members of the Italian school, including Gaspar Poussin (1613–1675) and Salvator Rosa (1615–1673), were to have a profound influence on the English Landscape movement.

John Claudius Loudon (1783–1843). Writer, encyclopaedist and editor, whose capacity for work was prodigious. *An Encyclopaedia of Gardening*, which he published in 1822, packed more information into a single volume than any previous horticultural book and in this respect has never been surpassed. He founded *The Gardener's Magazine* in 1826, the first popular journal of its kind. His influence on gardening was considerable, though more by precept than by example. He favoured a style he called 'gardenesque', which might be briefly described as designing gardens to display plants and the varied arts of the gardener to the best advantage. He designed Derby Arboretum, possibly the first municipal park in Britain.

Sir Edwin Lutyens (1869–1944). Architect and garden designer who exercized a great influence in both fields in the early twentieth century. Very early in his career he met Gertrude Jekyll, they became close friends and he relied greatly on her to plant the gardens which he designed. Examples of his work can be seen at Castle Drogo, Folly Farm (Sulhamstead, Berkshire), Great Dixter and Hestercombe. *See also* page 49 *et seq.*

John Nash (1752–1835). Architect, town planner and garden designer. He entered into partnership with Humphry Repton in the 1790s. He planned Regent's Park and redesigned St James' Park. Regent Street is his and so is the oriental pavilion at Brighton. Work of his on a very different scale is to be seen at Blaise Hamlet (Henbury, Avon).

William Andrews Nesfield (1793–1864). Engineer, who in later life turned to painting and garden designing. He favoured the neo-Italian style of symmetrical plans and geometrical terraces laid out as parterres, and on several occasions collaborated with Sir Charles Barry. Examples of his work can be seen at Castle Howard, Kew and Trentham.

André Le Nôtre (1613–1700). Greatest of the seventeenth century French garden designers. He worked for most of his life for Louis XIV, and exercized an enormous influence on garden design throughout Europe. Some gardens in England are attributed to him, e.g. Bicton; however there is no evidence for this, nor is there any record that he even visited the country.

Andrea Palladio (1518–1580). Italian architect whose ideas for a very regular style, based on classical principles of proportion, were adopted by some British architects. Many buildings in the classical landscape gardens of the mid-eighteenth century are Palladian in style and three famous decorative garden bridges (at Wilton, Prior Park and Stowe) are based on his designs.

Sir Joseph Paxton (1803–1865). A gardener who became also an architect and an engineer. For many years he was head gardener to the Duke of Devonshire at Chatsworth, and made many additions there, including the Emperor Fountain and some of the massive rock work. He designed the great greenhouse at Chatsworth, since demolished, and then the even larger building for the Great Exhibition of 1851 in Hyde Park, which was later removed to Sydenham and became the Crystal Palace. Some other gardens or garden features are also attributed to Paxton, including the Italian terraces at Tatton Park.

Harold Ainsworth Peto (1854–1933). Architect and garden designer who admired the Italian Renaissance style and sought to adapt it to contemporary needs in the British Isles. His gardens have a highly distinctive mixture of for-mality and naturalism. Examples are to be seen at Buscot Park and Garinish Island. *See also* page 55 *et seq.*

Augustus Welby Northmore Pugin (1812–1852). Architect who played a leading part in the nineteenth century Gothic revival. He was a protégé of John Talbot, Earl of Shrewsbury, who, like Pugin, was a Catholic, and he worked for him at Alton Towers. For a few years before his death he assisted Sir Charles Barry in the design of the Houses of Parliament. He also worked at Adare House.

James Pulham. Garden designer and contractor of Chelsea, who traded from the 1860s until the Second World War as Pulham and Sons. He was particularly skilful at rock and water work and was a regular exhibitor of such gardens at the Chelsea Flower Show. He also invented an artificial rock known as Pulhamite. His work is to be seen at Batsford Park, Sandringham, Sheffield Park, Waddesdon Manor and Wisley.

Humphry Repton (1752–1815). Artist who turned to garden designing after the death of 'Capability' Brown. Though he was in sympathy with Brown's ideas, his own landscapes are quite distinctive, with more trees placed individually or fairly widely scattered, and often a degree of formality, including terraces, around the house. He also re-introduced the avenue in some of his gardens. It was his practice to produce water colour sketches with overlays of the gardens on which he was asked to advise, showing them as they were and as they would look after the alterations he recommended. These, with a description of the proposed work, were bound in red morocco leather and became known as Repton's 'Red Books'. They are now exceedingly valuable collector's pieces. *See also* page 19.

Nicholas Revett (1720–1804). Architect and painter who accompanied James Stuart to Greece to make measurements and drawings of classical buildings there. Later they both became members of the Society of Dilettanti and jointly published their Grecian findings in a book which appeared in 1762 entitled *The Antiquities of Athens measured and delineated by James Stuart, FRS, FSA, and Nicholas Revett, Painters and Architects.* Stuart seems to have gained most of the fame for this but Revett was possibly ahead of him in designing buildings actually based on these measurements. His work can be seen at West Wycombe Park.

William Robinson (1839–1935). An Irish gardener who came to London in 1861 and worked in the Royal Botanic Society's garden in the Inner Circle, Regent's Park, where the Queen Mary rose garden now is. Here he made a garden of English wild flowers. Soon he was a regular horticultural correspondent for *The Times* and from this he moved on to found and edit several gardening journals, including *The Garden, Gardening Illustrated* and *Flora and Sylva.* He wrote numerous books of which one, *The English Flower Garden*, became a classic and went through many editions. Robinson was a forceful advocate of 'natural' methods of gardening and of hardy plants, particularly plants of the Northern Hemisphere. He moulded ideas both through his own writings and through those of the many writers he used in his journals, including Gertrude Jekyll. He spent many years developing his own garden at Gravetye Manor, Sussex, which, though now considerably changed, still displays a great deal of the Robinsonian style.

Lanning Roper (1912–). American born garden designer and writer who has lived in England since 1948 and done much of his work there and in Ireland. Examples of his work may be seen at Claverton Manor and Wisley.

James Russell (1920–). After leaving Eton he became a nurseryman and set about rebuilding the old, but derelict, Sunningdale Nurseries, now part of the Waterer Group. He has always been keenly interested in garden design and planting and has worked in greater or lesser degree in nearly 200 gardens in all parts of the British Isles. These include Achamore House, Crathes Castle, Tyninghame, Castle Howard, Bramham, Brodick Castle, Rudding Park, Arley Hall, Culzean Castle and Hidcote.

Anthony Salvin (1799–1881). Architect who trained under John Nash. He became the leading authority on mediaeval military architecture. Examples of his work as an architect may be seen at Muncaster Castle and Scotney Castle.

Sir Eric Savill (1895–). Chartered surveyor and garden designer whose name is indelibly associated with the creation of the Savill Garden and the Valley Gardens in Windsor Great Park. He was Deputy Surveyor to Windsor Parks and Woods from 1931–1959 and Deputy Ranger from 1937–1959, when he became Director of Gardens, Windsor Great Park.

James Stuart (1713–1788). Architect and painter. He visited Athens with Nicholas Revett (q.v.), and subsequently produced a book with him describing the measurements and drawings they had made of classical buildings. This earned him the nickname 'Athenian' Stuart, and greatly influenced architectural styles. Examples of his work can be seen at Mount Stewart and Shugborough.

Graham Stuart Thomas (1909–). Garden designer, writer and artist, and, for many years, Garden Advisor to the National Trust. He has designed features for many gardens, including a canal and new planting at Sezincote, one of the yew enclosures at Knightshayes Court and much new planting at Wallington and Mottisfont Abbey.

Sir John Vanbrugh (1664–1726). Actor, playwright, architect in the baroque manner and garden designer. He made an enormous impact on English architecture and garden making in the early eighteenth century, two of his most notable works being Castle Howard and Blenheim Palace.

John Van Nost. A late-seventeenth/early-eighteenth century craftsman in lead, who cast many of the statues, urns and other ornaments that decorate gardens of the period. He worked in London and his yard and many of the moulds from which he worked were eventually taken over by John Cheere, who continued to make similar ornamentations for many of the mid-eighteenth century landscape gardens. Examples of his work may be seen at Melbourne Hall.

Veitch. The Veitches crop up again and again in the British garden story. First to come to notice was John Veitch (1752–1839), a Scot who came to Devon to work for Sir Thomas Acland at Killerton and in 1808 founded a nursery at Budlake which was later moved to Exeter. Under his son, James (1772–1865), and grandson, James (1815–1869), the business expanded into orchids and other tender and semi-tender plants as well as trees, shrubs and hardy herbaceous plants, and adopted the style James Veitch and Sons. The firm began to send out collectors to foreign countries to extend the range of their plants. It also acquired a nursery in Chelsea and in 1863 the firm split into two, James Veitch and Sons trading from the Royal Exotic Nursery, King's Road, Chelsea, with several other nurseries in nearby Surrey, and the Exeter firm changing its style to Robert Veitch and Son after Robert Toswill Veitch (1823–1885). In charge at Chelsea were John Gould Veitch (1839–1870), Arthur Veitch (1844–1880) and Harry James Veitch (1840–1924), who was knighted in 1912. Both firms not only continued to breed,

Quarrelling cherubs by Van Nost, Melbourne Hall

Four Seasons urn by Van Nost, Melbourne Hall

Japanese garden by Edward White at Samares Manor, Jersey

collect and grow large collections of plants, but were also engaged in planning and planting gardens for their clients. An example of planting by Robert Veitch and Son can be seen at Exeter University and of James Veitch and Sons at Ascott.

Simon Verity. (1945–   ). Sculptor and garden designer. Examples of his work can be seen at Barnsley House and Wilton House. Nephew of Oliver Hill, the architect, in whose Cotswold manor house he lived for several years. He likes to create with English stone.

Edward White (1872–1951). Garden designer who was president of the Institute of Landscape Architects from 1931 to 1933. He was apprenticed to H. E. Milner, civil engineer, who later took him into partnership. He worked mainly for large estates and town councils, designed gardens for government buildings in Ottawa and also planned the first Chelsea Flower Show, the great Royal International Horticultural Exhibition of 1912. He advised Pulhams in the construction of the Wisley rock garden and also made the large rock garden and Japanese pavilion at Samares Manor, Jersey.

James Wyatt (1746–1813). Architect who built country houses in Romantic or Gothic-revival styles. In 1796 he succeeded Sir William Chambers as Surveyor General to the Board of Works. An example of his work is Dodington House, where he also designed the conservatory.

Sir Jeffrey Wyatville (1766–1840). Architect and nephew to James Wyatt. He altered his name to Wyatville. The greenhouse at Woburn Abbey is his and he designed the north wing at Chatsworth as well as other Italian style buildings for the garden. He also designed a temple in Kew gardens and picturesque ruins at Virginia Water.

Index

Main entries appear in heavy type; photographs in italics; (*pl.*) refers to colour plates.